A Plurilingual Approach for Foreign Language Education in Japan

Enriching Learners' Metalinguistic Awareness through
Comparative Sino-Japanese EFL Textbook Research

Linfeng WANG

KAZAMA SHOBO

About the Author

Linfeng WANG is an Associate Professor at Osaka Kyoiku University, specialized in the teaching of curriculum and instruction subjects to both graduate and undergraduate students. She received her MA in Education from Southwest University's Faculty of Education (Chongqing, China) and a PhD degree in Education from the Graduate School of Education at The University of Tokyo (Tokyo, Japan). Her recent research interests include lesson study, teachers' learning, global education and foreign language education.

Copyright©2025 by Linfeng WANG
All rights reserved.

ISBN978-4-7599-2528-9
Printed in Japan

Published by KAZAMA SHOBO Co., Ltd.
34 1-chome Jimbocho Kanda Chiyoda-ku
TOKYO 101-0051 JAPAN

ABSTRACT

This study analyzes a set of English textbooks used for foreign language education in Japan and China to clarify their character as unfulfilled manifestations of national curriculum guidelines. It explores how these guidelines are reflected in the actual textbooks, identifies the common challenges that English textbooks currently face as foreign language instructional materials, and proposes a plurilingual approach that takes each country's native languages into account, so as to enrich learners' metalinguistic awareness.

Chapter 1 reviews the existing literature to underline the significance of textbook research and examines recent trends in English language textbook research, providing an overview of the historical development of English textbooks in Japan and China. It highlights the need for further research on the characteristics of English as a Foreign Language (EFL) textbooks.

In Chapter 2, this study outlines a framework for the descriptive analysis of English textbooks, to elucidate how certain educational philosophies embedded in the curriculum guidelines have come to be manifested within the textbooks. Furthermore, it analyzes the interactions between learners and textbooks by categorizing the components of learning units into three elements: information related to learning; core contents; and practice activities. Each component in the textbooks is further examined through metadiscourse analysis (Chapter 3), rhetorical pattern analysis of the texts (Chapter 4), and content analysis of the practice activities (Chapter 5). The analysis focuses on 42 units extracted from the English language textbooks used in Japan (published by six companies) and China (published by eight companies) in 2012, centered on themes such as "school," "family," and "events," which are particularly relevant to first-year middle school students.

Chapter 6 discusses the extent to which the qualities and competencies that the textbooks aim to instill in learners reflect the policy directions of national curriculum guidelines, while examining the distinct features and issues related to English language textbooks as foreign language resources.

Chapter 7 presents a set of classroom practice case studies using a plurilingual approach that integrates both native and foreign languages in language education. These include: a lesson targeting first-year middle school students, which focuses on the notion of "Awareness of Japanese, English, and Chinese through Classical Poetry;" a lesson for fourth-grade elementary students titled "Exploring Japanese, English, and Chinese through Word Formation," and online lessons for first- and second-year middle school students centered on "Learning Multiple Foreign Languages Beyond English." The reflection notes gathered from participating students revealed a number of insights related to the enrichment of learners' metalinguistic awareness.

Finally, this book concludes by discussing the study's overall significance and implications, while advocating for further research on the inherent traits of foreign language textbooks, as well as the development of instructional materials and practices that closely interrelate foreign languages with native ones.

INDEX

ABSTRACT ··· i

Chapter 1╱Research Background: Textbook Research in an EFL Context ·· 1

1.1　Introduction to English Textbook Research ······························· 1

1.1.1　General introduction and outline of this book ···················· 1

1.1.2　Textbook research: from the perspective of curriculum and instruction theory ·· 2

1.1.3　English textbook research in an EFL context ···················· 3

1.2　English Textbooks in Japan: An Overview ···························· 6

1.2.1　Meiji period (1887–1894): imported English textbooks were superior to domestic English textbooks ··· 6

1.2.2　From Meiji to Taisho period (1895–1924): the start of state-approved English textbook entrenchment in schools ······························· 8

1.2.3　From Taisho to Showa period (1925–1939): improvement in English textbook compiling skills, and the establishment of a stable model for English textbooks in the post-war era ··· 9

1.2.4　Showa period (1940–1946): a crucial time for textbooks during the Second Sino-Japanese War ·· 9

1.2.5　Post-war era (1947–1956): the beginning of the nation's gradual recovery from war damage with a newly-developed national textbook ············· 10

1.2.6　Economic recovery period (1957–1976): emergence of innovative textbook models ··· 11

1.2.7　Relaxed-education period (1977–1997): a growing awareness of Japanese identity and softening of textbook contents ·······································11

1.2.8 'Zest-for-living' period (1998–2007): emphasizing a global perspective while encouraging the cultivation of practical communication ability ·············12

1.2.9 Globalized period (2008–present): highlighting the integration of the four skills ···12

1.3 English Textbooks in China: An Overview ······························13

1.3.1 The late Qing dynasty (1840–1911): reliance on the introduction, translation, and adoption of foreign textbooks ·······························14

1.3.2 Republic of China period (1912–1948): rapid development of textbooks compiled by Chinese scholars ···15

1.3.3 From the founding of the People's Republic of China until the 1970s (1949–1978): temporary shortage of learning materials and the politicization of English textbooks ··16

1.3.4 Chinese economic reform period (1978–1988): development of national English textbooks based on a constructivist theory of language teaching and learning ··17

1.3.5 National teaching guidelines period (1988–2001): cooperation with foreign publishers with a focus on language structure and function ············18

1.3.6 2001–2010: increased diversity of English textbooks at the onset of the 21st century ···19

1.3.7 2011–present: towards textbooks with Chinese characteristics in fulfilment of 2011's revised national curriculum ·······························21

1.3.8 Summary and discussion ···22

1.4 A Descriptive Analysis of Japanese and Chinese English Language Curricula ···25

1.4.1 Framework for curriculum analysis······································25

1.4.2 Analysis of the 2008 English National Curriculum for junior high schools in Japan 27

   ① Curriculum documentation and origins (JPN) 28

   ② The curriculum proper (JPN) 35

   ③ The curriculum in use (JPN) 41

   ④ Critique (JPN) 44

1.4.3 Analysis of the 2011 English National Curriculum for compulsory

education in China 44

   ① Curriculum documentation and origins (CHN) 47

   ② The curriculum proper (CHN) 58

   ③ The curriculum in use (CHN) 67

   ④ Critique (CHN) 70

1.4.4 Summary and conclusion 70

1.5 Core Focus of This Study 76

1.6 Purpose of the Present Study 79

1.7 Thesis Outline 81

Chapter 2 ╱ Literature Review: Towards a Descriptive Model for EFL Textbook Unit Analysis 85

2.1 Introduction 85

2.2 A Review of Descriptive Models 86

2.3 A Descriptive Model for EFL Textbook Unit Analysis 90

  2.3.1 Messages from textbooks to learners: metadiscourse analysis 92

  2.3.2 Understanding the comprehensibility of texts through rhetorical

pattern analysis 98

  2.3.3 Looking at 'what learners are required to do': practice activity analysis

.... 102

2.4 Conclusion 110

Chapter 3∕Metadiscourse Analysis in Japanese and Chinese EFL Textbooks ·· 113

3.1 Introduction ·· 113

3.2 Adaptations to Crismore's Methodology ························ 113

3.3 Examples of Metadiscourse Subtypes Found in EFL Textbooks···· 118

   3.3.1 Informational metadiscourse ····························· 118

   3.3.2 Attitudinal metadiscourse ······························· 124

   3.3.3 Other tags ··· 126

3.4 Description of Steps Used for the Metadiscourse Analysis and
Other Methodological Considerations ···························· 129

3.5 Main Findings from the Metadiscourse and Non-Metadiscourse
Analysis of Japanese and Chinese EFL Textbooks ················ 138

   3.5.1 Voice and target-native language (non-metadiscourse) ·········· 138

   3.5.2 Voice and target-native language (metadiscourse) ············ 139

   3.5.3 Diversity and balance of metadiscourse subtypes ············ 140

   3.5.4 Extra materials ··· 142

3.6 Discussion and Conclusion···································· 143

Chapter 4∕Rhetorical Pattern Analysis in Japanese and Chinese EFL Textbooks ···································· 151

4.1 Introduction ·· 151

4.2 Main Issues Related to Text Comprehensibility and Objectives of
This Analysis·· 152

4.3 Analysis Framework: Merits and Previous Experiments with
Rhetorical Patterns ·· 155

   4.3.1 Merits of rhetorical patterns ····························· 156

   4.3.2 Experiments involving easy-to-understand rhetorical patterns ········ 160

INDEX   vii

4.4 Method for Analysis of EFL Textbooks ···································· 164

4.4.1 List of textbooks whose units are to be analysed ···························· 164

4.4.2 Brief considerations on the analysis method and list of selected texts/

units·· 165

4.5 Results ·· 168

4.5.1 Main characteristics of rhetorical patterns in reading comprehension

texts·· 168

4.5.2 Rhetorical pattern analysis organized by unit theme ···················· 173

4.6 Discussion of Results·· 195

Chapter 5／Analysis of Practice Activities in Japanese and Chinese EFL Textbooks ··· 201

5.1 Introduction ··· 201

5.2 Overview of EFL Textbooks from the Viewpoint of Practice

Activities··· 202

5.3 General Aspects of Littlejohn's Framework ························· 203

5.4 General Methodological Choices and Procedures ····················· 205

5.4.1 Guidelines for distinguishing between different sub-categories ········· 212

5.4.2 Sequence of analysis procedures and other minor methodological

considerations·· 217

5.5 Results ··· 221

5.5.1 Learners' roles in regards to turn-taking ································· 221

5.5.2 Focus of practice activities ·· 223

5.5.3 Mental operations in practice activities··································· 226

5.5.4 General considerations about mental operations: diversity & frequency

·· 233

5.5.5 Modes of participation in practice activities ····························· 234

5.5.6 Input contents ·· 236

5.5.7 Output contents ··· 240

5.6 Discussion of Results and Conclusion ························ 244

5.6.1 Output: writing and speaking ····························· 245

5.6.2 Input: reading and listening ······························· 246

Chapter 6/Results of EFL Textbook Comparisons with the English Language Curricula of Japan & China ··············· 249

6.1 Introduction ·· 249

6.2 Main Objectives of Textbook Contents According to the Curricula

··· 249

6.3 Summary of EFL Textbook Characteristics ··············· 254

6.4 Adequacy of EFL Textbooks to the English Curricula of Japan and China ··· 257

6.4.1 Reading·· 258

6.4.2 Writing ·· 261

6.4.3 Listening ·· 262

6.4.4 Speaking ·· 263

6.4.5 Other aspects: moral education, cultural awareness, learning strategies, and mental operations ··· 265

6.5 Final Verdict: Balance of the Four Skills & the Role of L1 in EFL Education ··· 268

6.5.1 Balance of the four skills ····································· 268

6.5.2 Role of native language in the teaching of foreign languages ··········· 269

6.6 Applicability of the Analytical Framework of This Study ·········· 271

Chapter 7／Towards an Approach for Enriching Learners' Metalinguistic Awareness ································· 275

7.1　A Collaborative Approach for Enriching Metalinguistic Awareness
·· 275

7.2　Rationale Behind these Case Studies ································· 281

7.3　Action Research Initiatives Towards Metalinguistic Awareness
Development ··· 288

7.4　Case Study of an English Class for Grade-7 ··················· 289

　7.4.1　Lesson Implementation Process ····························· 291

　7.4.2　Analysis of Worksheet Answers and Reflective Writings ··············· 293

　7.4.3　Results & Discussion ··· 294

　7.4.4　Summary ·· 297

7.5　Case Study of a Foreign Language Activity Class for Grade-4 ······ 298

　7.5.1　General Description of the Lesson ····················· 300

　7.5.2　Results ··· 304

　7.5.3　Reflections from the Teacher ···························· 306

　7.5.4　Summary ·· 308

7.6　Case Study of Online English Classes for Grade-7 ··················· 310

　7.6.1　General Background ··· 310

　7.6.2　Guest Teachers ·· 312

　7.6.3　Pre-lesson Phase ·· 313

　7.6.4　Lesson Example: French ··································· 314

　7.6.5　Selected Comments from Students ····················· 315

　7.6.6　Summary ·· 316

Chapter 8 / Conclusion ⋯⋯ 321

8.1 Conclusion: Changes and Prospects for Newly-Revised Textbooks ⋯⋯ 321

   8.1.1 Significance of This Study ⋯⋯ 325

   8.1.2 Scope and Limitations of This Study ⋯⋯ 327

   8.1.3 Recommendations for Future Research ⋯⋯ 327

   8.1.4 Final Remarks ⋯⋯ 330

BIBLIOGRAPHY ⋯⋯ 333

   List of government-approved EFL Japanese Textbooks analysed in this study ⋯⋯ 333

   List of government-approved EFL Chinese Textbooks analysed in this study ⋯⋯ 333

   List of Reference Works ⋯⋯ 333

ACKNOWLEDGEMENTS ⋯⋯ 355

Chapter 1／Research Background: Textbook Research in an EFL Context

1.1 Introduction to English Textbook Research

1.1.1 General introduction and outline of this book

In this thesis, I argue for the importance of investigating the core characteristics of authorized EFL textbooks, and their relationships with national curricula. Because it is assumed that authorized textbooks adhere to the national curriculum, they often play a key role in classroom teaching and learning. This research seeks to explore an approach that addresses the weak points and discrepancies found between the authorized textbooks and national curricula. This is achieved through a critical textbook analysis methodology, which employs both descriptive and quantitative methods.

Another point argued in this thesis is that EFL textbooks should be distinguished from ESL textbooks, even though the globalized English textbook publishing market tends to confuse them. As a result, the key problems and characteristics of EFL textbooks must be identified and discussed. Until now, the two main trends of English textbook publishing were either to produce general globalized materials (i.e., 'one-size-fits-all' materials) which are sold to several countries in order to save costs, or create materials that focus too narrowly on the contexts and needs of a specific country. Throughout this thesis, Japan and China are selected and analyzed as two examples of EFL textbooks for two main reasons. One is that they share a common cultural heritage in the form of Kanji logograms as well as other linguistic traits. Despite the grammatical differences, this shared linguistic heritage of Kanji may provide a helpful foundation on which to build a new framework for learning English as a foreign language. The other reason is that Japan and China have implemented systems for authorizing textbooks and selecting them.

1.1.2 Textbook research: from the perspective of curriculum and instruction theory

Textbook research has drawn increased attention as an autonomous academic research field within curriculum and instruction studies since the 1970s, when the field of Sociology of Educational Knowledge emerged as a new direction within the 'New Sociology Education' initiatives (Young, 1971; Bernstein, 1971; Gorbutt, 1972). It aimed to apply a sociological approach to the study of curricula and textbooks, focusing on the control and management of knowledge, especially in regards to the complex relationships between knowledge and power. In the domain of textbook analysis, debates have been taking place about how public educational knowledge is selected, classified, distributed, transmitted, and evaluated, thus reflecting the realities and rules of social power distribution and social control.

Apple (1979, 1991) examined the curriculum and the textbook critically from the viewpoint of ideology and politics, to answer the classic question 'whose knowledge is worth the most?' He pointed out that legitimate knowledge in textbooks was determined by interactions among political, economic, and cultural variables. Although he criticized textbooks as controlled by mainstream ideology, he never denied the value and significance of textbooks. Furthermore, the textbook was considered to serve as the preferred medium for the intended curriculum, and it played a key role in connecting curriculum theory with practice.

Apart from ideology in textbooks, the functional aspect of textbook usage has also been identified as one of the main categories of textbook research. Given its long historical existence and strong influence in classroom practices, the textbook has been viewed as the concrete materialization of curriculum and instruction. There have been studies that illustrate to what extent textbooks can support teachers' teaching and learning, in addition to the teachers' role in curriculum development in classroom practices associated with educational reform settings (Davis & Krajcik, 2005; Remillard, 2005).

In recent studies on the importance of textbook research, Oates (2014) clarified why textbooks mattered by showing that high-quality textbooks lead to higher performances in regards to international standards of education. He showed that the extent of textbook use in science classes could be attributed to differences in educational performance. He pointed out that textbooks had been largely abandoned in England, to the extent that only 4 per cent of teachers claimed to use textbooks, in contrast to 68 per cent in Singapore and 94 per cent in Finland, that lie among the top-ranking countries of PISA. Based on such arguments, restoring the primacy of high-quality textbooks as a key part of the classroom experience has been a crucial aspect to achieve the highest-performing standards of school education.

1.1.3 English textbook research in an EFL context

In the field of English language education, the development of English textbook research coincides with that of textbook research in general. However, the distinction between English as a Second Language (ESL) and English as a Foreign Language (EFL) is a predominant issue that relates to the region in which English language is taught. In consistence with the focus of this chapter, an ESL classroom is narrowly defined as one in which English is the native or official language of the country, such as the United Kingdom and the United States, where the original purpose of learning English is to survive in the target society. On the other hand, an EFL classroom is one in which English is not the country's native language, such as Japan or China, where the meaning of learning English is embedded into the national curriculum as a school subject. Since the two settings differ in educational goals, learning environments, and educational systems, it is important to distinguish them and duly consider about how to apply the appropriate methodology for the proper context. Therefore, EFL textbooks are expected to have characteristics in clear contrast to ESL textbooks (Nakamura, Minemura & Takashiba, 2014); this is an important aspect which is nevertheless often left understated.

The distinctions between EFL and ESL started to take shape in the 1960s (Okihara, 2011). Different terms were used to make such distinctions, in accordance with the prevalence of English teaching in a worldwide context. Kachru (1982, 1992) classified 'world Englishes' into three concentric circles to demonstrate different socio-cultural environments where English is used and taught (Figure 1.1). Similarly, Holliday (1994a, 1994b) used the two terms BANA and TESEP to make a distinction between two types of educational contexts in various countries: BANA refers to countries such as Britain, Australia, and North America, where English language teaching is mostly of a private nature much like a daily commodity product, which is like Kachru's concept of 'inner circle' within his established circles of English. TESEP refers to state education, either in tertiary institutions, or secondary and elementary schools in countries where English teaching is associated with national public education, which relates to Kachru's defini-

Chapter 1 / Research Background: Textbook Research in an EFL Context   5

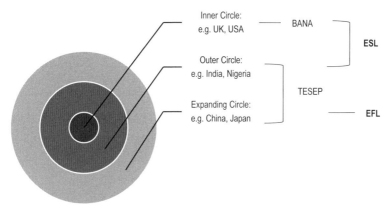

Figure 1.1: The concept of 'World Englishes' according to different interpretive frameworks (made by the author).

tions of 'outer circle' and 'expanding circle'. Figure 1.1 illustrates the above terms used to identify various contexts in regards to their characterization as ESL and EFL. Both China and Japan are ascribed to the notions of expanding circle, TESEP, and EFL.

It is argued that the above distinctions among terms are not clear-cut, in that exceptional cases can be found beyond or between the categories. In fact, it is worth looking at these various distinctions in order to stress the difference between ESL and EFL. However, two internationally influential associations, IATEFL (International Association of Teachers of English as a Foreign Language, based in the United Kingdom) and TESOL (Teachers of English to Speakers of Other Language, an international association centred in the United States) are attempting to devise an inclusive, unifying term to diminish the distinctions between ESL and EFL. One of the reasons attributed to this agenda might be an attempt to keep their dominant supremacy in English language teaching and learning. This may entitle them to the convenience and benefits of promoting standardized global textbooks all over the world, which also brings with it an inevitable influence on the socio-cultural aspects of regional English education. This point suggests the need to conduct research on local EFL textbooks to figure out the idiosyncrasies of EFL contexts.

1.2　English Textbooks in Japan: An Overview

The diverse body of literature regarding the history of English textbooks in Japan has been summarized in various published studies. This includes not only content analyses of textbooks (Kihei, 1988; Yamada, 1998; Ishii, 2002; Ozasa, 1995), but also investigations of rare historical materials, namely: collections of old textbook copies (Omura, Takahashi & Deki, 1980; Takahashi & Deki, 1992; Imura, 2003; Ito, 2003; Erikawa, 2008), interpretations of textbook features in different historical periods (Takahashi & Deki, 1993), and the establishment of databases of old textbooks (Erikawa, 2003).

Saito (2003, 2006, 2007) has provided a unique perspective to examine classic English learning experiences in Japanese history. Ozasa & Erikawa's (2004) insightful historical periods have helped to unfold a chronological picture of textbook development. Moreover, they stress the significance of learning from history to figure out solutions to current challenges and problems. The following part is intended to provide an overview on how English textbooks have been developed since the textbook approval system was established, in reference to Ozasa & Erikawa (2004).

1.2.1　Meiji period (1887–1894): imported English textbooks were superior to domestic English textbooks

The emergence of English textbooks in Japan began with textbooks imported from Western countries during the Meiji period. Given their overwhelming popularity, the number of printed imported English textbooks reached its peak from 1885 to 1888, during which English became a hot topic due to the controversial process of Westernization in the Rokumeikan period (Ozasa & Erikawa, 2004). The importance of imported English textbooks paralleled that of domestic-approved textbooks for a while, even after the textbook approval system was established in 1886. The leading imported English textbooks were *New National Readers, Longmans' readers, Swinton Readers, Union* and *Wilson*. Most of them were English-language textbooks made for English native speakers. One of the main features of these textbooks was that their corpus of literature readings was varied and of high quality, but with less focus on grammar. Being widely used at the time, they have had a heavy influence on the development of both approved English textbooks and Japanese textbooks.

There were 20 approved English textbooks in the first two years of the approval system, but it was eventually made extinct in 1894. One-third of approved English textbooks were written by foreigners, and some imported textbooks were authorized as approved English textbooks. The former Ministry of Education, Culture, Sports, Science and Technology (MEXT) issued a textbook named *The Monbusho Conversational Readers*, which represented the first concrete step towards making English textbooks specifically for Japanese learners. The grammar in it was sequenced and was recalled repeatedly so that readers could master it more thoroughly. Basic and short sentences were chosen so that they could be understood without notes or interpretations written in Japanese. It is worth noting that the level of post-elementary school (10–13 years old) was newly-set up in 1886, and English education was further promoted. Thus, most approved English textbooks were made for post-elementary schools. However, English education in post-elementary schools fell abruptly into decline from 1890, which caused a slump in textbook numbers.

1.2.2 From Meiji to Taisho period (1895–1924): the start of state-approved English textbook entrenchment in schools

The number of secondary school students sharply increased as the result of a series of educational reforms that were implemented in 1899. With steadily growing numbers, approved English textbooks re-flourished in 1901. Around the same time, the Copyright Act was promulgated, which contributed to the disappearance of pirated versions of imported English textbooks, and stimulated the development of domestic English textbooks. The most used textbooks at the time were *Kanda's New Series of English Readers* that notably specialized on balancing the four skills, and *Standards Choice Readers* that selected contents from leading imported English textbooks, arranging them in a way that catered to Japanese learners.

As imported English textbooks made their gradual exit, the Japanese started to explore ways to compile textbooks appropriate for Japanese learners. Unlike the difficult-to-understand imported English textbooks, domestic textbooks attempted to set reasonable learning objectives which could more realistically be achieved by Japanese learners. This may be considered to mark the start of textbook designing within the context of English as a foreign language. What was mainly adopted in textbooks at this time was to control the exposure of grammatical items and vocabularies, to make them easier to learn, and then gradually build up from there. One potential downside is that restricted and limited grammars can easily lead to simplistic and uninteresting language materials. In sum, the key

Chapter 1 / Research Background: Textbook Research in an EFL Context 9

concern was how to balance between simplicity and authenticity when composing and selecting language materials.

1.2.3 From Taisho to Showa period (1925–1939): improvement in English textbook compiling skills, and the establishment of a stable model for English textbooks in the post-war era

In 1931, English was made a compulsory subject in teachers' schools, and in 1932, occupational schools began to adopt state-approved textbooks. These reforms expanded the demand for textbooks. The most representative textbook at the time was *The Standard English Readers* by Palmer. He invented the Oral Method, believing that English can be learnt by repeating oral practices. Due to growing requests for a large quantity of textbooks, scientific investigations were carried out to select frequently-used vocabulary words, and the effective sequencing of language materials was taken into consideration.

1.2.4 Showa period (1940–1946): a crucial time for textbooks during the Second Sino-Japanese War

Textbooks were restricted to 5 titles for each subject in 1940. Among these, *The New Monbusho English Readers for Elementary Schools* were published for usage in national 2-year post-elementary schools. The publisher known as Secondary School Textbooks Publishing, resulting from the merging of multiple publishers into a national company, exclusively produced approved textbooks for secondary schools. Not only the topics of British meals, Christmas, and Aesop's Fables were included in textbooks, but also some contents relevant to war were featured. Instead of state-approved English textbooks, some alternative textbooks were used in Navy and Army preparatory schools. Even as the operation of regular schools was ceased during wartime, some of the Navy and Army preparatory schools, whose soldiers were fighting against western military forces, kept teaching English. Right after the war, some schools used the so-called *su-mi-nuri* textbooks, in which sensitive war-related contents were covered with black ink.

1.2.5 Post-war era (1947–1956): the beginning of the nation's gradual recovery from war damage with a newly-developed national textbook

In the immediate post-war era, the junior-high school level became a part of the compulsory education system, which contributed to the popularization of education. This surge in demand made it necessary to cut off textbook contents, resulting from requests to simplify teaching materials. The national textbook *Let's learn English* developed by MEXT focused on reading, which went contrary to the structure of previous oral-centred textbooks. On the other hand, the approved textbook *Jack and Betty* continued with the oral-centred approach, depicting American middle-class life. In fact, textbooks in the post-war era adopted a grammar-controlled approach, which focused on clear-cut objectives, dominated by a carefully-restricted and sequenced grammar. From this period onwards, textbooks established a tendency to obey the stipulations of the national curriculum, which ruled with a heavy hand both teaching methods and teaching materials. This phenomenon resulted in a high level of homogeneity among textbooks, standardized with restrictive lists of grammar and vocabulary items.

1.2.6 Economic recovery period (1957–1976): emergence of innovative textbook models

In 1965, a textbook labelled as ground-breaking at the time, *The Junior Crown English Course* by Sanseido, caught people's eyes. Its featured storyline was centred on the Browns, namely Tom and Susie. A Japanese painter visited their town, and they reunited once again when the Browns stopped by Japan on their way to India and Africa, resulting in a storyline which differed from then-current Western-dominated textbooks. It inserted a foldout page with a drill chart as appendix, a feature which was copied by other publishers. In the era of high-speed economic growth, the theme of Japan's growing worldwide presence was reflected into the contents of English textbooks, such as Mujina from Koizumi Yakumo's Kwaidan, a Japanese character who attended American schools. Reading-centred textbooks lost their edge, since the time allotted for English classes was shortened, and a number of textual contents in language materials had to be cut off.

1.2.7 Relaxed-education period (1977–1997): a growing awareness of Japanese identity and softening of textbook contents

To alleviate school violence and failures in classroom discipline, a more relaxed education policy was introduced in 1977 that reduced curriculum contents and overall class time to make education freer from emotional pressure. This resulted in a decrease of vocabulary and language materials in English textbooks, especially reading-centred textbooks. Textbook contents tended to shift from cultural Western dominance to the stressing of multiculturalism and Japanese identity. Contents such as saving African children were included in *New Horizon*, and the number of Japanese culture-related contents (such as an interview with *kyogen* performer Izumi Junko, or explanations of Japanese calligraphy and the culture of Ainu people) was also increased in other English textbooks.

1.2.8 'Zest-for-living' period (1998–2007): emphasizing a global perspective while encouraging the cultivation of practical communication ability

The predominant stance of the aforementioned 'relaxed-education' period continued after the turn of the millennium, as Western-centric perspectives in state-approved English textbooks became less dominant, and characters from Asian countries, like Thailand, China, and Korea, were brought forth to communicate with Japanese characters about Japanese Manga. Topics of national relevance such as *shamisen* music, greeting customs, or 'Japanese' manners of thinking were arranged in textbooks with the aim to help learners rethink their identities as conforming to a state-approved, uniform notion of what it is to be 'Japanese'. Ethnic minorities, like those from the Bhutanese kingdom, were included in English textbooks to convey the message that understanding minority cultures is essential. Each textbook made efforts to design situations close to learners' real lives, in order to provide practical settings to which they could relate to for enhancing their communicative ability, including references to conversations with foreign students, gathering information on the Internet and travelling abroad.

1.2.9 Globalized period (2008–present): highlighting the integration of the four skills

The national curriculum was revised towards developing the communicative ability of Japanese learners, to better enable them to survive in these global times throughout the elementary, junior high and senior high school systems. Featuring an additional emphasis on listening and speaking activities, the English teaching materials *English Notes* and *Hi, friends!* were distributed to elementary schools. In secondary schools, language learning activities were devised to integrate the four skills in a synergistic manner, rather than developing them in isolation; as a crucial foundational basis for communication, grammar is to be learnt through communicative activities overall. In high school, the aspect of communication is so heavily emphasized, that the names of compulsory and selective English subjects were defined as *Communicative English*, *English Conversation*, and *English Expression*.

1.3 English Textbooks in China: An Overview

The history of English textbooks in China has not yet been fully studied. There are few published studies that address textbooks prior to the founding of the People's Republic of China in 1949. Liu (2011) briefly reviewed the last 150 years of history of English textbooks used in China throughout five historical periods, but for certain periods, accurate sources or evidences were not made fully clear. While taking into consideration the results of previous literature reviews (Liu, Gong & Zhang, 2011; Dong, 2013; Qin, 2014; Liu & Wu, 2015; Sheng, 2016) and looking at existing documental sources, I intend to represent in this section a historical overview of the vicissitudes of English textbook development in China in reference to Liu (2011).

1.3.1 The late Qing dynasty (1840–1911): reliance on the introduction, translation, and adoption of foreign textbooks

English language education was officially established in China during the 'Self-Strengthening Movement' in the late Qing dynasty. It was the nation's first coordinated attempt to learn a Western language after years of reluctance, in order to improve its weakened position when negotiating with military Western powers. China had been forced to sign a series of unequal treaties as the result of military defeats that granted territorial and legal concessions to various Western countries. The final, ultimate interpretations of the legal dispositions in the treaties were ascribed to the texts in the English versions, and this was specified as one entry in the treaties (Li, Zhang & Liu, 1988). A government school for teaching foreign languages, Tongwen Guan, was founded in Beijing in 1862; this signified the start of English education in modern China. The textbooks used in Tongwen Guan were mostly imported textbooks from overseas (i.e., *The Mother Tongue, School Reading by Grades: Baldwin's Readers*), along with Chinese translations as complementary materials. Given their large quantities of repeated sentence pattern drills, without any vocabulary or grammar explanations, they imply a preference towards the Direct Method as their main teaching approach.

The growing needs for translating Western books led to a thriving situation for publishers, one of which was Commercial Press. It published the very first English textbook series *English and Chinese Primer* and *English and Chinese Readers* for Chinese students in 1898, which were translated and adjusted from the textbook series *Primer* that the British originally developed for Indian students in India during its colonial period. Another influential translated textbook series was *Nesfield's English*

Chapter 1／Research Background: Textbook Research in an EFL Context   15

Grammar Series, originally used in secondary schools in the U.K., and subsequently brought to India by the East India Company, before being passed along to China.

1.3.2 Republic of China period (1912–1948): rapid development of textbooks compiled by Chinese scholars

The number of textbook series compiled by Chinese scholars grew rapidly during the 1920s and 1930s. In 1922, it was decided that the new school system would feature English classes from junior high school, and guidelines for textbooks and teaching methods were enacted to regulate textbook publications. The most representative textbook series can be grouped into three clusters (Liu & Wu, 2015), as follows:

① Grammar-centred textbooks: *Kaiming English Books* (1927) and *Kaiming English Grammar* (1931), *English Reader and Grammar* (1923);
② Direct Method textbooks: i.e. *The Direct Method English* series (1930), and *Model English Readers* (1930);
③ Comprehensive textbooks: *The Standard English Readers* (1930, 1935), and *Comprehensive English Readers* (1933).

In contrast with secondary school, the English textbooks used in higher education were mostly imported ones; so were the textbooks of other subjects. This situation made grammar-translation approach the main teaching method in universities. English literature books were widely used under the belief that language should be learnt through the study of classic literary works.

1.3.3 From the founding of the People's Republic of China until the 1970s (1949-1978): temporary shortage of learning materials and the politicization of English textbooks

At the onset of the founding of the People's Republic of China (PRC), Russian became dominant as a foreign language at universities, while English was replaced in high school, and suspended at the junior high school level. This was the result of a national diplomatic strategy for establishing stronger ties with the Soviet Union against the capitalist camp led by the United States. All development of English textbooks was ceased until 1956, when English regained its position of priority as the country's main foreign language. During the period of 1956 to 1963, several national common textbooks were designed for the secondary school level by People's Education Press, and English textbooks were made for the university level as well. However, the Cultural Revolution movement brought tremendous setbacks to the production of English textbooks, through its claims that revolutionary ideals and contents ought to be added onto formal textbooks, while any capitalist or traditionalist pre-revolution elements should be deleted from all textbooks. As a result, political slogans such as "Long Live Chairman Mao" were included in English textbooks.

Along with the strong growth of the country's socialist-focused development since 1957, English regained its former importance. English classes in secondary school increased from 749 periods in 1953 to 1238 periods in 1963, during which textbooks intended for the senior high school level and above were developed, as well as a 10-year and 12-year curriculum.

1.3.4 Chinese economic reform period (1978–1988): development of national English textbooks based on a constructivist theory of language teaching and learning

The famous policies for economic reform promoted by Deng Xiaoping (often referred to in Chinese language as the 'reform and opening-up' period) viewed English as the international medium of scientific and technological knowledge that held the key to China's modernization. Thus, the revival and expansion of English language education were crucial steps to allow more people to access and reap the benefits of advanced science and technology developed worldwide. The national English textbook committee drafted a tentative 10-year English teaching guideline in 1978, and compiled 6 textbooks for elementary and junior high school and 2 textbooks for high school. Each textbook was accompanied by a teachers' book. This textbook series led to the improvement of teaching quality and played a significant role in bringing forth a sense of order out of the previous chaotic situation caused by major historical events, when policies were heavily influenced by political priorities, rather than sound language-learning principles.

The Ministry of Education released another tentative 10-year English teaching guideline in 1980. The newly-compiled textbooks were put into use from 1982 until 1998. They were the longest-running set of textbooks in use after the formal declaration of the People's Republic of China in 1949. During this period, the teaching guideline was adjusted a couple of times, but textbooks were merely amended towards a slight decrease of contents. There was a need in 1986 to lower the difficulty of textbooks (to decrease the burden on learners) and clarify teaching requirements, which was reflected into new guidelines for teaching. It also defined two starting points for English learning: one was from junior-high school, and the other one from high school. To cater to high-school starters, new English textbooks for learners who only started to learn English in high school were compiled. The same national English textbooks were used nationwide from 1978 to 1992, during which its editors applied a constructivist theory of language teaching and learning when compiling them, based on their assessment of a few imported language materials.

1.3.5 National teaching guidelines period (1988–2001): cooperation with foreign publishers with a focus on language structure and function

In 1988, the first edition of the National English Teaching Guideline for 9-year Compulsory Education was released. To cater to varied needs from different areas, the Ministry of Education encouraged the editing of various styles of textbooks in line with national guideline requirements. Namely, the version of People's Education Press was used nationwide, but there was also a 'Shanghai version' used in Shanghai, a 'Guangdong version' used in Guangdong and Fujian, a 'Beijing Normal University version' used in Shangdong, and finally the 'Sichuan version' used in Sichuan in 1993. This established the start of the period known as 'multiple versions under one guideline'. Even though these different versions varied in overall features, volume, difficulty level and sequence of contents, they all adopted a structural-functional approach.

The 'People's Education Press version' resulted from the cooperation between People's Education Press in China and Longman Publishing in the U.K. It was supported by the United Nations Development Programme. This was the first English textbook series produced in cooperation with a

Chapter 1 / Research Background: Textbook Research in an EFL Context   19

foreign publisher since the implementation of the economic reform policies in 1978. The textbook series of *Junior English for China* (JEFC) was first tried out in a limited number of cities, and afterwards was adopted nationwide (except for Shanghai) after being formally authorized by the textbook evaluation committee in 1993. Meanwhile, taking into consideration the context of high school education, *Senior English for China* (SEFC) was tried out in 1993, and then authorized for use across the nation (once again with Shanghai being exempted) by the same evaluation committee in 1996. These two series were used until 2005, with only minor adjustments taking place.

The functional approach, also known as communicative approach, was advocated by European linguists in the 1980s. They developed this approach by first analysing what learners can do with language, so that the necessary relevant language forms could be determined. Based on this foundation, notional-functional syllabi were made. The functional approach focuses on the essential functions of language and is inherently learner-centred. It pushes learners to acquire a language by using it in personal and practical ways in order to develop communication competency.

1.3.6　2001–2010: increased diversity of English textbooks at the onset of the 21ˢᵗ century

The tentative national curriculum issued in 2001 required elementary schools to start English classes from grade 3 (MOE, 2001). Three contributing sociocultural factors can be linked to this policy initiative (Hu, 2005). First, it was promoted by China's upcoming grand entry into the World Trade Organization. Second, it was intended to prepare Beijing to become the next host city of the 2008 Olympic Games. Third, it was expected to improve the quality of English language teaching from an earlier stage, since not much progress had been made at the secondary level despite considerable efforts, according to a large-scale survey of English language education quality conducted in the late 1980s (Hu, 2005).

Like the policy directive of introducing English classes into elementary schools in 1978, the expansion of English language education into the compulsory education system was faced with the challenges of acute shortages of competent teachers and appropriate teaching materials. There were multiple English textbook series published in the 1990s, but in most areas the 'People's Education Press version' was still used in practice except for Shanghai. The new batch of textbooks in use, which were made in line with the revised national curriculum of 2001, has brought out a diverse swath of publishers. All in all, there are thirty textbook series for elementary schools, ten textbook series for junior high schools, and seven textbook series for senior high schools that were authorized by the Ministry of Education's textbook evaluation committee. Among these, half of them are textbooks imported and adapted from foreign publishers, while some of them are co-edited by both Chinese and foreign experts, and a small number were originally made by Chinese experts and revised by foreign experts.

An examination of recently-renewed curriculum standards reveals that communicative language teaching has been given increased prominence, and task-based teaching is now strongly advocated as a form of communicative pedagogy. Furthermore, pedagogical recommendations are now written as guiding principles rather than as detailed prescriptions, while teaching objectives are furnished with detailed descriptions.

Overall, this ongoing process towards the diversification of textbook pub-

Chapter 1 / Research Background: Textbook Research in an EFL Context   21

lications has been taking place and realized since the late 1980s. On one hand, locally-produced textbook series are available to cater for varying local needs. On the other hand, due to outdated pre-service teacher preparation and inadequate in-service support, many teachers fail to understand the underlying principles of the textbooks and they end up using them in traditional ways, without realizing their full potential.

1.3.7 2011-present: towards textbooks with Chinese characteristics in fulfilment of 2011's revised national curriculum

After 10 years of accumulated experiences, a revision of the previously tentative national curriculum was released in 2011. While devoid of radical changes, two major points are reiterated from the previous curriculum. On one hand, there is an emphasis on core socialist values, as they became more comprehensively implemented and pervasive across the contents dealt with in the subject of English. As is common in all subjects, moral education and integrity of students should be given priority, with the vigorous promotion of a well-rounded education. English as a subject has a dual attribute, namely a humanistic feature and an instrumental feature. It means English does not only function as a communication tool, but also possesses a humanistic quality that helps to cultivate students' all-round development, providing them with opportunities to: broaden their horizons and enrich their life experiences; to develop their memory, imagination, and creativity; to simultaneously establish a notion of national identity, and an awareness of and respect for cultural differences; and to build moral integrity with a healthy outlook on life. In practice, such a human-oriented concept needs to be fulfilled in more depth. This requires the valuing of each student's feelings, a caring for individual differences, and addressing all students' needs in a balanced way.

On the other hand, to foster students' practical abilities, 'learning English by using English' is recommended once again for developing a comprehensive language competence that is comprised of five objectives: *language skills, language knowledge,* positive attitude towards learning, *acquiring learning strategies,* and *cultural awareness.* Task-based teaching is suggested as an approach for engaging students in situations relevant to their life experiences and cognitive level, to enhance their ability to use English to achieve various things. Nevertheless, this approach is also criticized as unsuitable for the Chinese context (Li, 2001; Zhang, 2005; Wen, 2016), in that there are problems and obstacles when conducting task-based teaching in practice. There are calls for more efforts in searching appropriate ways to address the characteristics and issues inherent to the Chinese educational environment. Furthermore, in a similar way to the 'Can-do' list, the objectives listed in the national curriculum are divided into nine ability levels, corresponding to the attainment targets of certain grades. At the same time, the contents for teaching and learning need to be reconsidered in order to alleviate excessive study loads.

1.3.8 Summary and discussion

To summarize the historical development of both countries in terms of textbook development practices, the most significant aspects are summarised in Table 1.1 as a comparative timeline. It shows that in the beginning, both Japan and China were strongly influenced by imported English textbooks. However, they recently seem to move in opposite directions. In opposition to imported ESL textbooks, Japan chose to change course and search for an original way which better suits the specific reality of Japa-

Chapter 1／Research Background: Textbook Research in an EFL Context   23

Table 1.1: Summarised timeline of English textbook development (Japan／China).

Time period	Japan	China
1800s–1890s	Imported English textbooks for native speakers dominated and influenced the development of domestic English textbooks.	Imported English textbooks along with Chinese translations were used in foreign language schools.
1900s–1920s	Due to copyright protection issues with imported textbooks, domestic ones were made that catered to Japanese learners.	Chinese scholars became mainstream developers of English textbooks under a set of regulated guidelines. A variety of textbook series were published with different features, while still complying with regulations. Unlike the case of basic education, textbooks for higher education in all subjects were still mostly imported ones.
1930s	Given the increased demand for textbooks, there was a concerted push for improving textbook compiling skills.	
1940s	Textbooks were restricted to a limited number of publications. Western-culture related materials were included in textbooks, as well as war-related topics.	
1950s	Textbook contents were simplified together with the expansion of compulsory education. Guided by national curriculum stipulations, textbooks tended to be standardized with designated grammar and vocabulary items.	Political concerns led to Russian being set as the main foreign language until English regained its position in 1956. National common English textbooks were published by People's Education Press. Revolutionary ideas and contents were added onto English textbooks during the Cultural Revolution period.
1960s–1970s	During the economic recovery period, innovative textbooks that focused on character storylines emerged, bringing some needed variety to the textbook industry.	
1980s–1990s	To cope with a worsening crisis in school failures, curriculum contents were reduced. Instead of the previous Western cultural dominance, themes of multiculturalism and Japanese identity were introduced into textbook contents.	English teaching guidelines were designed to improve textbook compiling. English textbooks were revised to lower the burden on learners. In reference to imported language materials, a constructivist theory of language teaching and learning was applied.
1998–2007	Textbook contents made increasing efforts to relate to learners' real lives, develop their communication ability and promote a Japanese identity.	Multiple textbook series existed in different regions, but the People's Education Press version (made in cooperation with Longman Publishing) was the most popular and the longest one in use. English textbooks were introduced in elementary schools in 2001.
2008–present	Integration of the four skills is now a highlighted feature of textbooks, in accordance with national curriculum stipulations. A new set of authorized English textbooks will be introduced in elementary schools in 2020.	Regarding the development of English textbooks, each region is starting to choose different publishers to better suit their specific needs.

nese learners. China has decided to borrow the dominant features provided by imported ESL textbooks, believing that these can be adjusted to meet the needs of Chinese learners.

These different decisions have resulted in an enduring legacy. The currently-authorized English textbooks in Japan are made by independent domestic publishers. On the other hand, most authorized English textbooks in China are all the result of cooperation with foreign publishers. The process of curriculum revision and textbook renewal has continued for decades, but both nations are still facing the challenge of developing more effective EFL materials to meet societal demands and learners' needs.

One of the crucial reasons why the teaching of EFL has not reached a satisfactory outcome is that EFL education lacks a vision for language education which can articulate learners' first language (L1) with foreign languages. Therefore, it is urgent to develop teaching materials that articulate L1 and EFL. One of the ways in which this can be achieved is by focusing on metalinguistic awareness. Otsu (2009; 2010; 2011) conducted some classroom experiments that aimed to provide learners with improved metalinguistic awareness by directly comparing aspects of Japanese and English. The results of recent action research initiatives also suggest that comparing two different languages helps learners to fully grasp metalinguistic concepts in a clearer way, which should then have a positive effect on their linguistic skills (Saito et al., 2012; Akita et al., 2012; Saito et al., 2013; Akita et al., 2013; Akita et al., 2014; Wang, 2017a; 2017b; 2018a; 2018b; 2019; 2020). Otsu (1989) and Otsu & Kubozono (2008) argued that both mother tongue and foreign languages could be cultivated synergistically and effectively by encouraging learners to become aware of linguistic commonalities as well as the unique characteristics and mechanisms of each language. In addition, Candelier (2007) has also argued that the multilingual and multiculturalist education that is being increasingly cultivated in Europe can be applied to foreign language activities in EFL contexts.

For future endeavours in comparative textbook research, I argue that a more detailed analysis of textbooks needs to be conducted at each stage, in reference to the social-cultural contexts in both countries. Ideally, similarities and differences as well as chronological changes should be interpreted from various perspectives. Having realised that textbooks are primarily the materialised products of the national curriculum, the gap between what textbooks contain and what the curriculum requires should be examined, to shed light on the process of textbook evaluation and selection.

It is also worth noticing the significance of L1 use when conducting future studies of EFL materials development. According to an international survey targeting 120,000 learners in 18 countries, it was found that the more they talk about their mother tongue together with their target language, the better their academic abilities at school will be (Agirdag & Vanlaar, 2016). Also, when mastering a foreign language, Ortega (2018) has pointed out that we should place more importance on the value of the native language. Given this increasing awareness of the importance of L1 for EFL learning (Cook, 2010), a push for new language materials development along with action research programmes in real classrooms should be encouraged.

1.4 A Descriptive Analysis of Japanese and Chinese English Language Curricula

Authorized textbooks are assumed to reflect the contents embedded in the national curriculum. An analysis of the national curriculum is a prerequisite for investigating how its principles are materialized at the textbook level. This curriculum analysis also provides a base for comparison with the results of the textbook analysis that will take place in the following chapters, and allows us to check if the curriculum's requirements are being fulfilled in practice.

1.4.1 Framework for curriculum analysis

To provide better information about the foundational aspects of curriculum literature, as well as to present the practical application of valuable ideas in the process of curriculum development, Posner (1995) proposed a comprehensive framework for conducting curriculum analysis that is still well-regarded and widely taught in higher-learning institutions. His framework represents a set of questions pertaining to essential curriculum components in a manageable and coherent way. This framework derives from four fundamental questions posed by Tyler (1949) in his theory for curriculum planning, and from Johnson's (1977) improved model for the analysis of formal curricula.

Posner (1995) proposes four main parts for a successful curriculum analysis process: (1) analysis of the curriculum's documentation and origins, (2) analysis of the curriculum proper, (3) analysis of the curriculum in use, and (4) the curriculum critique.

'Curriculum documentation and origins' refers to how the curriculum is currently documented and what situations resulted in the decision to develop the curriculum in the first place. The first step is to specify the list of available documents and resources for analysis, clarify the curriculum's stated focus and look at the individuals who drafted the curriculum. Regarding the contextual issues pertaining to the curriculum, Posner asks us to describe the political, economic, social, and educational problems that prompted the formulation of the curriculum. This allows us to understand the necessity of developing a curriculum, and encourages us to consider any theoretical perspectives that were in vogue during its development.

'The curriculum proper' is concerned with the purpose, content and structure of the curriculum, as well as any underlying assumptions about it. This is meant to capture the process of designing and developing the curriculum, which requires a close examination of its educational aims, goals, and its learning objectives. By understanding how the full contents of the curriculum are organized, we can bring to the forefront the epistemological and psychological views that are embedded in it.

'Curriculum in use' is designed to help us detail the issues of curriculum implementation and evaluation. In this part, we take into consideration the requirements for implementing the curriculum in line with the values that it espouses. We also seek to answer questions about which evaluation approach should be adopted. In other words, this section is intended to help us learn about the curriculum as it is being used, from an evaluation viewpoint.

'Curriculum critique' tells us about the strengths and limitations of the curriculum that may potentially lead to its revision. It is at this phase that any concerns, critiques, and judgements about the curriculum are put forth, and in so doing, this helps us to adapt it to maximize its strengths and minimize its limitations.

1.4.2 Analysis of the 2008 English National Curriculum for junior high schools in Japan

The contemporary junior high school English curriculum in Japan was originally released in 2008, but only began to be implemented nationwide from April 2012. A four-year period was set up to allow local institutions and individual schools to have enough time and assistance to prepare for a smooth transition. The first approved textbooks based on the 2008 curriculum were only published and officially put into use in Japanese schools in 2012. It is stipulated that a comprehensive textbook revision should be carried out every four years, and therefore the 2012 textbooks were newly-revised in 2016.

Nevertheless, the 2016 textbooks were still fully based on the 2008 curriculum, which means that the 2008 English National Curriculum for junior high schools issued by MEXT is the main object of analysis in this section.

We will now delve into each of Posner's four-part framework in detail, starting with the Japanese curriculum.

① *Curriculum documentation and origins (JPN)*

The core documents that serve as basis for this analysis are the 2008 English national curriculum for junior high school (Course of Study), and other officially-released documents featuring additional explanations related to the teaching of foreign language disciplines. Although the relevant section in the curriculum is titled as 'foreign languages', it actually refers exclusively to the teaching of English; the teaching of all other foreign languages should follow the same regulations. The basic procedures for elaborating the Japanese curriculum are shown in Figure 1.2.

Every 10 years, the curriculum is revised. In response to an advisory request from the minister of MEXT, the Japanese Central Council for Education submits a deliberation report after a continuous process of meetings. A list of items marked for revision is proposed according to the findings of the deliberation report. Once there is a general agreement on the revisions that should be made, there is a period in which public comments and ap-

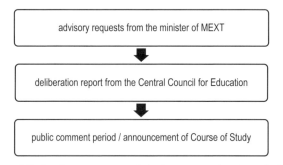

Figure 1.2: Development stages of the Japanese national curriculum.

Chapter 1 / Research Background: Textbook Research in an EFL Context   29

praisals can be submitted, and after taking such comments into account, a final version of the new curriculum is released. For this reason, I have taken into consideration a few additional materials, which are preliminary documents pertaining to the curriculum's revisions, including the most recent advisory requests from MEXT and subsequent deliberation reports from the Central Council for Education.

2008 English national curriculum for junior high school (MEXT, 2008a) defines the objectives, contents and considerations that relate to lesson plan design. Its contents consist of language activities and language elements, as well as instruction suggestions of how to implement them in practice. *Explanation of English discipline* (MEXT, 2008b) explains the background, basic intent and key points of the changes made to the curriculum. It also provides a thorough elaboration on the curriculum's contents and how to treat them. *Deliberation report from the Central Council for Education* (Central Council for Education, 2008) states some essential points related to general curriculum changes, revised principles for each subject, and requests for implementation depending on the educational context.

Identifying the curriculum developers enables us to grasp which areas of expertise were brought into the development phase. There is no direct nor explicit information provided about the curriculum developers, but a list of members comprising the foreign language division within the Central Council for Education is publicly available. It is assumed that these members are involved with English curriculum development, since the Central Council for Education is the main advisory body for curriculum design. There are 21 members in the foreign language division, as listed in Table 1.2. They gathered for 18 meetings to discuss issues related to the English language curriculum from 2004–2007.

30

Table 1.2: Members of the foreign language division, Central Council of Education (2004-2007).

Names	Affiliation	Specialty area
Hideo Oka	Professor, University of Tokyo	English education
Osamu Kageura	Professor, University of Miyazaki	English education
Ken Kanatani	Professor, Tokyo Gakugei University	English education
Tsuyoshi Kanamori	Professor, Ehime University	Language policy
Yukiko Shima	Professor, Sanyo-Onoda City University	Linguistics
Yoshimi Sugimoto	Assistant Professor, Kyoto University of Foreign Studies	Classroom teaching
Tetsuo Tamura**	Principal, Shibuya Junior & Senior High School	Education
Haku Taroura	Principal, Kasai Junior High School	Classroom teaching
Mineo Nakajima*	President, Akita International University	Social studies
Tomoko Nakano	Advisor, Council on International Educational Exchange	English education
Suzuko Nishihara	Professor, Tokyo Woman's Christian University	Linguistics
Hiroko Hakiwara	Assistant Professor, Tokyo Metropolitan University	Linguistics
Reiko Matsukawa	Professor, Gifu University	Education
Shigeru Matsumoto	Professor, Tokai University	Communication
Takashi Muto	President, Shiraume Gakuen University	Psychology
Shibuyuki Honna	Professor, Aoyama Gakuin University	Linguistics
Kouichi Monma	Principal, Narita Elementary School	Classroom teaching
Kenji Yamaoka	Vice Principal, Kusatsu Higashi High School	Classroom teaching
Kensaku Yoshida	Dean of Faculty of Foreign Studies, Sophia University	Linguistics
Hirohiko Yoshida	Director, NPO Supporting Union for Practical Use of Educational Resources	Education
Yoji Tanabe	Professor, Tokyo International University	Linguistics

* Chief **Deputy Chief

Schwab (1971) stresses that, ideally, five types of interested parties should be involved in curriculum development: learners, teachers, academics related to the subject matter, representatives from the educational milieu, and curriculum coordinators. As shown in Table 1.2, the specialty area of each member was gathered from their personal introduction pages at the websites of institutions to which they are affiliated. Four members specialised in classroom teaching have former experience as English teachers, so they can also be considered as representatives for the teacher community. There are six members specialised in linguistics, and four members specialised in English education that represent the subject matter at hand. Team members that have majored in psychology, social studies and communication can be said to represent the educational milieu. The other four members linked to education and language policies may function as

Chapter 1 / Research Background: Textbook Research in an EFL Context   31

coordinators, or contribute to discussions about the milieu as well. Since there are no clear accounts of each person's specific roles in the development of this curriculum, it is not appropriate to speculate on what exactly each representative did, but we can still become aware of any potential blind spots that were not represented in the meetings. In this case, we find that no representatives from the learner community were found to be directly involved in the process of curriculum development. This is an important issue, since the curriculum was designed in the first place to target all students in the country, and it constitutes compulsory education.

Any brand-new curriculum, or its revision, can be thought of as an attempt to respond to a set of increasingly disruptive problems or situations. This means that the solutions proposed in the curriculum provide certain clues, from which we can deduce the problematic issues that are meant to be addressed. In fact, as a common reason for changing the national curriculum for all subjects (and not just that of English), the *deliberation report* states that efforts must be made to better mobilise the country's present resources pertaining to students, teachers, and schools, based on societal changes and the actual situation of students, in order to attain universal education goals. In reference to the OECD PISA scores, there are five issues that have been made apparent (CCE, 2008).

① MEXT did not sufficiently clarify the significance and necessity of the 'zest for life' concept, resulting in a lack of general recognition and understanding.

② There is a real possibility that teachers have over-valued the autonomy of their pupils, resulting in their hesitance to discipline some children.

③ Poor implementation of measures that could improve the synergies between 'knowledge / skill attainments' for each subject, and 'exploratory activities / problem-solving endeavours' during periods of integrated study.

④ There are not enough classes that allow for the cultivation of applied learning skills within each subject, such as: observation, experimentation, reporting, and dissertation.

⑤ Insufficient attention was paid to the fact that a significant number of homes and communities no longer have enough educational capacity to nurture a rich spirit and healthy body.

In accordance with these five problems, *Explanation of English Discipline* provides remarks of a similar nature that justify the need for revisions. In the current paradigm of a globalised knowledge-based society, there is an acceleration of international competition for knowledge and highly-skilled human resources. This increases the need for better co-existence and collaboration among different cultures, which requires learners to cultivate a zest for life comprising of solid academic prowess, an enriched humanitarian spirit and a concern for maintaining one's personal health & fitness. Furthermore, it is recognised that the teaching system has faced difficulties in encouraging students to incorporate the individual skills that they acquire at school into comprehensive strategies for solving more complex problems. Therefore, the document concludes with four principles aimed at revising the English curriculum.

① It is necessary to promote instructions aimed at balancing the four skills in a comprehensive manner, so that learners can effectively convey messages through communication.

② It is important to select teaching materials that can enhance students' motivation for learning, and enrich the expressiveness of their contents in order to cultivate the four skills in a comprehensive way.

③ As a basis for communication, grammar instruction should be conducted together with language activities in order to gain better communication abilities.

④ In addition to listening and speaking, reading and writing should be carried out in a balanced way; in doing so, it is important to connect the knowledge that students have already achieved during elementary school with the basic aspects that they need to master for further learning in high school.

In order to realize these principles, one class per week in each grade year was added (thereby increasing the total number of yearly classes from 105 to 140), and the number of vocabulary items required to study was also increased from 900 to 1200 for junior high school. This boost in the number of classes and vocabulary items is meant to expand students' awareness of various topics and scenarios in which communication activities can take place, which is expected to make the language activities at school more enriching and meaningful. In sum, it can be said that the main point of change in this curriculum is to provide learners with enough language activities that focus on balancing the four skills.

The way in which the curriculum is structured and the amount of emphasis given to each of its categories both reflect the planning elements that developers choose to prioritise. In the English curriculum document itself, it is the contents of language activities and language elements that dominate the planning scheme. There is one overall objective which is for learners to develop the four skills, while improving their understanding of language and culture, and developing a positive attitude towards learning and communication with others. The basic structure of the curriculum is presented in Figure 1.3.

The curriculum provides a list of language activities that should be conducted over the total period of three years in order to develop a practical command of English; these activities are distributed according to each of the four skills. The reason for the use of a global three-year period is so that each school can have the freedom to assign learning contents for each year, according to its possibilities. The characteristics of the target students are also considered, in the sense that in each of the three grade levels, there are special recommendations for teachers to follow when planning and carrying out language activities.

As for language elements, these include *speech sounds, letters, symbols & words, collocations & common expressions*, and *grammatical items*. Teachers are supposed to select from the list of language elements the

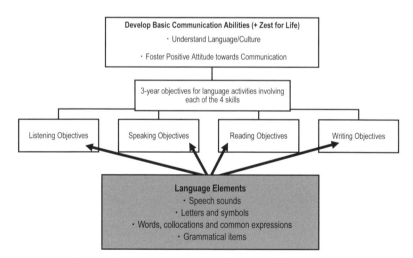

Figure 1.3: Basic structure of the Japanese EFL curriculum.

Chapter 1 / Research Background: Textbook Research in an EFL Context   35

items that are most suitable for designing language activities related to the four skills. The emphasis given in the curriculum to these language contents and activities shows that they were the dominant elements in the planning process.

② *The curriculum proper (JPN)*

When designing a curriculum, some of its parts may offer help and guidelines intended for the *training* of students, while other parts are intended for the *education* of students. To clarify, *training* and *education* are terms used to make a distinction between predictable situations and unpredictable situations that the students are expected to deal with when learning. 'Training' refers to contexts of predictable situations in which students will use what they learn. In this case, the curriculum provides a list of specific tasks that students are expected to perform in pragmatic situations, such as daily activities (ex: asking and giving directions, travelling, ordering in restaurants, answering phones, etc.) or what is called 'familiar language-use situations'.

As for 'education', this term refers to contexts of unpredictable situations in which students must apply what they learn. As opposed to the more pragmatic aspects of 'training', 'education' is about cultivating all-round reasoning skills such as critical thinking, and language learning, which usually requires students to deepen their understanding of Japanese language as well. In essence, 'education' deals with skills that will prove to be useful to the learner when dealing with unexpected situations. In this aspect of education, the stipulations of the curriculum are presented in a much more broad and general way.

The purpose of the English curriculum is to develop students' basic communication abilities, to deepen their understanding of language and culture, to foster a positive attitude toward communication using English, and to be able to communicate Japanese culture to foreigners. Due to its position in compulsory education, English is one of the subjects that students must engage with in order to prepare themselves for future jobs (and other pragmatic situations), which places it within the purview of 'training'.

For students to express themselves in English, there should be situations outside of the classroom where they can use their language skills; however, not all students are meant to involve English in their daily lives or jobs. English is not used daily in EFL countries like Japan; therefore, what students learn in the classroom can hardly be employed in the real world, unless English communicative needs are demanded by most of the job market, or unless there are drastic changes in the demographics of the country's population. To cater to those students who don't use English after graduating, the curriculum needs to include educational purposes, rather than focus on 'training' aspects related to pragmatic situations.

Societal and administrative goals are not explicitly addressed throughout the English curriculum; most of its goals are expressed at the level of educational aims, educational goals, and learning objectives. According to Article 1 of the first chapter in the *Basic Act on Education* (MEXT, 2006), the general educational aim of the Japanese government is to cultivate both mentally and physically healthy citizens and develop their individual character, which are crucial steps for forming a peaceful and democratic society and nation. The following three purposes of English curriculum as a subject are stated as educational goals:

① To deepen students' understanding of language and culture;

Chapter 1 / Research Background: Textbook Research in an EFL Context　　37

② To foster a positive attitude toward communication;
③ To develop students' basic communication abilities such as listening, speaking, reading and writing.

The more detailed learning objectives are enumerated in the four points below. They describe the learning objectives for a total of three academic years, to allow each school to determine the most suitable grade objectives for their students' levels. We can see that there is a clear emphasis here on language use for communication.

① To enable students to understand the speaker's intentions when listening to English.
② To enable students to talk about their own thoughts using English.
③ To accustom and familiarize students with reading English and to enable them to understand the writer's intentions when reading English.
④ To accustom and familiarize students with writing in English and to enable them to write about their own thoughts using English.

The 2008 English National Curriculum for junior high school focuses on Bloom's (1956) cognitive domains. Of the six cognitive classes, the curriculum focuses on *knowledge, comprehension,* and *application.* Regarding knowledge, it lists out a few language elements suitable for the attainment of its learning objectives, including speech sounds, letters and symbols, words, collocations and common expressions, and grammatical items. To improve learners' comprehension rates, language activities are required to consider the circumstances of students and the local community. To further encourage the application of these language elements in schools, the curriculum suggests that teaching materials and learning activities should consider actual language-use situations and functions of language in order to comprehensively cultivate communication abilities.

The term *hidden curriculum* refers to norms, values and beliefs that are not openly stated in the curriculum, but are nevertheless implicitly conveyed in classrooms, textbooks and in the social environment. Since most aspects of a hidden curriculum relate to its implementation phase, and there is still a lack of evaluation data and academic studies, it is hard to provide any definitive statements on this issue. There are some studies dealing with aspects of 'hidden curricula' within the Japanese Course of Study as a whole (Hishikari, 2018; Ujihara, 2011 and 2013; Takahiro, Kohei and Fumio, 2015), but if we search only for studies that discuss the English curriculum, there is much less information available. One might point out a short study of two series of EFL textbooks conducted by Jackie F.K. Lee (2014) with results that suggest the existence of gendered messaging and imbalances in gender representation in textbooks, but the most relevant study for our purposes is that of Urata and Kojima (2016). It points out how ingrained cultural behaviours are preventing Japanese learners from acquiring healthy habits that can allow them to thrive in a globalised world. According to the authors, Japanese children refuse to clearly say either 'yes' or 'no'; if they are asked a question, they remain silent; they avoid taking the initiative to start a conversation; they avoid looking at the other person; they tend to adopt a sad or depressed posture; and they feel nervous and anxious when talking in front of other people. All these ingrained cultural behaviours are trespassing into the domain of English education, which severely hampers the learners' chances of improving their communication skills.

As possible suggestions for improvement, Urata and Kojima recommend creating learning practices in which children can fully realise that their behaviours are 'Japanese-like', and therefore are not typical of most Western cultures; and understand that such behaviours are ingrained and can be changed depending on the context. It seems that a direct comparison of ingrained behaviours that hamper personal development could be done in a way that does not attribute any degree of superiority to either the Japanese or Western cultures.

As a government-issued policy document, the curriculum is expected to play a leading role in the implementation of changes in English education. It already determines the main contents of English language skills, which constitutes the core part of language learning; but for most other aspects, there are only recommendations for best practice, and schools have a good degree of freedom to decide class schedules, as well as the details of lesson plans and learning activities that best fit the characteristics of the educational milieu. Nevertheless, it is fair to say that the Japanese curriculum is unmistakably a top-down document, since it does not make any explicit mention of any other organizations that can unilaterally modify it. The only entity that can implement changes to the curriculum is MEXT itself, although we can expect that it will conduct surveys regularly in order to gather external opinions. On the other hand, according to Paul Underwood (2012) the implementation process is likely to face significant obstacles due to systemic problems with the Japanese educational system (ex: excessive workload, etc.) and a 'generational clash' between younger teachers and their seniors.

Morris and Adamson (2010) have summarized a list of five main ideologies that are dominant in the curricula of most nations. These are the following: *academic rationalism; social and economic efficiency; child-centred ideology; social reconstructionism;* and *orthodoxy/ideological transfer.* In the Japanese curriculum, I find that its focus lies on 'child-centred ideology', combined with elements of 'academic rationalism' (scientific, fact-based learning). This is made clear by the curriculum's statements, which promote: the personal and intellectual development of learners; a focus on 'knowledge' as a holistic domain (instead of transmitting knowledge to learners as fragmented and disconnected pieces within each subject); a focus on teaching learners how to learn; and a focus on activities.

Regarding the aspect of activities, the curriculum argues that learning is best achieved by *doing,* and learning should be based on content that is *meaningful* to learners. Learners should make use of their whole bodies by participating in simulated situations that provide context for the words they pronounce. Under this rationale, a learner will memorize and understand a sentence pattern much more effectively if he/she pronounces it within a simulated context (based on a real-life situation that they are familiar with), compared to a learner that tries to memorize that same pattern by merely reading it from a textbook. Likewise, a new vocabulary item is best remembered by studying it within the context of a full sentence that is meaningful to the learner. This means that the learner is trying to embed a new, unknown piece of information into a memory (of an experience) that is already well-established in the learner's mind. This sort of learning is generally known in scientific literature as 'mnemonic strategies' (Thomas E. Scruggs *et al.*, 2010).

Two topics that are often discussed when addressing the relationships between curricula and the human psyche are those of identity and mental well-being. Multiculturalism (as proposed by North American societies) is

Chapter 1 / Research Background: Textbook Research in an EFL Context   41

not a concept strongly espoused by the Japanese EFL curriculum; it clearly states that, although learners should develop respect for other cultures and ways of viewing the world, the teaching materials should also heighten the 'students' awareness of being Japanese citizens living in a global community'. Therefore, the curriculum aims to reinforce a strong sense of Japanese national identity in learners, but tries to balance it respectfully with other national identities in a positive manner through the idea of cooperation. The fictional situations shown in textbooks therefore should stress the idea of cooperation and comparison of cultural differences. This does not necessarily mean that, for example, Japanese learners are to be exposed to the diverse cultures and identities that exist within the United States, Canada, or Australia, nor discuss their social problems. It is implied that, whenever possible, the learning contents should focus on *positive values* when discussing cultural differences.

Besides this, the curriculum tries to balance the importance of individual development with that of cooperating with other learners through pair work and group work. It recommends that learners discuss ideas with each other, and suggests that differences between people should be seen in a positive light. Furthermore, the learner-centred approach promotes the importance of maintaining the mental and physical well-being of students.

③ *The curriculum in use (JPN)*

The curriculum only provides language-skill objectives for a total of three academic years, and allows schools to design syllabi and lesson plans that distribute those objectives for each year as they find most suitable. Also, the number of required classes per year has been stipulated as 140. It does not make any demands in terms of physical spaces, other than imply that language activities are to take place at schools, and that teachers should take advantage of school facilities such as libraries when designing tasks and learning activities, if possible.

The curriculum states the importance of moral education and the teaching of Japanese cultural identity, but it is not clear how in practice this will affect minorities such as the Ainu and migrant communities. Likewise, it argues for the respect of cultural differences, but does not state explicitly what Japanese cultural values should be. It is assumed that local schools will use the Moral Education Act as a basis for adapting the curriculum to suit their local demographic contexts.

The analysed documents do not provide much clear information from which we can fully understand the approaches towards curriculum change. In a report on the elaboration of a reform plan for English education (MEXT, 2014), it is said that the ongoing phenomenon of globalization and the incoming Olympic Games of 2020 have prompted the urgent improvement of the communicative competence of Japanese citizens. The document states the following:

> *Japanese people should expect to achieve top-level English proficiency in Asia. Under the reform of English education, not only the cultivation of fundamental knowledge and skills, but also such abilities as to reason, make decisions or express oneself in order to solve problems by oneself will be inevitable.*

As a result, the revision committee elaborated 5 major revision points:
① *Goals presented by the government and the improvement of the contents of education.* The aim is to provide coherent education goals so that there is a smooth transition between elementary, ju-

Chapter 1／Research Background: Textbook Research in an EFL Context   43

nior high and high school education. The standard for measuring students' proficiency is the result of official tests such as Eiken or TOEFL iBT, which can better reflect the needs of the job market around the time that students graduate from high school.

② *Improvement of teaching and evaluation at school.* Schools must encourage students so that they do not become afraid of making mistakes. Instead of elaborating only 'Can-do' lists, schools may include attainment descriptors in the lists that express students' attempts to achieve something, such as 'the student tries to do…using English'.

③ *Improvement of English proficiency evaluation and entrance examination at high schools and universities.* The government will encourage the use of English language certifications and qualifications that focus on a balanced use of the four skills, and likewise it will encourage entrance examinations at high schools and universities to evaluate communication skills in terms of the four skills. The reason for this is to improve the degree of consistency among all examinations.

④ *Improvement of textbooks and educational materials.* Teaching materials should contain elements that help teachers devise language activities, such as presentations, and offer more explanations, which can improve learners' reasoning skills and digital literacy skills.

⑤ *Enhancement of the education system at schools.* This means the improvement of regional education systems by conducting more training seminars in cooperation with local universities and other relevant institutions. Another measure is to arrange for temporary teacher exchanges between elementary school and junior high school to create a smoother transition for students. Attempts will be made to allow for more ALT participation in elementary English classes whenever possible. And finally, there is a clear need to develop better university curricula for training school teachers.

From these five revision points, the clear mainstays are that the results of official English certification tests and entrance examinations should represent the standard of proficiency to which learners should aspire, and that all efforts should be made to mobilize schools, teachers, ALTs, exam planners and textbook designers to design learning activities and exams that balance the four skills adequately. These revisions strongly suggest that the current problems are not necessarily related to the curriculum's chosen approach, but rather that there has been some systemic resistance on behalf of schools and teachers towards adopting the approach and goals of the curriculum.

④ *Critique (JPN)*

If one were to point out a limitation of the curriculum, it is that it does not try to include more explanations and suggestions of how to create learning activities that make full use of the communicative approach. There is also a need to provide professional development programs for teachers to become more comfortable in implementing the curriculum. Furthermore, the curriculum does not sufficiently detail the issues caused by ingrained Japanese behaviours in students that hamper the development of their communicative skills.

1.4.3 Analysis of the 2011 English National Curriculum for compulsory education in China

The current junior high school English curriculum in China was originally released at the end of 2011, but only began to be fully implemented nationwide in September 2012. Both elementary schools and junior high schools are covered in the same curriculum for compulsory education. It is the revision of a former document that had been adopted on a trial basis in 2001, which included stipulations for all school subjects. The first batch of approved textbooks based on the revised 2011 curriculum were published in 2012, which are still used in schools today.

Perhaps the most important development of the 2011 curriculum was a push towards *quality-driven education* as opposed to *exam-driven education*. The term 'quality' means that English education should play a role in the all-round development of learners, as they try to develop cognitive and reasoning skills that can help them to become more informed citizens, who can better deal with unexpected situations. This required a shift towards acknowledging the importance of developing learners' moral character, interest for learning, and cultivating good habits (MOE, 2012). It also includes the teaching of core socialist values such as 'equality', 'justice' and 'rule of law'. Accordingly, the 2011 curriculum attempts to integrate the teaching of English language skills with positive values/moral aspects, and lowered the difficulty requirements for some of the language skills to reduce the burden on students.

Another major change in the 2011 curriculum was a shift from 'content standards' to 'graded standards'. In other words, language contents such as vocabulary and grammar items represented the standard by which the knowledge of learners was evaluated. These language contents are usually conveyed by the teacher to students in a passive manner, which is a defining characteristic of an education system focused on preparation for exams. Although such language contents are still present in the 2011 curriculum, now the focus lies on mastering abilities/skills that can be applied outside of exams. For each language skill, there is a list of short sentences that define the concrete targets or objectives for each ability in the form of a 'Can-do' list. These learning objectives are generally named as either *targets* or *attainment descriptors* (or merely 'descriptors'), and are ordered by grades/levels of increasing difficulty. The language contents are also organised by grades.

Based on early investigations conducted by the curriculum revision team (Wang Q., 2012) it is known that most surveyed individuals held positive attitudes towards the 2001 curriculum, and therefore it was decided that the 2011 curriculum would keep the same basic structure and system with graded objectives. The same investigations pointed out that there were difficulties in applying the curriculum, and that there was a need for clear teaching instructions to help teachers prepare their activities. In response, the 2011 curriculum added more detailed descriptions of learning contents, and provided teaching instructions along with examples of activities, lesson plans and evaluation guidelines for elementary school.

Based on the results of the investigations, it can be said that since 2001 there have been meaningful improvements in English education. However, in the 10 years that followed the implementation of the 2001 curriculum, five main issues remained unsolved:

① The main concept of the new curriculum, which is *quality-driven education*, has not yet been fully manifested into meaningful learning activities in classrooms;

② There are still strong imbalances and development gaps among various schools and regions;

③ The professional development of teachers needs to be taken into better consideration, since there is a need to ensure more consistency in the quality and quantity of teachers at elementary schools;

Chapter 1 / Research Background: Textbook Research in an EFL Context   47

④   More attention should be given towards improving teaching quality and assessing its effects on learners;

⑤   There is an urgent demand for reforming the current evaluation system.

In the same manner as the Japanese curriculum, Posner's framework (1995) will be used to produce a descriptive analysis of the Chinese curriculum. Due to lack of data, not all questions can be fully answered, and in some cases I have resorted to studies from the period of 2001 to 2012 in order to provide some hypotheses that could clarify about the current situation of the English curriculum.

① *Curriculum documentation and origins (CHN)*

The main object of analysis in this section is the *2011 English National Curriculum for Compulsory Education* for junior high school, issued by the Chinese Ministry of Education (MOE). Another important document that was consulted is the *Explanation of 2011 English National Curriculum for Compulsory Education.*

The process of how this curriculum was revised is shown in Figure 1.4. After the trial version was released in 2001, surveys were carried out with students, parents, teachers, and principals in 2003 and 2007 to better understand how it was being implemented in practice. Based on the survey results, the revision team made a list of major principles and core points that needed to be revised. In essence, the priority of moral education throughout all the subjects was emphasised, and the quantity of curriculum contents had to be adjusted to alleviate the burden of students.

MOE set up three divisions (Leadership Committee, Consultant Commit-

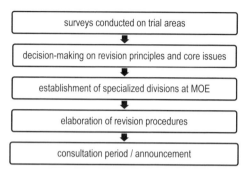

Figure 1.4: The development process of the 2011 Chinese curriculum.

tee and Executive Committee of Basic Education Curriculum and Teaching Materials) comprised of 172 experts that contained curriculum revision teams for each subject. Throughout the revision period, the revision team members held various consultation meetings and received comments and feedback from teachers, administrative departments, educational research centres, textbook publishers, and other relevant parties.

As secondary documents, I have consulted for this analysis section a conclusive report written by the English curriculum revision team, and a few papers published by the revision team members (these documents will be described later in this section). It is worth noticing that the names of the curriculum revision team members have not been made clear publicly, although some of them could be identified through media interviews and self-reported claims in public lectures and publications.

2012 English National Curriculum for Compulsory Education (MOE, 2012a) defines the following aspects: the main features of English as a school subject; the principles of curriculum design; overall objectives and graded objectives; standards for each educational level; and suggestions for teaching, evaluation, compilation of teaching materials and development of curriculum resources. In addition, nine appendixes are provided with the curriculum, including lists with phonetic items, grammatical items, vocabulary items, notional-functional items, topics, lesson demonstration examples, evaluation examples, and recommendations for teaching skills in classrooms.

Explanation of 2011 English National Curriculum for Compulsory Education (MOE, 2012b) begins with a review of achievements made during the last 10 years of English curriculum reform, then introduces the core principles and processual stages of the curriculum's revision. Apart from this, it also gives a thorough elaboration of each part of the revised curriculum.

A conclusive report for approval, written by the English curriculum revision team in August 2010, presents the results of preliminary surveys, as well as revision principles and revision contents. Two published journal papers, *Meanings of Learning English* (Wang Q., 2012) and *What is New in English Curriculum Revision* (English Curriculum Revision Team, 2012) were authored by the English curriculum revision team. Another published journal paper, *English Education for Students' Life-Long and Full-Person Development* (Chen, 2011), was written by Chen Lin, who is the leader of the English curriculum revision team. These three journal papers allow us to interpret the main changes and significant points of this curriculum revision.

Like Japan, no officially-written descriptions were found that clarified the rationale or philosophy behind the commission's choices in terms of learning objectives and contents, or why they are important. Likewise, there are no explanations for why the standards for different levels were established in this way. Finally, there are no mentions about the sequencing of contents (that is, in what order the contents should be learnt).

There is no direct nor explicit information about the curriculum developers, but Qiang Wang, a core member of the English curriculum revision team, revealed in one of her lectures (Wang Q., 2012) that there were 10 members in the team, of which five came from the former curriculum development team, and the other five were new members. They gathered 21 times to discuss issues regarding English curriculum revision between 2007 and 2010. It was possible to positively identify five individuals, since they reported to be team members in some of their publications. Their names, affiliations, and specialty areas are listed in Table 1.3.

The specialty areas of each member were gathered from their self-introduction pages attached to the websites of their affiliated academic institutions. Four of the members who are specialized in the field of English education are professors at universities, and for the most part, that is where their teaching experiences come from; their academic credentials and achievements allow us to place them as representatives for the subject matter of English. Jingchun Li has had a long teaching experience within schools, which makes him a suitable representative for teachers. Because so little information has been made publicly available, it was not possible to find representatives of the educational milieu, or any representatives of the

Table 1.3: Incomplete list of members of the 2011 English curriculum revision team (2007-2010).

Names	Affiliation	Specialty area
Lin Chen*	Professor, Beijing Foreign Studies University	English education
Qiang Wang	Professor, Beijing Normal University	English education
Xiaotang Cheng	Professor, Beijing Normal University	English education
Lianzhong Zhang	Professor, Beijing Foreign Studies University	English education
Jingchun Li	Researcher, People's Education Press	Classroom teaching

* Chief

Chapter 1／Research Background: Textbook Research in an EFL Context   51

learner community that were directly involved in the process of curriculum development.

Given the large size of the country, the difficulties of implementing educational reforms at such a large scale, and the fact that the revision incorporated the results of surveys in test areas, we must admit the possibility that no such representatives were ever a part of the revision team. This assertion is supported by a paper written by Yongqi Gu (2012) stating that in previous years, there has been very little cooperation between the various interested parties; because most of Chinese society considers entrance exams to be the best way to ensure a fair result in terms of university admission, test developers tend to conduct their work in secrecy and avoid sharing information with the other main parties, which are curriculum developers and classroom teachers. Gu further states that communication channels between these three parties tend to be very limited and inadequate, which has made it difficult to implement the curriculum standards adequately. No data or studies are available from recent years, so it is unclear at this stage whether the situation has improved or not.

In the same way as other subjects, the English curriculum is meant to be revised after a ten-year period. Based on a series of school visits, investigation surveys and interviews, the English curriculum revision team listed three problems that had to be addressed (English curriculum revision committee, 2010). First, the former curriculum had a lack of instructions and suggestions for English teaching in elementary schools. The former curriculum for compulsory education included both the elementary and junior high school levels, but no separate vocabulary nor grammatical items lists were ever provided for each level. Responding to this point, the revised English curriculum consists of separate content lists and adaptable suggestions and examples.

Second, the revision team received conflicting feedback regarding the quantity and difficulty of learning contents. For example, some stated that writing requirements for a certain level were too high, while others thought it was low. The unbalanced distribution of the country's economy and educational resources results in different satisfaction rates and diverse attitudes towards the former curriculum. Regarding this point, the revised English curriculum lowers the requirement level for some basic knowledge and skills, but also increases the flexibility of the curriculum by creating attainment targets for each administrative area. The third issue was that the statements and descriptions in the curriculum had to be made more accurate and rigorous. Accordingly, the revisers of the English curriculum made a concerted effort to clarify the text.

During the revision period, a fundamental education policy titled *Outline of China's National Plan for Medium and Long-term Education Reform and Development (2010-2020)* (State Council, 2010) was released. It points out the following three strategic themes to guide the process of education reform and development, by focusing on putting people first, and fully implementing quality-oriented education (as opposed to exam-oriented education).

①　*Always put moral education first.* The core socialist values, expressed in 12 keywords or phrases,[1] should be incorporated into the national education standard.

②　*Emphasise the building of capabilities in students.* It is essential to enhance the students' capability to learn, practice, and innovate

---

[1]　These 12 Chinese terms can be translated as: *prosperity, democracy, civility, harmony, freedom, equality, justice, rule of law, patriotism, dedication, integrity,* and *friendship.*

in order to enable them to adapt to the society on their own and create a beautiful future.

③ *To focus on the all-round development of learners.* Students' overall qualities and character should be well-developed through moral education, intellectual education, physical education, and aesthetic education.

In accordance with these three strategic themes, the revised English curriculum states the significance of English curriculum for the whole nation's development as well as that of individual students. By stressing both the instructional and humanistic functions of learning English, it declares that learning a foreign language means not just learning a communication tool, but it also should facilitate the all-round development of the learners. This notion is written in the preface as follows (MOE, 2010:1):

With the tendency of global multi-polarization and a globalized economy in the advent of the information age, there are radical transformations undergoing. As a major country committed to peaceful development, China is responsible for contributing to this historical mission and international duty. Being the most widely spoken language all over the world, English is the dominant carrier of information. Therefore, an English curriculum in compulsory education can enhance the quality of national citizens, cultivate innovative and cross-cultural communicative talents, and strengthen China's international competitiveness and the communication capability of Chinese citizens. At the same time, it plays an essential role in fulfilling the potentials of individual students. Learning English can not only help them to know the world and connect with foreign people, but also assist them to activate their thinking skills, and form a correct perspective of the world, of life and of values. This enables them to adapt to

the changing international society and work out a brighter future.
(Translated by the author)

In the same way as Japan, the Chinese government's concerns for the effects of globalization on its society were a pressing factor in their planning decisions for the curriculum. If there is one aspect that should be singled out from the whole curriculum, it is that learners must become independent, self-reliant agents who can devise strategies to adapt to a rapidly-changing world, and not overly depend on the government for support. Since the populations in both countries are decreasing (which also reduces tax revenue), and their economies are transitioning from agriculture and manufacturing towards services, the respective governments find themselves struggling to invest in infrastructure and public service jobs as ways to absorb low-skilled labour. This correlates with the adoption of recent immigration policies that are designed to attract more highly-skilled foreigners into China, in detriment of unskilled labourers. Therefore, the Chinese curriculum is asking learners to become more innovative and seek their own development by creating (or proactively seeking) their own means of sustenance.

One more crucial aspect in which the curriculum seems to be influenced by the needs of a globalised job market is the growth of English in East Asia as a non-Western-centric language. This means that English is not necessarily used by Chinese to talk to Westerners, but to talk to other East Asians, which means that during such interactions, the Western cultural overtones of English play a reduced role. David Gradoll, in an analysis of trends in English learning across the globe for the digital publication *English Next* (2008), argued that there is a global form of English emerging

Chapter 1 / Research Background: Textbook Research in an EFL Context   55

in Asia, because the number of Asian speakers of English is growing expo-
nentially in India and China. On one hand, the fact that the English language is distancing itself from a Western-centric perspective poses a great
concern for the British and North Americans, since due to complacency,
few of them have bothered to master a second language, and are therefore
not prepared to complete in the global market. On the other hand, it means
that for Asians, just knowing basic English grammar is no longer enough
to guarantee a higher-level job. Having relationship-building skills, a desire
for learning new skills, and a resilient spirit have become crucial factors for
achieving success in the international job marketplace.

Even though the curriculum aims to promote the understanding and respect of cultural differences, the fact is that these cultural differences no
longer mean 'Asians vs. Westerners', but primarily cultural differences
within Asia itself, especially as China ramps up its infrastructure-building
projects across its neighbouring countries as part of the 'Belt and Road' initiative. As a result of these developments, we can expect to see soon some
clashes between Western-centric and Asian-centric teaching approaches, as
textbook publishing companies and higher-learning institutions of both regions fight for dominance in the global stage.

The curriculum claims to follow the international practice of dividing
overall objectives into different ability levels. The five overall objectives for
developing students' comprehensive language competence are: 1) language
skills, 2) language knowledge, 3) attitudes towards learning, 4) learning
strategies and 5) cultural awareness.

Figure 1.5 shows the structure of the five overall objectives, and Table
1.4 shows the correspondence between grades and levels in compulsory
and non-compulsory education.

Each of these five overall objectives are further divided into five ability levels within compulsory education (nine in total, if we include non-compulsory education), and descriptors for each level are provided, which function

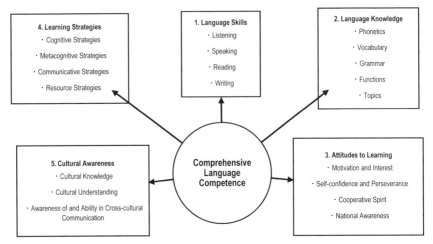

Figure 1.5: Diagram of the five general objectives and sub-objectives in the Chinese EFL curriculum.

Table 1.4: Correspondence between grades and ability levels in compulsory (Grades 3–9) and non-compulsory education (Grades 10–12) in China. Based on Gu (2012: 43).

Senior Secondary	Grade 12 (Foreign Language Schools)	Level 9	External Exam
	Grade 12 (Senior Secondary 3)	Level 8	External Exam Level for University Entry
	Grade 11 (Senior Secondary 2)	Level 7	External Exam Level for Graduation
	Grade 10 (Senior Secondary 1)	Level 6	
Junior Secondary	Grade 9	Level 5	External Exam Level for Graduation
	Grade 8	Level 4	
	Grade 7	Level 3	
Primary School	Grades 5-6	Level 2	
	Grades 3-4	Level 1	

Chapter 1／Research Background: Textbook Research in an EFL Context   57

as graded attainment standards. To achieve these attainment standards, the revised document provides suggestions regarding instruction, evaluation, teaching materials and curriculum development.

There are two lists of descriptors: *overall descriptors* and *detailed descriptors.* 'Overall descriptors' are general descriptors of attainment standards for comprehensive language competence (ex: students can read and understand short stories and other simple written material; students can perform simple role plays, etc.). This is a single list, in which the descriptors are distributed according to the nine ability levels.

A list of 'detailed'-level descriptors is available for each of the five general objectives. In each of these five lists, the detailed descriptors are distributed according to two aspects: ability level and sub-objective. For example, in the case of the first overall objective known as 'language skills', it has a list organized by ability level (1–9). Then, within each level, the descriptors are distributed according to the sub-objectives *listening, speaking, reading, writing, and other.* These detailed level descriptors are presented in the form of a 'Can-do' list (ex: students can read and organize all words studied; can copy example sentences, etc.). The emphasis that the curriculum devotes to objectives and graded attainment standards shows that they constitute core aspects of its planning.

The revised English curriculum reflects the perspectives from behavioural and cognitive perspectives. As mentioned above, for compulsory education, the five general objectives are broken down into five ability levels, and for each level there is a bullet-point list with descriptors. These descriptors are basic descriptions of attainments, and are shown in the form of a 'Can-do' list, indicating what students should be able to do, in order to reach each level (ex: sing simple English songs; write letters and words,

58

etc.). Processing information adequately using cognitive skills is now much more important than simply memorising and repeating information.

In essence, the provided suggestions for implementing the curriculum reflect a learner-centred perspective that incorporates activity-based interaction and a communication-oriented approach which puts a focus on experiential and participatory learning.

② *The curriculum proper (CHN)*

Regarding the aspects of 'training' and 'education', the curriculum certainly provides examples of expected situations in which English language skills should be employed, and as for unexpected situations, there is a list of objectives related to a student's all-round development, such as: developing good study habits, learning/research strategies, and a positive attitude towards learning; use English to develop creative thinking and a sense of inquiry and discovery towards the world; encourage learners to assess themselves; develop students' self-confidence, courage and ability to cooperate with others (especially in the case of introverted learners); and encourage learners to better understand cultural differences.

However, although the curriculum certainly claims to value the aspect of all-round education, it does not provide much concrete advice on how to achieve the above-mentioned objectives. There are a few suggestions for teachers, such as 'give students plenty of space for self-development' and 'create conditions that allow students to explore questions they are personally interested in and solve problems by themselves', but there are no specific examples of learning activities designed to nurture these qualities. Although the curriculum does value the importance of talking about cultural differences, there is no specific mention of developing debate skills, or en-

Chapter 1／Research Background: Textbook Research in an EFL Context   59

gaging in critical thinking in the way that is normally defended by Western educators.

Much like its Japanese counterpart, the Chinese curriculum does not make explicit claims in the domains of societal goals and administrative goals, preferring to stay within those of educational aims, educational goals, and learning objectives. Learners are expected to develop themselves not just in terms of English ability, but also in terms of all-round development. One can summarize its main points as follows. Students are expected to:

①   Attain a reasonable level of comprehensive language competence and the ability to use language for real communication;
②   Master a reasonable amount of basic language competence;
③   Master the skills of listening, speaking, reading, and writing;
④   Have an increased interest for learning English, and become more self-disciplined, perseverant, and self-confident;
⑤   Improve their own abilities for cooperation, investigation and thinking, while developing their memory, imagination, and creativity;
⑥   Adopt good study habits, effective learning strategies, moral integrity, and a healthy outlook on life, while developing as autonomous and lifelong learners;
⑦   Simultaneously nurture a national spirit while understanding and respecting cultural differences, so that they can broaden their horizons and enrich their life experiences;
⑧   Actively participate in cultural life and develop as individuals.

(MOE, 2011)

In the Chinese curriculum, the mastery of the four skills is just one objective among the five that constitute 'comprehensive language competence' which is the core priority of the curriculum: the four skills are defined as *language skills*, while *language knowledge* includes the aspects of phonetics, vocabulary, grammar, functions, and topics. The other three general objectives are related to the all-round development of students, and are titled as *attitudes to learning* (self-confidence, motivation, etc.), *cultural awareness* (for cross-cultural communication) and *learning strategies* (cognitive, metacognitive, communicative and resource strategies).

Another priority of the curriculum is to encourage the formative assessment of students while also including summative assessments, by promoting student participation in classes, developing continuous feedback loops between teachers and students in order to design better learning activities, and improving students' ability to do self-assessment. The use of summative assessment is limited to testing students' integrated language skills and their ability to use language mostly through exams.

The learning objectives stated in the curriculum relate to the cognitive and affective domains. In the former case, we can identify references to all six categories in Bloom's (1956) taxonomy of cognitive processes: *knowledge, comprehension, application, analysis, synthesis,* and *evaluation.* However, just like the Japanese curriculum, there is much more detailed and specific information available for the first three categories, (ex: list of vocabulary items and sounds, etc.) while in the case of analysis and synthesis, which refers to things such as creativity and ability to combine pieces of information into a coherent whole, it is not very clear how the objectives are supposed to be achieved, and it passes the burden of deciding the implementation details to teachers and textbook designers. In this respect, the curriculum provides only a few points of advice for teachers, which encourage them to: use Task-Based Learning methods when designing learning activities that develop students' cognitive abilities; to develop cross-curricular activities; and provide clear instructions to students about what they are expected to achieve during the tasks.

Within the overall objective of 'learning strategies', there is a sub-section called 'metacognitive strategies' with attainment descriptors that ask learners to become aware of their own progress and shortcomings, share their study experiences with teachers and classmates, and understand their own learning needs clearly, among other attainments.

As for the affective domain, the curriculum stresses the importance of encouraging students to develop positive feelings toward each other, and gives a couple of suggestions to teachers on how to achieve that result, such as respecting students' emotions, integrating English education with their emotional education, and pay special attention to the needs of introverted learners and weak learners.

The curriculum does not try to force teachers into a single method for presenting English learning contents to learners, but it does suggest the Task-Based Learning approach as one useful tool for designing learning activities, and it recommends the use of cooperative classroom tasks as a preferred method for engaging students in the use of English language, instead of focusing on individual text-based drills. Overall, the curriculum states a preference for communicative language learning, and it primarily reflects *behavioural, cognitive,* and *affective* perspectives in its design. To a smaller extent, it also contains a few suggestions that present *collaborative* and *psychomotor* perspectives, by focusing on activities such as group presentations, songs, and performances.

Native proficiency in English is no longer the main target for Chinese learners; they must evolve towards becoming confident speakers and competent users of English. The underlying idea is that traditional language teaching is quickly becoming irrelevant for international communication within the Asian continent, because most of its tourists and speakers are non-native speakers of English. Furthermore, merely knowing a foreign language for communication purposes is not enough: English must be used as a tool for problem-solving, creativity, innovation, collaboration and acquiring digital literacy skills in this age of information. In addition to these requirements, we can mention the development of life and career skills such as flexibility and adaptability to unexpected situations. The development of these skills is therefore very much a crucial part of the curriculum. It should be learners who take the initiative in developing such skills, and they should visit places where large amounts of knowledge are accumulated (libraries, internet, etc.) to pick out the pieces of knowledge that can help them to improve themselves.

In theory, the teacher is no longer a figure of absolute authority that merely presents pieces of knowledge to the learners, but is now a facilitator/mediator between learners and learning contents; furthermore, the teacher now has the added responsibility of closely monitoring students' needs and desires, and respond accordingly with carefully-tailored learning activities.

It is hard to discuss the issue of a 'hidden curriculum', because the unwritten aspects of a curriculum only become visible when they are put into practice, and it is still too early to assess the full effects of the curriculum on educational practices across the country. Just like in the case of Japan, there is a notable shortage of recent studies concerning the problems of hidden curricula. The few studies available so far have chosen to focus on the hidden curriculum as a tool for the acculturation of ethnic minorities so that children are encouraged to adopt the cultural identities of the majority Han group (Minhui Qian, 2007; Zhang Donghui & Luo Yun, 2016). Seonaigh Macpherson and Gulbahar Beckett (2008) have argued that deceptively-neutral ideas such as 'modernization' and 'globalization' were being employed in China to dismiss cultural and language variations within the country.

As for studies specifically related to the effects of hidden curricula in English language education, the most relevant one is by Guangxiao Shi (2010), who conducted a short meta-analysis of previous studies on the subject. The results suggest that current practices in Chinese schools are inhibiting learners' enthusiasm for English, as well as the development of effective communicative learning approaches. The main reason for this is that teachers are still choosing to maintain their position as authority figures, which undermines the idea that teachers and learners should collaborate as equal partners in the construction of language activities. Many schools have developed the habit of establishing after-school activities in which students must use English to produce an argumentative text related to a given topic, and the results of this activity are considered when calculating the students' overall performance in English as a subject. Because not all students choose to participate in these activities, this leads to increased disparities in the quality of their learning.

Furthermore, some schools tend to assign students to specific classes according to their English language abilities based on Classroom Heterogeneity Theory. On one hand, any mistakes in this assignment process might hamper student mobility, especially if many weak learners get grouped together; but on the other hand, if there is a big disparity in the abilities of students within a single classroom, this can also negatively affect the teachers' ability to cater to the needs of each student, because there is too much variation. The last point brought up by Shi in his meta-analysis is that parents' insistence in sending their children to private tutors and cram schools is exacerbating the problem, because these educational contexts are strongly oriented towards achieving exam success rather than teaching for overall language competence.

If we look exclusively at the curriculum itself and deduce its main underlying principles, one can see that there are two main shifts in paradigms about learning. The first shift is from formal grammar and functional grammar to a humanistic view on grammar learning. In the current information age, students are not supposed to learn English just to pass exams, but to communicate, interact and learn from foreigners. Learners are expected to develop a range of positive emotional expressions (ex: enthusiastic, warm, and humorous, business-like, flexible character, etc.), which is an important factor for making alliances in the work place, as well as gaining promotions. At the same time, students should be able to create presentations and talk with others in a logical, clear, and persuasive way by using short, concise statements that go to the point quickly.

The second shift is from a teacher-centred perspective to a learner-centred perspective. The basic procedures of the traditional 'PPP' model (presentation-practice-production) are no longer considered relevant. According to a paper by Prof. Zhang Lianzhong (Zhang L.Z., 2011) from Beijing Foreign Studies University, the new model of PPP is more akin to something like 'process / problem-solving / progress' which puts the learner at the centre of the learning process.

The curriculum is supposed to lead the way in implementing these changes in learning paradigms, but it is very likely that it will face significant oppositions and obstacles in its implementation across the country,

Chapter 1／Research Background: Textbook Research in an EFL Context   65

due to regional disparities in education standards, and difficulties in training teachers to implement these new principles. The basic contents for language skills are well-defined in the curriculum, and not much leeway is provided for teachers to deviate from these stipulations. But in other domains, such as 'attitudes to learning' and developing the humanistic character of learners, the provisions are much more open to broad interpretation, so we should expect to see a lot of regional disparities in this respect.

At the macro-level, the content is organized in a hierarchical manner. While the five general objectives are laid out in a horizontal way, and are supposed to be equally important, it is arguable whether that will truly be the case during actual implementation, or if we will see a dominance of language skills in detriment of other general objectives, because language skills are much better-defined in terms of language contents such as vocabulary items. For each of the five general objectives, we then have various vertically-organized layers of attainment descriptors, organized by ability level. Learning contents are also mostly organized in a vertical manner, according to categories such as 'grammar' and 'functions'.

The Chinese curriculum actively encourages teachers to make use of audio-visual materials, the Internet, and multi-media software to enrich the learning experiences of students, if possible. Teachers are also encouraged to find ways to make learners consult print media and libraries as resources for knowledge. However, there are no further guidelines about how to make this work in practice, and this is not a mandatory requirement, because of disparities in regional development. The most likely scenario is that teachers will continue to rely excessively on textbooks and printed teaching materials as a basis for developing learning activities.

In a similar way as the Japanese curriculum, we find that the Chinese curriculum progresses from a set of language skills, as well as cognitive and affective skills, towards a list of desired learner behaviours (described by attainment descriptors); these behaviours are organized by level of ability, and a set of suggestions/advices is provided for achieving those aims.

Unlike the Japanese curriculum, the Chinese curriculum does not mandate any specific topics as purpose of practical usage (ex: school life, shopping, answering the phone, etc.), but asks teachers to develop learning activities with contents/topics relevant and meaningful to their students. In sum, the organizational principles we find here are: learner-centred learning; activity-based learning; focus on practical use of language; contents structured by levels of difficulty; and the principle of correlation between English contents and contents from other subjects. More importantly, the curriculum is trying to distance itself from grammar-based teaching and repetitive drills.

Just like the Japanese curriculum, the concepts of child-centred ideology, activity-based learning and task-based learning are prominently featured in the Chinese curriculum. In other words, learners *learn best by doing* and teachers should be attuned to the specific needs of each learner by introducing *meaningful* contents. On a much more subtle basis, the curriculum suggests that learners should share their experiences and learning strategies with each other. Therefore, they are encouraged to *learn by teaching others*, instead of passively absorbing knowledge from the teacher as an authority figure.

The next aspect is how learners can *learn to think*. In this respect, we can contrast the traditional notion of 'academic rationalism' and its positivist, fact-based approach to learning, with the notion of 'social reconstructionism' based on equality and social justice that is currently on the rise in

Anglophone countries: this new stance prefers to focus on 'speaking truth to power' or challenging established power structures. As argued by Hu and Adamson (2012), the Chinese curriculum clearly favours the learning of English in the sense of social and economic efficiency (i.e., mastering useful skills for the job market). They also found elements of academic rationalism (which helps students understand the world from a scientific and empirical perspective), especially in terms of student assessment.

Here too, the Chinese curriculum specifically asks learners to deepen their knowledge of Chinese culture, while at the same time seeking to respect cultural differences. This stance belies the curriculum's belief in cross-cultural communication while still maintaining a strong sense of a unified national identity, just like its Japanese counterpart. To be clear, the curriculum does not make any explicit mention of political contents or Marxist ideals such as revolution. The use of the expression 'Chinese culture' means that political themes are not explicitly mentioned, but a sense of 'collectivist identity' is nevertheless palpable, due to the mention of core Socialist ideals in the main curriculum documents (i.e., the list of 12 terms/phrases defined by the Chinese government). The 2011 revision specifically contains the following description: "the purpose of the English curriculum is to cultivate a high moral spirit and social applicability, in order to improve the quality of national citizens, to encourage technological innovation and cross-cultural talents." Likewise, the mental and physical well-being of learners and motivation towards learning are prime concerns of the curriculum.

③ *The curriculum in use (CHN)*

Yongqi Gu (2012) and Ran Hu and Bob Adamson (2012) have made it clear that many teachers have expressed considerable resistance to the 'quality-driven learning' approach, because they believe that students don't like learning about things that don't appear in exams. Also, a significant portion of the teaching community prefers to teach contents strictly related to exams because of the 'one-test-determines-life' problem (i.e., national university entrance examinations).

We can understand the term 'cultural values' in terms of both *educational culture* and *cultural identity*. Regarding educational culture, as mentioned in the previous question, there is a clear confrontation between the new educational value based on 'quality' and all-round development of learners, and the traditional view focused on test results that is still dominant in Chinese society. This means that clashes between both perspectives will continue to take place in the foreseeable future. Furthermore, Gu (2012) has clarified that cooperation between interested parties such as textbook compilers and test developers, teachers, and curriculum developers has been generally poor.

As for cultural identity, the curriculum is considerably vague in this respect, because it merely asks learners to respect cultural differences and nothing else. China has 56 ethnic groups, but the English curriculum documents make no mention of this fact. This strongly suggests that the Han ethnic identity will continue to be the predominant cultural identity represented in educational materials. Just like in the case of Japan, the recent revisions made to the curriculum do not imply any real change in methodology and approach: the changes are designed to clarify certain points and push forward with the original objective of 'quality-driven education'.

The official curriculum documents themselves do not explicitly mention how the results of the curriculum's implementation are to be evaluated. According to Gu (2012), the curriculum might be intentionally worded in a way that conveniently overlooks the very real tension between high-stakes exams and the demands of a quality-driven education. But in practice, the results of exams will continue to be the primary yardstick by which the English proficiency of learners is measured. Besides this, we may assume that MOE will continue to conduct surveys across the country as a way of collecting useful data.

In the same manner as Japan, the primary concern is the real difficulty of implementing a 'quality-driven' education policy when large sectors of Chinese society are driven by test results. It will be crucial to conduct surveys with test developers and universities to reduce the barriers towards an education system that considers the all-round development of students.

As mentioned before, until this curriculum came into legal force, the primary method for student evaluation was *summative assessment* (i.e., standardized test results), but this curriculum places a much higher importance on *formative assessment* which focuses on all-round development and integrated qualities of learners. In practice, summative assessment is still predominant, but at the very least the current curriculum is eclectic in its approach since it includes both perspectives.

The Chinese curriculum is a clear attempt to reform educational institutions and practices, but has not achieved its full objectives yet because it has adopted vague wording and avoids addressing the very real clashes between institutionalised practices and its new ideals. A new approach to the evaluation system would involve improving cooperation and communication channels between interested parties (i.e., curriculum developers, teachers, textbook compilers and test developers), and it would be advisable to involve IT companies in the development of innovative learning products

70

that can provide personalised guidance in real time, while reducing bureaucratic practices at schools so that teachers have more time to receive training and develop better lesson plans and learning activities.

④ *Critique (CHN)*

The basic principles of the English curriculum (comprehensive language competence; activity-based learning; communicative learning; learner-centred teaching; graded standards) seem to enjoy widespread support by the academic community. Yet once more, the big question is how to overcome institutionalised teaching practices and implement the curriculum in an effective manner. On one hand, there are no obvious issues with the learning contents associated with the four skills and grammar teaching. But the contents related to other overall objectives such as 'attitude to learning' are still somewhat vague. The suggestions and instructions that are currently present in the 2011 revision do not seem to be sufficient to help teachers transition to a new teaching style. Other apparent limitations of the curriculum seem to be its ambiguity towards the issues of national cultural identity and ingrained cultural behaviours.

1.4.4 Summary and conclusion

Throughout this long descriptive analysis, it has become clear that the Japanese and Chinese EFL curricula share much more similarities than differences. To begin this summary, I will present the main common aspects and differences in Table 1.5, so that the reader can grasp them more easily.

At a quick glance, we can see that both countries see 'knowledge' and 'ways of thinking' as the most valuable assets for learners in the 21st centu-

Chapter 1／Research Background: Textbook Research in an EFL Context   71

Table 1.5: Summary of similarities and differences between the Japanese and Chinese EFL curricula.

Curriculum Analysis	Aspects of Curriculum Analysis	Similarities Japan & China	Differences Japan	Differences China
① Curriculum Documentation and Origins		Globalization pressures / Need to nurture global workforce	Zest for Life	Achieve Quality-driven education (not exam-driven)
		Gradual emergence of International English / Global English	Develop basic communication skills	Develop comprehensive language competence (5 overall objectives)
	Context & Societal Needs that Curricula Must Address	Irrelevance of traditional English teaching Irrelevance of achieving native proficiency		
		All-round development / Self-reliant learners		
		Improve mental and physical health of learners		
		Digital literacy / Information literacy		
② The Curriculum Proper	Underlying Assumptions in the Curricula	English as a tool for general problem solving		
		Teacher as facilitator/mediator, not as authority figure		
	Planning Elements in Curricula	'Can-do' lists (Lists of targets for learners, expressed in terms of desired abilities & skills)	Balancing the 'Four Skills' →Reading →Writing →Listening →Speaking	**Five Overall Objectives (Comprehensive Language Competence)** →Language Skills (Reading + Writing + Listening + Speaking) →Language Knowledge (Phonetics + Grammar + Vocab + Functions + Topics) →Attitudes to Learning (Moral Education + Affections, etc.)
				→Learning Strategies (Cognitive + Metacognitive + Communicative + Resources) →Cultural Awareness (Knowledge + Understanding + Awareness)
			Predominance of language elements & language objectives	Overall descriptors + Detailed descriptors (Graded standards; 5 ability levels)
			3-Year list of objectives / targets (organized by Grades 1-3 & difficulty level)	
	Organization & Structure of Curricula	Mostly top-down / hierarchical organization of learning objectives + contents	Horizontal organization: equal importance of the four skills	Horizontal organization: equal importance of 5 overall objectives
		Textbooks as primary teaching materials		
	Perspectives & Ideologies on Learning Found in the Curricula	(Behavioural + Cognitive + Affective) > Collaborative + Psychomotor		
		Meaningful content / Mnemonic Strategies		
		Child-centred ideology / Learner-centred approach		
		Social & Economic Efficiency (job market-oriented education)		
		Academic Rationalism (positivism / empiricism / fact-based learning)		
		Activity-based learning / Task-based learning		
		Communicative language teaching		
	Epistemological Assumptions Found in the Curricula	Learn by Doing (with meaningful content)	Learning by Contrast (Japanese vs. English)	Learn by Teaching Others
		Learn to Learn + Learn How to Think		
	Main Cognitive Domains Favoured by the Curricula	(Knowledge + Comprehension + Application) > Analysis + Synthesis + Evaluation		
		Focus on Educational Aims & Educational Goals & Learning Objectives	Focus on Training (predictable situations)	Balance between Training & Education (predictable & unpredictable situations)

	Main Approaches & Purposes	Understand & respect cultural differences	Foster positive attitudes towards learning & communication	
		Balance of Formative Assessment with Summative Assessment		
	Main Cultural Values Espoused by Curricula	Moral Education & Sense of national identity (acculturation)		
		Cross-cultural communication / Respect for differences + positive values		
		Encourage cooperation and mutual affection		
		Prevalence of grammar-focused methods	Gendered messaging in textbooks	
		Deficiencies in debate skills & critical thinking	Minor regional disparities in learning ability	Strong regional disparities in learning ability
		Ingrained cultural behaviours that hamper communication		
		Influence of tutors & cram schools in training for exam success		
	Aspects of Hidden Curricula	Teachers will not let go of their role as authority figures		
		Students will not let go of their role as passive learners		
		Society favours exam results over all-round development		
		Possible degradation of ethnic cultural values due to acculturation		
③ The Curriculum in Use	Approaches Towards Curriculum Revision	Focus on reform of institutional practices		
	Method of Curriculum Evaluation	Results of entrance exams & language proficiency certificates + surveys		
	Method of Student Evaluation	Both (Measurement-based + Integrated Approach)		
④ Critique	Potential Risks of Implementation	Possible decrease in overall test scores in the short-term		
		Possible clash between Anglo-centric and Asian-centric values		

ry, rather than mass production of physical products and reliance on low-skilled labour. For example, if we look at the transformations in the Chinese curriculum in the last decades, we find that before the 1980s, it was only necessary to understand the form and structure of English to incorporate foreign technologies; but after the 1990s, it was a tool for basic communication, which led to a functional view of English; finally, it is now currently seen as a means for thinking, which requires us to consider the importance of learning processes. The current Japanese curriculum appears to share similar concerns as the Chinese one.

Another crucial point is that both countries assume that the main challenges of this era can no longer be solved strictly at the national level. By using English, citizens will have to collaborate at a global/international level, whether it is by aiding the global spread of Japanese corporations, or by participating in the academic world, or merely by having a heightened understanding of how current issues are interrelated with those of other countries, and support international collaboration efforts to address such issues.

Regarding the chosen approaches of both countries to learning, it might appear in the surface that they align closely with Western approaches, but there are some differences. There are no explicit references to critical thinking, debating opposing ideas, or social justice, although it is implied that free inquiry by means of media literacy (i.e., listening to all points of view concerning a given issue, or exploring various possibilities through the scientific method) is to some extent desirable.

Both curricula attempt to shed away the past of burdening learners with excessive drilling, but they also carefully try to minimize external cultural influences using a 'respectful standpoint' perspective. Therefore, both countries wish to reap the socio-economic benefits of innovation and globalization without absorbing too many Western ideals and losing their own cultural identity. Learners are not expected to internalize foreign cultural values, but rather they must act as mediators between their countries' values and those of the West. They must be attuned to changes and developments in other countries, and if necessary, find ways to adapt them to the contexts of their own countries and vice-versa.

Although the purpose of this study is to analyse textbooks regardless of how they are implemented in practice, one cannot avoid mentioning once more the obstacles presented by hidden curricula. In Japanese society it is considered inappropriate to voice one's opinion too vehemently, or establish too much eye contact with others, but such behaviours are having a negative influence on students' ability to develop their communication skills and develop alliances and stronger relationships. Many senior teachers in both countries are not convinced that communication-based methods can lead students to be successful in exams, since that is what they will ultimately be judged on. The ranking of schools is also partially dependent on the yearly results of exams. Therefore, school administrators also feel pressured to cater to parents' expectations that their children must achieve high scores in exams.

As both Underwood (2012) and Gu (2012) state, no meaningful progress can be made until exams are changed to focus more on communication skills. In the case of Japan, Underwood further states that despite the general beliefs of school teachers and administrators, studies suggest that few of them have a clear understanding of what recent exams look like. For some years now, university entrance exams have already been slowly shifting towards featuring a better balance between the four skills, which makes the *yakudoku* approach increasingly ineffective. Although there is still a long way to go until that balance is reached, it is a fact that exams have started to introduce listening and have been featuring less and less translation-based exercises, and including more lengthy texts with a relatively high level of difficulty in terms of reading comprehension.

The Chinese curriculum explicitly promotes the importance of professional teacher development and tends to provide more explicit instructions and suggestions for teachers. In a section called 'Teaching Suggestions', it says: 'self-reflection on one's teaching practices is a continuous process for spotting out problems, analysing and solving them, which makes it a significant approach for promoting the professional development of teachers'. It also stresses the importance of setting up a teaching group with mecha-

Chapter 1 / Research Background: Textbook Research in an EFL Context   75

nisms for collaborative learning and inquiry. By doing so, it can encourage the sharing of useful experiences and teaching, inspire deeper communication, and help teachers to be more creative.

Having said this, in both countries, teachers are generally overworked and are not very receptive to changing their teaching methods, to the point that they may even discourage younger teachers from exploring communicative learning approaches. In order to cope with the demands of knowledge-oriented exams, it is necessary to dabble with long texts, complex grammar, and a wide range of vocabulary items. Furthermore, teachers often experience serious difficulties in understanding what are the best 'teaching points', and in distinguishing between real-language-use and pattern drills. They also feel that their own language abilities are not sufficient to carry out CLT activities adequately, and even doubt the efficacy of the method, especially in large-size classes that surpass 40 students.

In terms of differences between Japan and China, the main one is that Japan is focusing mostly on improving the 'basic communication skills' of students while China is promoting the notion of 'comprehensive language competence'. The former gives predominance to language skills (four skills) while the latter makes language skills just one of the five components that characterise the ideal communicative abilities of students. To be clear, it is not the case that Japan completely neglects aspects such as 'learning strategies' or 'attitudes to learning', but rather that the Chinese curriculum is more explicit in arguing for the importance of these additional aspects. And in any case, both curricula provide much more explicit information and recommendations for the improvement of language skills and knowledge, while the other aspects do not receive as much attention.

Based on the above issues, at the very least, textbooks should play a role in improving the reading abilities of students towards more complex texts, and ideally, teaching materials should help learners to develop the four skills in a balanced manner, using meaningful learning activities. Teaching materials are required to rely on the 'Can-do' lists with targets/descriptors provided by both curricula for several purposes: to select appropriate language items for each practice activity; categorise expressions; tell students about the objectives of each section using metadiscourse; practice various types of skills; and promote the cognitive internalisation of language contents. In this manner, the 'Can-do' lists are expected to contribute to the use of language to do things in the real world and solve real problems.

1.5 Core Focus of This Study

The historical review of EFL textbooks and national EFL curricula analysis in Japan and China suggest similar contexts in both nations in terms of English learning and teaching. Most importantly, the Japanese and Chinese languages bear one essential similarity, in that they both employ Chinese characters. This is significantly different from English, which makes use of phonograms, whereas Chinese characters have evolved from logograms. In fact, Japanese and Chinese are the only two currently-used languages in the world that employ Chinese characters. By understanding better how Japanese and Chinese speakers learn English, it becomes possible to contribute to the whole English language-teaching profession by both adding variety to textbook contents and find out whether some strategies that have long been used in each country may have limited effectiveness. Thus, from the view of logographic mother tongues, it is meaningful to build up a comparison of English textbook designs between Japan and China.

Furthermore, it is assumed that it is difficult for both Japanese native speakers and Chinese native speakers to learn English as a foreign language due to their respective linguistic distance with English. Linguistic distance is a concept to show the degree of similarity and disparity of two languages, which is widely used as an influential factor that impacts on the proficiency of the target language (Chiswick & Miller, 2004). The Foreign Service Institute of the U.S. Department of State classified Japanese and Chinese languages as category 4 (FSI, 2020), meaning that they are among the most difficult languages for English native speakers to learn, and linguistic distance can be considered as one of the reasons for this. Swan & Smith (2001) illustrated the linguistic distances between various mother tongues with English to call for increased attention when teaching English to non-native speakers. The same authors noted in particular the features of 'respect language' and visual decoding which present vast differences between Japanese and English, apart from other grammatic, lexical, and phonetic disparities. English belongs to the Indo-European language family, while Chinese belongs to the Sino-Tibet family. Although there is a very limited number of similar syntactic structures between Chinese and English, most of them are strikingly different. In addition, disparities in phonology and grammar show that Chinese is fairly distant from English. Thus, it can be said that there is difficulty in learning English for both Japanese and Chinese speakers from the perspective of linguistic distance.

Regarding the institutional frameworks and entities for selecting textbooks, three main patterns can be recognized by reviewing the Japan Textbook Research Centre's (2020) report series from an international survey. The first pattern is that schools or school districts, like in the U.S., Canada, and Germany, decide which textbook should be used in classrooms, according to state or school district guidelines. The second pattern is that teachers, like those in the U.K. and France, are entitled to select textbooks upon their professional understanding of how to achieve the expected educational goals. The third pattern is that prefectural or provincial boards of education, such as in Japan and China, choose textbooks from an authorized list.

Both Japan and China possess the same textbook approval system, by which textbooks are evaluated as to whether they comply with national curriculum guidelines. There were no approved English textbooks for elementary schools in Japan until April 2020, because English was not an official subject in elementary schools. Rather, English as a foreign language was introduced as a formal subject only from the secondary school onwards, thus making English textbooks for the first grade (i.e., seventh grade) the first official ones that Japanese learners encountered. As for China, English is taught from the third grade in elementary schools, in accordance with the current national curriculum. Although there are approved English textbooks for elementary schools in China, this study will focus only on textbooks for the first grade in secondary school, mainly to have the same point of comparison with Japan, since learners in both nations share the same age. In doing so, this can provide useful insights on English language learning.

The materials selected for this study are approved English textbooks published after 2012. In Japan, the currently-used six English textbooks are based on the 2008 national curriculum that only began to be implemented in 2012. These textbooks were revised in 2016, since revisions usually take place every four years in Japan. Thus, the revised 2016 editions will be examined and discussed.

Chapter 1 / Research Background: Textbook Research in an EFL Context   79

Table 1.6: List of approved English Textbooks featured in this study.

Japan		China	
Series Title	Publisher	Series Title*	Publisher
New Crown 1	Sanseido	Renjiao ban 7	People's Educational Press; Cengage Learning
New Horizon 1	Tokyo Shoseki	Beishida ban 7	Beijing Normal University Publishing Group; Pearson Education
Sunshine 1	Kairyudo	Ren'ai ban 7	Popular Science Press
Total English 1	Gakko Tosho	Yilin ban 7	Yilin Press; Oxford University Press
One World 1	Kyoiku Shuppan	Jijiao ban 7	Hebei Education Publishing House; DC Canada Education Publishing
Columbus 21 1	Mitsumura Tosho	Waiyanshe ban 7	Foreign Language Teaching and Research Press; Macmillan Publishers
		Shangwai ban 7	Shanghai Foreign Language Educational Press
		Shangjiao ban 7	Shanghai Educational Publishing House; Oxford University Press

*In reality, English textbook series in China are all titled with the common word *English*, so here they are named after their respective publishers' names in order to distinguish them from each other.

In China, the English textbooks employed now are based on the 2011 national curriculum, which received final approval in 2012. Table 1.6 shows the list of approved English textbooks for the first grade of secondary school, which constitute the main object of this study.

As can be seen from Table 1.6, there are six series of approved English textbooks in Japan and eight series in China. It is immediately noticeable that 6 out of 8 publishers in China chose to cooperate with foreign publishers (especially well-known publishing houses in English-speaking countries) to produce their approved English textbooks, whereas all the Japanese publishers are local and independent ones. So, this study may also provide insights in regards to the impact that partnerships between local and foreign publishers may have on textbook characteristics.

1.6 Purpose of the Present Study

Based on the need to raise awareness about the differences between EFL and ESL, and to distinguish them in terms of teaching and learning, Japan and China are chosen here as two case studies of EFL textbook countries. As mentioned previously, these two countries represent Japanese and Chinese speakers who use the common logograms of Chinese characters in their activities as English learners. Global English textbook publishers from BANA countries have sought to promote their products in EFL markets, while ignoring or dismissing the fact that speakers of different mother tongues learn English in different ways, with different purposes. A global English textbook which aims to fit in each cultural market is unlikely to work well in the long run. Even when cultural differences are considered by inserting illustrations and pictures that reference each local region in which they are published, global English textbooks lack at their core the view of incorporating EFL contexts and specific needs into the processes of English teaching and learning.

Considering the above, this study offers an East-Asian EFL textbook development perspective. It proposes a micro-view of unit/lesson designs, which altogether comprise the structure of each textbook. In other words, it looks at language learning materials and activities in individual units and deconstructs them into their basic constituting components, which are then analysed in detail; afterwards, by looking at the global results, the entire textbook is discussed as a teaching and learning resource. It is worth noting that this research is restricted to textbook descriptive analysis rather than textbook use in classrooms. Based upon these findings, we will verify whether the textbooks truly adhere to the requirements and goals of national English curricula in both countries, since textbooks are supposed to be the materialized forms of the same curricula. To summarize, there are three main objectives to this study:

① To inquire about the idiosyncrasies of EFL textbooks by looking at both case studies;

② To verify if there is a gap between national curricula and approved English textbooks;

③ To explore optimal approaches towards improving the development of EFL textbooks.

1.7 Thesis Outline

In this Chapter 1, I have presented the origins of the field of textbook research from the perspective of curriculum and instruction theory, and identified the need for a form of textbook research that considers the distinctions between EFL and ESL. By reviewing the general histories of English textbooks in Japan and China, I drew attention to the similarities in their respective processes of gaining independence from foreign publishers, and looking continuously for ways to cater to domestic learners. As two representative examples of countries with EFL textbooks, I justified the inclusion of Japan and China in this study, and why I chose to particularly focus on the first grade of secondary school. Furthermore, I respectively analysed the national English curricula of Japan and China, in order to establish a referential basis from which to compare the results of the approved textbook analysis.

In Chapter 2, I introduce a literature review, aimed towards elaborating a descriptive model of EFL textbook unit analysis, by considering different perspectives about how to analyse English textbooks. To address the gaps in previous research that this study intends to fill, I present a path for viewing textbook contents at the micro-level, namely to examine each "unit" (or lesson) which is the chief constituent part of a textbook. Then, I examine literature that is relevant to each sub-part within the unit, pointing out

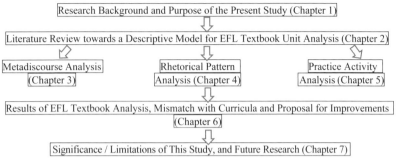

Figure 1.6: Outline of this study.

how these various elements may facilitate learners to learn. Lastly, a descriptive model of EFL textbook unit analysis will be presented, based on the viewpoint of learners as textbook users.

Chapters 3 to 5 present the core findings of this study, in which I analyse and begin to discuss the data from selected units of all the currently-approved English textbooks in Japan and China. These findings include: metadiscourse messages transmitted from textbooks to learners (Chapter 3), rhetorical patterns in the main reading comprehension texts (Chapter 4), and the main mental operation requirements embedded within learning activities (Chapter 5).

In Chapter 6, I discuss the overall findings considering the idiosyncrasies of EFL textbooks. This discussion will be divided into three parts. First, I will review the results of the analysed curricula, revisit the three analyses of the descriptive model identified in Chapter 2, and explore the novel contributions of this study for each type of analysis. Second, I will also verify if there are gaps, incongruences or inconsistencies between national curricula and the approved English textbooks. Third, I will point out some factors that are absent in EFL textbooks, and propose an approach to remedy

Chapter 1 / Research Background: Textbook Research in an EFL Context 83

this situation along with two case studies of teaching practice.

Chapter 7 provides a compilation of three case studies as action research, carried out in real classrooms. These small-scale studies are intended to demonstrate ways in which the teaching of English as a foreign language can be interconnected with the teaching of Japanese and other foreign languages, so as to help learners gain a better understanding of meta-grammar, as well as language in general. This chapter also includes a literature review that explains the guiding rationale behind these case studies.

Finally, in Chapter 8, I will provide a summary to this study, along with considerations of potential directions for further research. The scope and limitations of the study will also be discussed, followed by a set of explanations related to its significance for the domains of textbook research and language learning.

Chapter 2/Literature Review: Towards a Descriptive Model for EFL Textbook Unit Analysis

2.1 Introduction

As stated in the previous chapter, this study does not attempt to address the production and implementation stages of textbooks, i.e., how textbooks are produced, how they are used in classrooms, and what outcomes occur when they are used. The enactment of these stages is dependent upon various contextual factors, the analysis of which goes beyond the scope of this study, and are therefore not included.

Instead, the focus of the present thesis is the inherent nature and characteristics of currently-approved English textbooks as they are in themselves; in other words, the study of their internal organization and structural aspects. In order to examine the nature of English textbooks, it is necessary to decide which interpretive model should be applied. Therefore, this chapter is mainly concerned with evolving a framework for describing and analysing English textbooks, which can be applied to the 14 sets of EFL textbooks that constitute the core body of data for this thesis.

To begin with, I will review several existing approaches towards the description of English textbooks, to identify what scholars consider to be the defining components that have shaped the structure and nature of foreign language textbooks (section 2.2). I will then draw upon the insights gained through this review, to suggest a list of significant aspects that should be addressed when attempting to describe and characterise the textbooks discussed in this thesis.

Given the absence of a micro-scale approach in current textbook analyses, we will zoom in to the level of the individual unit as a fundamental structure for examination, which is itself comprised of: metadiscourse; main texts; and learning activities. The metadiscourse analysis highlights messages transmitted from textbooks to learners (section 2.3.1). Rhetorical pattern analysis shows how the main texts are designed for learner comprehension (section 2.3.2). Finally, of central concern is the analysis of what learners are required to do through the various learning activities proposed in the textbooks (section 2.3.3). I will conclude by proposing a model that synthesises these significant features and that can be applied towards the examination of units (section 2.4).

2.2　A Review of Descriptive Models

In order to build a framework for the description of the EFL textbooks discussed in this thesis, we may refer to several models, suggesting various aspects that must be described and inferred. Among these, many models are used to guide the procedures for evaluation and selection of textbooks for groups (Harmer, 1983, 2001; Williams, 1983; Cunningsworth, 1984; Dougill, 1987; Sheldon, 1988; Skierso, 1991, McDonough & Shaw, 2003).

However, when we start to look at preferences concerning the suitability of textbooks, we find that these models do not seek to examine in depth the actual characteristics of textbooks and textbook contents. For my purpose of analysing the nature and essential qualities of textbooks, I have chosen to review two models which propose a more analytical approach relevant to the content analysis of English textbooks: Littlejohn's (1992) model for analysis of language teaching materials, and Gray's (2010) model for description of language systems and contents related to skills.

While referring to four previously-existing analysis models (Mackey,

Chapter 2 / Literature Review: Towards a Descriptive Model for EFL Textbook Unit Analysis   87

1965; Corder, 1973; Breen & Candlin, 1980, 1987; Richards & Rodgers, 1982, 1986), Littlejohn's (1992) model for analysis of language teaching materials centres on describing the explicit and implicit nature of the materials as a teaching and learning resource. It has three levels of analysis that answer these three questions accordingly: *What is there? What is required of users? What is implied?* (Table 2.1)

By making a strong effort to maintain a neutral stance, Littlejohn's model describes teaching materials as they are, as objectively as possible, without favouring analysis categories attached to any theories of language, learning or teaching. It is useful for examining what kind of tasks learning

Table 2.1: Littlejohn's (1992:47) model with three levels of analysis.

PROCESS	PRODUCT
Levels of inference	Related aspects of the material
	Realisation
Level 1: 'What is there?'	Place of learners' materials in set
	Published form of learners' materials
	Subdivision of learners' materials
	Subdivision of sections into sub-sections
	Continuity
	Route
	Access
	Design
Level 2: 'What is required of users?'	Subject matter and focus
	Types of teaching/learning activities
	Participation: who does what with whom?
Level 3: 'What is implied?'	Aims
	Principles of selection
	Principles of sequencing
	Teacher roles
	Learner roles (classroom/in learning)
	Role of materials as a whole

activities *require users to do*, which then allows us to infer the aims, principles of selection and sequencing that are implied by the textbooks themselves. By looking at the instructions given in each learning activity included in a textbook, and decomposing the various sequences of tasks, practices and roles that are embodied by the learners, it puts into relevance how many times learners have to do certain things, and clearly exposes the types of content that learners are requested to focus on. Therefore, this aspect constitutes a significant part of the analysis framework for practice activities provided by this study (see 2.3.3).

Developed for the purpose of analysing the textbook as a cultural commodity, Gray's (2010) model adopts an inductive approach to explore common elements within textbook contents, such as language systems and texts for developing language skills. In this case, 'language systems' refers to the aspects of grammar, lexis and phonology. Given Gray's arguments in favour of greater inclusivity regarding race, gender, and disabled people, he sees it as important to ask to what extent different varieties of English—as spoken by different types of social groups in the UK—are represented in textbooks. This requires the identification of such distinct representations of the grammar of spoken (written) English, in terms of: variety; register and idiomaticity of lexis; and accents used in Received Pronunciation.

Featuring a similar interest on the cultural content of textbooks, Gray looked towards Sercu's (2000) analytic framework, which was designed to evaluate textbooks' capacity to develop intercultural communicative competence. He pointed out some issues in Sercu's approach, in terms of featuring limited cultural themes and having a strong quantitative focus. Rather than discussing how culture is taught, Gray is interested in how cultural elements are selectively used in textbooks to construct a commodified, marketable reality of what it *means* to be 'English'; in other words, this selective process deliberately *creates specific meanings* about 'Englishness' and circulates them in the global marketplace. He sees culture as a process of 'meaning-making' and 'meaning-taking', which when applied to textbooks, gradually constructs their 'representational repertoires'; that is, the sets of cultural elements imbued with specific meanings that when taken as a whole, convey—represent—to learners *what is deemed appropriate* of being considered 'English' (or not).

One crucial problem which can be identified in both models, however, is that they are designed for global English textbooks that are produced by U.K. publishers and used across ESL countries. The models are therefore fully weighted in the universe of ESL textbooks and are clearly inadequate as a basis for describing EFL textbooks, which are developed for local markets under one common educational curriculum.

Furthermore, the emphasis in both models is still tied to the overall picture that is portrayed by a relatively narrow set of textbooks, for example in terms of broad cultural representations, or their general modes of organization; in other words, they lack a micro-scale view on the design struc-

Table 2.2: Gray's (2010:51) descriptive framework model.

Elements of content	Representational repertoire
Language systems Grammar	Which varieties of English are represented? Is the grammar of spoken English distinguished from written grammar?
Lexis	Which lexical fields are taught? What purpose does the lexis serve?
Phonology	Is phonological variation represented? Which aspects of pronunciation are addressed?
Skills content Texts to develop reading/listening/speaking/writing	What topics are addressed? Who are the characters? What types of activities are used to practise speaking? Which genres are practised? Are formal/informal registers addressed?

ture of specific units in a textbook, or do not attempt to look at the same thematic units among different textbooks.

Moreover, the methodological aspects of how learning materials transmit knowledge remain under-explicated. Both models, therefore, leave unconsidered one important aspect: the interactions between textbook and learners. That is, what messages are sent from the textbook to learners, to assist their learnings? What kind of texts are provided as the main language materials?

In constructing and applying a model for the description of English textbooks, it is important to ensure that there is as much as possible a distinction between the explicit nature of the textbooks, and the subjective nature of the researcher's inferences. This is illustrated as the distinction between reporting and interpreting (Littlejohn, 1988). Of course, it may be argued that reporting also involves a selection of information, which once again falls back into the domain of subjective judgements. However, even while taking this caveat into account, the mere description of the explicit aspects of the textbooks is more likely to achieve a general level of agreement, whereas the interpretations of these descriptions can often devolve into different views and arguments. A crucial problem that arises from textbook content analysis is therefore how to clarify the fundamental evidences provided by textbook descriptions (on which scientific discussions are based on), so that a wider number of scholars may have more productive debates, and potentially reach a consensus on the presuppositions made from the body of fundamental evidences.

2.3　A Descriptive Model for EFL Textbook Unit Analysis

As I have just argued, these two models bring into relevance some im-

Chapter 2 / Literature Review: Towards a Descriptive Model for EFL Textbook Unit Analysis   91

portant aspects of textbooks, but they do not offer further guidance for describing the design or structure of a unit at a micro-level. Unit/Lesson is a basic constituent part of a textbook, on which the lesson plan is based on. What seems to be needed here is a model which looks at a basic unit in detail, from which researchers can then describe, identify, and infer the organizational and structural nature of the textbooks. Equipped with such a model, it should then be possible to grasp the defining features of unit design in individual textbooks, which would then coalesce into overarching features of a group of EFL textbooks. It is necessary therefore to attend to the construction of a model to guide us during the descriptive process of individual unit analysis.

In EFL textbooks for secondary schools, there are three common elements within a unit, which can be identified as: *indirect messages, main texts*, and *learning activities*. 'Indirect messages' refer to descriptions that do not contain in themselves any obvious referential information for language study (i.e., grammar points, etc.), but instead provide accounts that can help to facilitate the learning process, such as statements of learning objectives, and tips for learning strategies. These messages from the textbook/author towards learners can be analysed through the lens of metadiscourse studies (Wang, 2012).

'Main texts' refer to direct language learning materials expressed in written form that contain a number of target linguistic items for study. They are often divided into several parts within a single unit, accompanied by learning activities between parts. How learners understand these main texts can be examined by the method of rhetorical pattern analysis (Wang, 2014).

As for 'learning activities', these refer to practices that are specifically

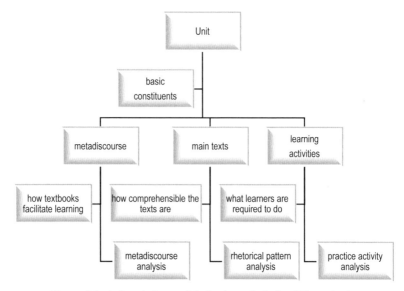

Figure 2.1: A descriptive model of unit analysis for EFL textbooks.

designed to develop one's language skills. They are mostly centred on specific language contents related to the unit's theme or objectives. Learning activities can be looked at through Nation's (2007) principle of four strands (Wang, 2015) and Littlejohn's framework for task analysis (1992).

Taking into consideration the above, a general model for unit analysis is summarised in Figure 2.1 which I will proceed to respectively justify and illustrate in the following sections.

2.3.1 Messages from textbooks to learners: metadiscourse analysis

School textbooks should be interesting and engaging for children, to help them learn the content of school subjects, develop a positive attitude towards studying, and learn how to learn as well. Yet, reality has not always corresponded to this ideal. As a result, in recent years there has been a move towards purposely enhancing the rhetorical characteristics of text-books, in order to aid students in their learning. This approach derives from speech communication studies, wherein certain characteristics of effective speech (such as explaining a goal, how to put emphasis on a portion of text/speech, etc.) have been found to help learners in acquiring a critical attitude toward the material, implying that rhetoric could result in a deeper mutual understanding and more positive attitudes on the students' side (Crismore, 1985). Considering how such spoken rhetoric may also be used in written texts, their study became somewhat of a trend, reflecting a growing interest on the interaction between readers and writers, parallel to the interactive process between reader and content.

Interaction between the learner and the textbook

Among the studies related to this trend, the use of metadiscourse is one aspect in which scholars have focused on. Besides the descriptive and contrastive perspectives, metadiscourse has been studied as an important interactive feature that is believed to facilitate the reading process (Camiciottoli, 2003). A text is composed of two parts: propositional content and metadiscourse features. Metadiscourse is defined by Vande Kopple (1997:2) as 'discourse that people use not to expand referential material, but to help their readers connect, organise, interpret, evaluate and develop attitudes towards that material'. In other words, metadiscourse refers to facets which make the text more explicit and accessible to the reader, and engage the reader during the process of interaction.

Metadiscourse has been traditionally considered as an instantiation of metalanguage (Aguilar, 2008); yet, there are different approaches to viewing metadiscourse. Etymologically, it is defined as discourse about dis-

94

course; however, the difficulty in categorizing metadiscourse items caused early studies on metadiscourse to lack taxonomy and a thorough elaboration of its deeper aspects. Although researchers have studied it for different purposes, much attention has been given to the role of metadiscourse in interaction.

Within the mainstream currents of metadiscourse research, we find that most of it is inspired by the same rationale: that it is defined as discourse detached from (and subordinate to) propositional discourse. A functional classification on two planes has been proposed, and research about the role of metadiscourse in writing and reading comprehension, as well as the use of metadiscourse in different genres, has been conducted (Aguilar, 2008).

In a textual context, the positive effects of metadiscourse on reading comprehension have been discussed in several studies by Crismore (1989), showing that it can guide and help readers to organise content, thus fostering further comprehension. Moreover, these studies suggest that it can promote critical thinking, further inspiring readers' opinions. Since its main function is rhetorical, metadiscourse is used to produce a desired effect, by meeting readers' expectations using explanatory and persuasive elements (Hyland, 2000). In other words, metadiscourse can be helpful in convincing readers to accept and understand what the text is aiming for, which can also influence readers' reaction to the text.

Additionally, metadiscourse can help the reader get a clear idea about goals, topics, text structure and organization, not only easing the reader's entry into a text, but also providing them with background information. Readers need ways to represent and encode the content into long-term memory. Metadiscourse can be considered as an inputting device or strategy that facilitates this representing and encoding, by providing a context in which the primary discourse can be embedded—in other words, a context for the text (Crismore, 1983).

When it comes to EFL instructional contexts, metadiscourse has proven to be useful in assisting non-native speakers of English, who often have difficulties in grasping the writer's stance when reading challenging authentic materials. It has been demonstrated that metadiscourse can benefit non-native learners dealing with argumentative texts (Bruce, 1989); also, the specific instructions of metadiscourse can be helpful for L2 readers in distinguishing factual content from the writer's commentary (Vande Kopple, 1997). Furthermore, the results of action research indicate that L2 readers can better understand a text containing more metadiscourse than one with less (Camiciottoli, 2003).

Overall, metadiscourse can be viewed as the direction or guidance that the author uses to help readers understand and comprehend the text. In school education, textbooks are still the main teaching and learning materials used in class, and metadiscourse can play an important role in making textbooks more efficient and understandable for learners. This pedagogical function of metadiscourse is emphasised in this study, which looks at how English textbooks make use of various types of metadiscourse. The results suggest that there are considerable commonalities and differences between English textbooks in Japan and China regarding metadiscourse usage, which may be respectively due in part to their development as EFL textbooks and to differences in standards of national curricula.

Metadiscourse analysis of EFL textbooks

Several other studies have been undertaken to analyse textbooks, regarding metadiscourse as a prominent feature (Crismore, 1983, 1989;

Hyland, 2000); moreover, the differences in usage across cultures have been compared as well (Mauranen, 1993; Valero-Garcés, 1996). An analysis of informational and attitudinal metadiscourse instances in textbooks, representing levels from elementary school through college, was undertaken by Crismore (1983), wherein she attempted to investigate different usages of metadiscourse in social studies textbooks, as well as non-textbooks. In her findings, metadiscourse is presented as playing a facilitating role in improving comprehension; it helps students anticipate context, goals, text organization, and the author's perspective, resulting in texts that readers find interesting and easy to remember (Crismore, ibid.). The quantity and styles of metadiscourse can be designated as 'stylistic variables' (Crismore, ibid.), which have implications for texts, and might also have an influence on the pedagogical beliefs and values expressed within the field of language studies.

The 'stylistic variables' category has been questioned as being inconsistent or ambiguous, since the borderline between primary discourse and metadiscourse is often blurry; however, this category is based on two main metadiscourse functions: one is the informational function, and the other is the attitudinal function. The former serves to help readers understand the author's purposes and goals, while the latter serves to help them grasp the author's perspective or stance towards the primary discourse (Crismore, 1984). The most impactful research related to metadiscourse can also be traced back to Crismore (1982, 1983, 1984, 1989), who was the first to address the pedagogical function of metadiscourse; furthermore, she reported on its role in facilitating comprehension by demonstrating how textual cues are helpful in reading and writing.

She also began to examine its use in school textbooks, to make more

Table 2.3: Typology of Metadiscourse Analysis for EFL Textbooks (Wang, 2012:109).

Categories	Subtypes
Informational metadiscourse	Goals: unit goal and statements
	Pre-plans: preliminary statements about content and structure
	Post-plans: review statements about content and structure
Attitudinal metadiscourse	Salience: importance of idea
	Emphatics: degree of certainty of assertion
	Hedges: uncertainty
	Evaluative: attitude towards a fact or idea
L1 use	Mother tongue use: title; goal; instruction of practice; context introduction; interpretation

reader-friendly social studies textbooks that make use of appropriate meta-discourse; another of her studies (1985) states that one of its most important functions is to provide cues for relevant aspects in the texts. Finally, she raised a theoretical issue within the study of metadiscourse: that it is important to integrate the characteristics of discourse that is 'contentless' (such as metadiscourse) with other kinds of discourse.

Given Crismore's contribution to metadiscourse studies in terms of pedagogical function, the typology adopted in this study follows her classification (Crismore, 1983), which is based on the functions of language and rhetorical techniques within school textbooks, including the informational and attitudinal categories, and their associated sub-types. In addition, one other aspect which is representative of the characteristics of EFL textbooks was taken into consideration: the ratio of target-native language used throughout a textbook, which is considered to have an impact on the language use of both teachers and learners. The overall typology can be summarised as shown in Table 2.3.

2.3.2 Understanding the comprehensibility of texts through rhetorical pattern analysis

That which makes one passage easier to read than another is likely to be attached to simplistic readability formulas; simple words and short sentences usually contribute towards a more readable text. Nonetheless, simplicity is not the only way to produce texts that are more comprehensible than others. After distributing texts with differing features among school-age children, researchers found three general features that affected children's answers concerning reading comprehension: familiarity, personal interest, and structure (Bransford & Johnson, 1972; Garner, Gillingham & White, 1989; van Dijk & Kintsch, 1983). Among these, structure was found to have the strongest effect on comprehensibility, especially when readers need to recall and apply the materials in another situation (Chambliss & Calfee, 1998).

Text structure: linkages that organise the design of a text

Structure is the organization and sequencing of sentences, paragraphs and information that lead to the overall construction of a total discourse. Structure provides a set of linkages (systems of links) between informational elements that undergird or support the overall design of a text. Miller (1956) once argued that at any given moment, human beings had limited attention spans and limited access to memory; therefore, it is critical to provide coherent structures for learning and thinking. Compared to narrative writing such as storytelling that tends to be more exploratory in character, expository writing demands clearer and more effective linkages. There is a wide range of expository genres to which textbooks belong.

Main texts in EFL textbooks consist of passages designed and created to be used as language input. How to make a passage comprehensible is a problem of design. A coherent design requests the use of linkages that incorporate individual sentences into a thematic passage. A passage is composed of sentences, paragraphs, and sections. How these elements can be linked to produce a comprehensible passage is a significant aspect of comprehensibility research (Chambliss & Calfee, 1998; Chou Hare, Rabinowits, & Schieble, 1989).

Mackay (1987) claimed that grasping the connections established by the systems of links among sentences was a crucial precondition for comprehending texts. Such linkages refer to connections and relationships existing among different sentences, paragraphs, and sections, which when taken together constitute a structure. However, it has been argued that there are serious insufficiencies in language teaching concerning reading comprehension beyond the sentence level (Tanabe, 1991).

Linkages: rhetorical patterns in written exposition

Unlike other structural systems derived from linguistics (van Dijk & Kintsch, 1983; Meyer, 1985; Cook & Mayer, 1988), Chambliss & Calfee (1998) proposed a typology of linkages constituting rhetorical patterns that have their basis in composition courses. It is displayed in Figure 2.2, and is designed to include a wide range of expository genres such as textbooks.

As shown in the top level, three main purposes can be identified in textbook writings: *to inform, to argue* and *to explain*. Main texts in EFL textbooks are generally considered as exposition, which can be constructed using seven basic building blocks, as shown on the left-hand side. They can be used separately or in combination. Informational text structures are classified as either *descriptive* or *sequential*. 'Description' presents charac-

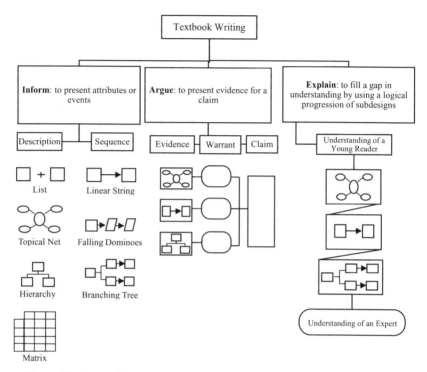

Figure 2.2: Types of design for rhetorical patterns (Chambliss & Calfee, 1998:32).

teristics fixed in each point in time; 'sequence' presents events progressing over time.

Within this set of descriptive patterns, that of 'list' stands as the one that provides the poorest amount of links. Conversely, 'hierarchy' and 'matrix' have the densest link networks and can coherently organise large amounts of contents. As for sequential patterns, the 'linear string' provides the least amount of structure, while the 'branching tree' can link several sequences coherently.

The two other purposes are 'to argue' and 'to explain'. An argument

Chapter 2 / Literature Review: Towards a Descriptive Model for EFL Textbook Unit Analysis   101

presents evidence for a claim. In complex arguments, evidence and claim are closely linked by an explicit warrant. Within logic theory as defined by Toulmin (1958), 'warrant' can be understood as 'analogous to the major premise in a classical syllogism' and is a 'law-like generalization that links the two' (see Chambliss, 1995:781).

As for 'explanation', it is meant to fill the gaps between a young reader's incomplete understanding of a phenomenon, and a more developed scientific explanation of it, using basic building blocks.

Text structure: how to distinguish between rhetorical patterns

These building blocks of informational patterns can be used and combined to form passages. They differ in the types of linkages that join the separate parts. Table 2.4 presents a set of guidelines for distinguishing between rhetorical patterns, by looking at the defining characteristics of the text; it is used to identify the structural designs of texts.

Table 2.4: Text characteristics of rhetorical patterns (Chambliss & Calfee, 1998:125).

Text characteristics	Building block design	
If the text presents		
attributes	then the design is	*Description*
events	then the design is	*Sequence*
Description		
If each subtopic deals with the same attributes	then the design is	*Matrix*
If subtopics present categories that are hierarchically related	then the design is	*Hierarchy*
If there are 3-5 main subtopics	then the design is	*Topical net*
If subtopics are none of above	then the design is	*List*
Sequence		
If there is more than one sequence covering the same period	then the design is	*Branching tree*
If there is a cause-and-effect relationship among events in a sequence	then the design is	*Falling dominoes*
If the events are linked by time only	then the design is	*Linear string*

2.3.3 Looking at 'what learners are required to do': practice activity analysis

In addition to metadiscourse elements and the main text, learning activities are a significant constituent part of a unit that provides learners with target language interactions: it offers additional opportunities for learning, and enables learners to practice together using language.

A well-balanced language course: the Four Strands principle

In regards to what constitutes a well-designed learning activity, Nation (1996, 2007) proposed a framework known as 'Four Strands' to ascertain if a language course provides an appropriate balance, in terms of equal amounts of time devoted to each strand, namely: meaning-focused input, meaning-focused output, language-focused learning and fluency development. The characteristics of the four strands (which are used to classify language activities) are summarised in Table 2.5.

As shown in Table 2.5, the 'meaning-focused input' strand involves learning through listening and reading, which are largely acts of incidental learning that focus on comprehending information and messages. 'Meaning-focused output' involves incidental learning through speaking and writ-

Table 2.5: Nation's (2007) Four Strands framework.

The Four Strands	Involvements	Typical activities
Meaning-focused input	Learning through listening and reading, using language receptively	Extensive reading, shared reading, listening to stories, watching TV, conversation listening
Meaning-focused output	Learning through speaking and writing, using language productively	Conversation talking, speech, writing a letter, keeping a diary, telling how to do something
Language-focused learning	Deliberate learning of language features such as pronunciation, spelling, vocabulary, grammar, and discourse	Substitution tables and drills, dictation, word cards, intensive reading, translation, memorizing dialogues, getting feedback about writing
Fluency development	The aim is to receive and convey messages, and make the best use of what learners already know regarding the 4 skills	Speed reading, skimming, and scanning, repeated reading, repeated retelling, ten-minute writing and listening to easy stories

ing. The 'language-focused learning' strand involves the deliberate use of attention towards language features, including spelling, pronunciation, vocabulary, grammar, and discourse, and is often referred to as 'form-focused instruction'. 'Fluency development' aims at helping learners to make the best use of what they already know at faster speeds, with a focus on receiving or conveying meanings.

Nation's work on the Four Strands drew from a few sources and preceding studies, namely the input hypothesis (Krashen, 1985), output hypothesis (Swain, 1985, 1995), form-focused instruction (Nation, 2001; Williams, 2005), and the development of speaking and reading fluency (Schmidt, 1992; Kuhn & Stahl, 2003). While claiming that every activity in a language course fits into one of these strands, Nation (2007) argued they should be evenly balanced in terms of class time, when designing a course that aims to cover both receptive and productive skills.

He justified the partitioning of total course time into 25% portions mainly based on the 'time-on-task' principle, which shows that more time spent on something leads to one becoming better at it. When describing the strands, he listed certain conditions that must be present in order to make each strand valid and effective, which stress the importance of large quantities of input and output.

Despite a lack of solid evidence for equal time allocation, the framework of four strands emphasises that the acts of learning from input and intensive deliberate learning are by themselves not enough. It highlights the need of designing a balanced set of learning activities that go through the requirements set by the four strands, including meaningful output and fluency development. The four strands principle can be applied for course design, autonomous learning, materials development, and pedagogy (Nation,

2009; Nation & Yamamoto, 2012), but it is not appropriate for analysing learning activities in a descriptive way.

Littlejohn's (1992) analysis of learning tasks

Instead, a method for analysing learning tasks, proposed by Littlejohn, is adopted in this study. Littlejohn's (1992) framework, which involves a detailed description of such 'tasks', examined the following aspects: the core nature of the processes through which learners are expected to go through; the level of classroom participation in which learners must get involved with; the type of content upon which learners are to engage with; and who decides what (See Table 2.6). In comparing Nunan's (1985) narrow definition of 'meaning-focused task' with the broader definition of Breen's (1987) 'task as work plan', Littlejohn defined 'task' as the configuration of three key elements: process, classroom participation and content. It re-

Table 2.6: Littlejohn's (1992:38) proposed basic method for initiating the analysis of learning tasks, with additional explanations by the author of this study.

I – What is the learner expected to do?

A *Turn-take (initiate language, scripted response, or none)*
B *Focus (meaning, form or both)*
C *Operation (list of mental operations carried out by the learner)*

II – Who with? (*participation*)

III – With what content? (*characteristics of learning contents*)

A *Form (graphics, sounds, text, speech, audio, etc.)*
→input given to learners
→output generated by learners
B *Source (from teacher, learner, textbook, dictionary, etc.)*
C *Nature (metalinguistic/linguistic items, fiction/non-fiction, etc.)*

IV – Who decides? (*parties responsible for decision-making*)

quires an introspective approach from the researchers, who must subdivide materials into constituent tasks: this activity demands a high degree of reliability, and is dependent on the researchers achieving a broad consensus among themselves on what those constituent tasks are.

By looking carefully at the purpose, usage, and definition of each component in Littlejohn's framework, I reconstructed it from the learners' point of view, when they are asked to do a learning activity. I made three major adjustments to it, by considering the defining features of EFL textbooks. Firstly, instead of 'task', we use here the term 'practice activity', referring to any activity that learners are asked to do with the use of language, to facilitate their language learning; this can be clearly identified in EFL textbooks.

Secondly, the category of *turn-take* has been modified. Among all the learning activities found in EFL textbooks, it is unlikely that learners are asked to *initiate language*, expressing what they wish to say without any kind of script to fall back on. Therefore, turn-take will only include the sub-categories of *scripted response* and *not required*.

Thirdly, in the context of EFL textbooks, *who decides* (what learners are to work upon and how they do it) overlaps with *source* (i.e., where content comes from: teachers, students or learning materials?). Textbooks normally don't make a distinction between these two aspects by identifying where the content of learning activities should come from, but it is solely the learning activities provided by EFL textbooks that are to be examined in this study. This means that the only source of contents must necessarily come from the textbook itself.

Taking into consideration the above modifications, the adjusted framework is summarised in Table 2.7.

106

Table 2.7: A framework for analysis of practice activities, adapted and modified from Littlejohn's research (1992).

Elements	Definition
① Turn-Take	*do learners produce language with or without guidance?*
initiate language (unscripted)	learner(s) initiate discourse without any prompt, script or guidance.
scripted response	learner(s) produce language under guidance by the textbook.
not required	textbook does not require direct production of language items / unclear.
② Focus	*where do learners need to concentrate/focus their attention?*
language system (form)	focus on grammar, pronunciation, sentence patterns, linguistic items.
meaning	focus on semantic aspects (ex: reading comprehension).
relationship of system and meaning	focus on the connections between meaning and language form.
A: Input to learners	*the form of content that is provided to the learner by the textbook*
1. graphic	pictures, illustrations, photographs, diagrams/tables, symbols, etc.
2. word/phrases/sentences: written	written letters/numbers/words/phrases/sentences without coherence.
3. word/phrases/sentences: audio/oral	spoken letters/numbers/words/phrases/sentences without coherence.
4. extended discourse: written	texts composed of more than one sentence/pattern which cohere (>30 words).
5. extended discourse: audio/oral	texts composed of more than one sentence/pattern which cohere (>30 words).
*. ask-and-answer: written	short dialogue with one question and one reply (can be repeated).
**. ask-and-answer: audio/oral	short dialogue with one question and one reply (can be repeated).
***. unclear	the form of input is not clearly specified in the practice instructions.
B: Expected output	*the form of content that is to be produced by the learner as a result*
1. graphic	pictures, illustrations, photographs, diagrams/tables, symbols, etc.
2. word/phrases/sentences: written	written letters/numbers/words/phrases/sentences without coherence.
3. word/phrases/sentences: oral	spoken letters/numbers/words/phrases/sentences without coherence.
4. extended discourse: written	texts composed of more than one sentence/pattern which cohere (>30 words).
5. extended discourse: oral	texts composed of more than one sentence/pattern which cohere (>30 words).
*. ask-and-answer: written	short dialogue with one question and one reply (can be repeated).
**. ask-and-answer: oral	short dialogue with one question and one reply (can be repeated).
***. unclear	the form of output is not clearly specified in the practice instructions.
C: Nature	*what is the nature of the content provided/created by learners?*
6. metalinguistic comment	comments on language use, structure, form or meaning.
7. linguistic items	words/phrases/sentences/symbols devoid of any global message.
8. non-fiction	factual sentences/texts/photos/graphics/audio with coherent meaning
9. fiction	fictional sentences/texts/photos/graphics/audio with coherent meaning
10. personal information/opinion	personal information about learner(s) or their own opinion(s).
D: Operation / Process	*which mental processes are involved while the activity is performed?*
11. repeat identically	the learner is to reproduce exactly what is presented.
12. repeat selectively	the learner is to choose before repeating the given language.
13. repeat with substitution	the learner is to repeat the basic pattern of the given language, but replace certain items with other given items.
14. repeat with transformation	the learner is to apply a (conscious or unconscious) rule to given language and to transform it accordingly.
15. repeat with expansion	the learner is given an outline and is to use that outline as a frame within which to produce further language.
16. retrieve from STM	the learner is to recall items of language from short-term memory, that is, within a matter of seconds.
17. retrieve from ITM	the learner is to recall items from intermediate-term memory, that is, within a matter of minutes.

Chapter 2 / Literature Review: Towards a Descriptive Model for EFL Textbook Unit Analysis   107

18. retrieve from LTM	the learner is to recall items from a prior lesson (long-term memory).
19. formulate items into larger unit	the learner is to combine recalled items in a way that requires the application of consciously or unconsciously held language rules.
20. decode semantic/propositional meaning	the learner is to decode the 'surface' meaning of the given language.
21. select information	the learner is to extract information from a given text/graphic/audio/talk.
22. calculate	the learner is to perform mathematical operations.
23. categorise selected information	the learner is to analyse, classify or organise selected information.
24. hypothesise	the learner is to hypothesise an explanation, description or the meaning of something.
25. compare samples of language	the learner is to compare two or more sets of language data on the basis of meaning or form.
26. analyse language form	the learner is to examine the component parts of a piece of language.
27. formulate language rule	the learner is to hypothesise a language rule.
28. apply stated language rule	the learner is to use a given language rule in order to transform or produce language.
29. apply general knowledge	the learner is to draw on knowledge of 'general facts' about the world.
30. negotiate	the learner is to discuss, decide or collaborate with others in order to accomplish something.
31. review own English output	the learner is to check his/her own foreign language production for its intended meaning or form.
32. attend to example/explanation	the learner is to 'take notice' of something.
*. translate	the learner is to translate between target language and mother tongue.
E: Participation	**who are learners expected to interact with during the activity?**
33. teacher and learner(s), whole class observing	the teacher and selected learner(s) are to interact together.
34. learner(s) to the whole class	selected learner(s) are to interact with the whole class, including the teacher.
35. learners with the whole class simultaneously	learners are to perform an operation in concert with the whole class.
36. learners individually simultaneously	learners are to perform an operation in the company of others but without immediate regard to the manner/pace with which others perform the same operation.
37. learners in pairs/groups; class observing	learners in pairs or small groups are to interact with each other while the rest of the class listens.
38. learners in pairs/groups, simultaneously	learners are to interact with each other in pairs/groups in the company of other pairs/groups.

An analytical framework of practice activities within an individual unit

Regarding the contents of practice activities, we are concerned here with the form of *input* presented to learners and the form of expected *output* from learners. When we say 'form' in this case, it can refer to *graphics* such as illustrations and videos, or *words/phrases/sentences*, or *aural/oral* sounds, which are presented to learners as a starting point (input), or as something that learners are expected to produce by the end of the learning activity (output).

In addition to graphic forms, we can look at words/phrases/sentences to verify if they are presented individually or as clusters. It has been argued that one of the main goals in language teaching should be the development of language use above the level of individual sentences (Cook, 1989). Considering the language levels of starters as being those of seventh-graders, I set forth the distinction between singular sentence and more than one sentence (*extended discourse*). But if it is an ask-and-answer pattern, such as *What's your name? –My name is Eva*, it is considered as one single pattern.

As mentioned before when introducing the *nature* of content, we are mainly concerned with the *place of focus*, or *where* learners should concentrate their attention. In a similar way to Nation (1996, 2007), we consider the distinctions between language of 'meaning-focused' and 'language-focused' nature. Contents of meaning-focused nature can be presented as factual texts, fictional texts, and personal information/opinion; language-focused nature can be subdivided into metalinguistic and linguistic items.

It is worth noting that metalinguistic awareness plays a significant role in learning foreign languages (Otsu, 2009, 2011, and 2017). Otsu (2009:247) stresses that the primary purpose of EFL in Japanese schools is to provide students with a viewpoint that is different from their mother tongue, thereby helping them enrich their metalinguistic awareness. Such enriched metalinguistic awareness would help students use their mother tongue and foreign languages such as English more effectively. A secondary purpose would be to help students understand the relativity of language and culture by learning and using English, thereby gaining a different, broader perspective of the world.

The significance attached to metalinguistic awareness in EFL learning originated from the linguistic interdependence hypothesis, purported by

Cummins (1978, 1979). It argued for the influence of first-language knowledge towards the learning of another language. This hypothesis represents L1 and L2 by using a 'dual iceberg' metaphor, which describes the two languages as being two tips of an iceberg which remain visible above the sea surface, but have a common basis that connects both languages below the surface. It suggests that every language presents its own unique features on the surface; however, they share a 'common underlying proficiency' (CUP). CUP refers to the interactions between the first and second languages. It is believed that what a learner knows in the native language can positively transfer to the second language that is being acquired. In sum, this means that CUP is transferable across languages, and metalinguistic awareness is one constituent part of it.

Regarding the aspect of psychological *operation*, it defines which mental processes are involved when performing the practice activity (i.e., what the learner is required to do in his or her mind while engaged in the activity). 'Learner operations' includes the aspect of learner strategies, which originates from information processing theory, as defined by authors such as O'Malley (1985); it uses the metaphor of the computer to describe the human mind's ability to cognize and solve problems, and it suggests that there are three types of memories involved in cognition: short-term, intermediate-term and long-term memory. Apart from memories, it is argued by most proponents that cognition also involves an 'executive function' structure (or executive control structure) that monitors and selects operations which are then applied to sensorial information. As these operations continue to process information, the 'executive function' structure develops within children, which results in the improvement of their cognitive competences and a greater ability to solve problems.

For Littlejohn, this conceptual framework provided by information processing theory provides some means for identifying several 'basic abilities' which learners may resort to, when developing a set of learning strategies for dealing with a new language. His framework requires researchers to conceptualize learner operations in this manner, so that they can find a way to describe the basic, elementary mental processes that are invoked when participating in a learning activity. As mentioned previously, the identification and categorization of these basic processes requires an effort of introspection by the researchers, as they attempt to find a reasonable degree of consensus among themselves as to which exact mental processes are invoked by the 'task' (or in the case of this study, by the 'learning activity').

As for *classroom participation*, this refers to the roles of learners and teachers when performing a practice activity. Along with the transition from 'teacher-dominated' classes to 'learner-centred' classes, scholars have called for increased collaborative learning during group work, to create a more positive environment for learners (Long, 1985; Richards & Rodgers, 2001; Storch & Wigglesworth, 2007). It is argued that this can develop not only language proficiency in regards to communicative ability, but also promote the cultivation of other competences such as self-disciplined learning (Erikawa, 2012; Sato, 2012).

2.4 Conclusion

Based on the discussion and review of previous literature presented in this chapter, I have sought to develop a descriptive model for EFL textbook unit analysis that allows us to understand textbook design from a micro-scale perspective. In addition to combining a few significant analytical

Chapter 2 / Literature Review: Towards a Descriptive Model for EFL Textbook Unit Analysis　　111

tools and components suggested by previous studies, the strength of the proposed descriptive model lies in the fact that it looks at unit analysis from the perspective of the learner.

Based on the analysis of the three constituent parts of a unit, which are metadiscourse analysis, rhetorical analysis of main texts, and practice activity analysis, we should be able to make concrete statements about: how learners' learning is facilitated by metadiscourse; the degree to which main texts become comprehensible to learners; and what learners are expected to do in learning activities, both mentally and physically. In doing so, it should then be possible to infer a few underlying principles that bear significant influence on the design of a unit.

Finally, further reflection on such underlying principles would allow us to make statements about what appear to be the overall aims of the textbooks and the basis on which learning activities are selected and sequenced within a given unit. It is crucial to notice here that the findings in this study about *what textbooks are ultimately designed to achieve*, may or may not be consistent with the guidelines given for textbook compiling by national governments. From Chapters 3 to 5, I will apply this descriptive framework for unit analysis to the 14 approved textbooks. According to the key features that emerge from the textbook analysis, we should then be able to discuss answers for the research questions posed at the start of this dissertation (Chapter 6).

Chapter 3╱Metadiscourse Analysis in Japanese and Chinese EFL Textbooks

3.1 Introduction

Having introduced in Chapter 2 the general analysis framework that will inform this study, this chapter will deal with the analysis of metadiscourse elements in 7th grade English textbooks from China and Japan. But before revealing the full details of the analysis, it is necessary to add some important explanations and additional details about the methodology employed here. As previously mentioned, it is based on Crismore's framework, which was originally devised for the analysis of high-school social studies textbooks written for native speakers (1983, 1984, 1988), as well as English materials for EFL university students in Malaysia and ESL undergraduate students in the States (2000). But there are important structural differences between English materials for university-level students and 7th grade EFL materials for Chinese and Japanese learners, where they are still dealing with the most rudimentary aspects of the target language. Therefore, it is necessary to make some adaptations to Crismore's framework.

3.2 Adaptations to Crismore's Methodology

For the sake of clarity and accessibility, we present in Table 3.1 the list of metadiscourse categories and sub-types first introduced by Crismore, and in Table 3.2 we present the modified list of categories and subtypes that is applied in this study. The principal reason for redefining the original elements and introducing new ones is that in Crismore's studies, the textbooks contained long-form texts intended either for native audiences or for

114

Table 3.1: Typology of metadiscourse as defined by Crismore (1984).

Categories	Subtypes
Informational Metadiscourse	Goals (preliminary / review): main goals that the learner is expected to achieve within the unit
	Pre-plans (integral / individual): preliminary statements about content and structure of textbook/unit
	Post-plans: review statements about content and structure
	Topicalizers: local shifts of topic; introduction of a new topic
Attitudinal Metadiscourse	Salience: ideas which are especially important or relevant
	Emphatics: how much the author emphasizes a given statement
	Hedges: reveals uncertainty/doubt in a given statement
	Evaluative: reveals the author's attitude towards a fact or idea

Table 3.2: Revised list of metadiscourse types which will be used in this study.

MD Category	MD Subtype	Code
Informational	Goals	G
	Pre-plans (Integral)	PP(Int)
	Pre-plans (Individual)	PP(Ind)
	Pre-plans (Individual): Context (Pre-Text)	PP(Ind)CPT
	Pre-plans (Individual): Context (Pre-Exercise)	PP(Ind)CPE
	Post-Plans (General)	PostP
	Post-Plans – Checklist	PostP(CL)
	Post-Plans – Exercises	PostP(EX)
	Topicalizer	Top
Attitudinal	Saliency (General)	S
	Saliency – Humor/Fun (songs, cartoons, etc.)	S(H)
	Saliency – Learning Strategies/Tips/Advices	S(LS)
	Saliency – Sentence Patterns	S(SP)
	Saliency – Word Lists/Vocabulary	S(WL)
	Saliency – Pronunciation	S(P)
	Saliency – Reference to Other Sections or Supplementary Materials	S(RSM)
	Emphatics *(not identified in EFL textbooks)*	E
	Hedges *(not identified in EFL textbooks)*	H
	Evaluative *(not identified in EFL textbooks)*	Eval
Other Tags	Culture Aspect (Native)	CA(N)
	Culture Aspect (Western)	CA(W)
	Voice (1st/2nd/3rd Person)	1P/1Pl/2P/3P
	Use of Target-Native Language	T/N/NT
	Supplementary Materials / Complementary Resources	SMCR

Chapter 3 / Metadiscourse Analysis in Japanese and Chinese EFL Textbooks   115

undergraduate foreign students who are expected to have mastered the basics of English. Such texts are not just *expository* and *descriptive*, but also *argumentative* in their nature. In other words, besides describing things and laying out series of facts, they can also state a case, or argue for a certain viewpoint.

In the case of these social studies textbooks, metadiscourse—the voice of the author speaking directly to the learner, thereby making his/her presence known—is primarily embedded into the main texts themselves, by using specific words and expressions such as: 'the objective of this chapter is/was...' (goals); 'in the next section, we will learn how...' (pre-plans); 'let us now turn to the issue of politics' (topicalizers); 'the main point that we wish to make here is...' (saliency); 'this is surely a problematic issue' (emphatics); 'it may be the case that the problem was more complex than anticipated' (hedges); 'interestingly (and ironically), the policies had the very opposite effect of what was intended...' (evaluative), etc. All these examples show the author's own intentions and opinions protruding from the text itself, which require a reasonable level of language knowledge in order to be properly understood.

To be clear, most of the textual passages in the materials analysed by Crismore were merely expository and descriptive, since they attempted to convey clear, objective facts to the learner by adopting an authoritative, impersonal stance. But she was especially concerned with the problem of preparing students for engaging with more complex writings, in which most facts are not as clear-cut as they seem at first. To her disappointment, most of the texts she analysed required learners to absorb facts passively, instead of promoting critical thought, argumentation, or debate. The types of metadiscourse that she categorises as being 'attitudinal' (i.e., which reveal the attitude of the author towards the presented information) are especially crucial for constructing argumentative texts: saliency, hedges, emphatics and evaluative, all of which were poorly featured in textbook materials. These are the elements that help to: express doubt and certainty; present the author's subjective assumptions and expectations about the learner's level of knowledge; or that try to 'guide' the learner into 'seeing things' from the author's standpoint, etc. She further argued (2000) that since learners from foreign countries generally have limited exposure to these types of metadiscourse, their ability to interpret and produce argumentative texts will suffer as a result.

To conduct this analysis, one must first learn to separate and distinguish metadiscourse from the following types of contents: reading comprehension materials, character dialogues, direct instructions for exercises and activities, and section titles. In doing so, it is inevitable to come across some contents which are ambiguous, or which may lie in the border between metadiscourse and non-metadiscourse. And even when they can be positively identified as metadiscourse, some doubts may linger about whether a certain element belongs to two categories at the same time. For example, in some cases it is not easy to properly distinguish between a very short sentence that sets the stage (context) for an exercise (which would fall under the pre-plans subcategory), and another short sentence that introduces the theme for a certain exercise (topicalizer subcategory). Another example would be the tenuous differences between goals and pre-plans, since textbooks do not always state goals clearly, and sometimes mix implicit goal statements together with other elements (which can be better classified as pre-plans).

In this study, the contents of 7th grade entry-level EFL textbooks are unmistakably descriptive and basic in nature. What happens in the case of these textbooks is that metadiscourse rarely arises from within the text passages themselves (such as reading comprehension texts or learning activity instructions), but mostly from side notes and small text columns adjacent to the main texts and exercises, that provide all sorts of hints, tips, advices, strategies, comments, sentence patterns, additional vocabulary, or simply motivational encouragement. These fall under the metadiscourse subcategory of salience, since the authors would not have included all these additional features if they did not think they would be especially relevant or useful for the learner. In textbooks, word limits are often strictly enforced and page space is limited, which forces authors to reduce the amount of superfluous information as much as possible. But in order to better conduct the micro-scale analysis of textbook units, it is necessary to add additional markers that can help distinguish between all these different aspects of 'salience' metadiscourse, as shown in Table 3.2.

Regarding the use of words such as 'but', which normally belong to the metadiscourse subtype of 'hedges', it was found that they are almost inexistent in the textbooks featured in this study, and they merely appear in some character dialogues or reading comprehension materials. Even so, the word 'but' is only used in a descriptive sense, not in an argumentative sense (for example, a sentence such as 'I did [this], but not [that]', is descriptive, while 'many authors defended this viewpoint in the past, but does it still hold up now?' is argumentative). For these reasons (scarcity of occurrences and descriptive character), and because such words are always included inside character dialogues or monologues, they do not truly convey the authors' attitudes towards the learning contents, and therefore were not counted as metadiscourse items. The last two types of attitudinal metadiscourse, emphatics and evaluative, are not found at all in the textbooks, which suggests that textbook design practices have not changed dramatically since Crismore's study.

3.3 Examples of Metadiscourse Subtypes Found in EFL Textbooks

We will now proceed to the list of the main categories and subtypes of metadiscourse used in this study, with explanations about how to distinguish between them to minimize ambiguities, while providing some examples for added clarity.

3.3.1 Informational metadiscourse

Goals: these indicate communication skills or aspects of the target language that the learner is expected to master by the end of the unit or the textbook. Although Crismore further divided this subtype into 'goals (preliminary)' and 'goals (review)', which respectively indicate goal statements presented at the start of a unit or at its end, it was considered best to consolidate them into a single 'goals' subtype. The main reason for this is that no goals were found at the end of units, and furthermore there are Japanese textbooks such as *One World* and *Sunshine 1*, which present new goal statements almost every two pages.

In fact, this study found that the EFL textbooks can present goals in very different ways. *Ren'ai, Waiyanshe*, and *Yilin* do not contain any goal statements inside the units themselves, although in the pre-plans sections at the very start of the textbooks, we can find a small number of very basic and formulaic expressions called 'Functions' that suggest the units' objectives, such as 'Greetings' or 'Describing appearances'. *Total English 1*

Chapter 3∕Metadiscourse Analysis in Japanese and Chinese EFL Textbooks   119

has clear goal statements only outside of the units, namely at the beginning of each main chapter. On the other hand, *Beishida, Renjiao, Columbus 21, New Crown 1*, and *New Horizon 1* present a very clear list of goals at the opening page of each unit, listed as '目標' or 'この科で学ぶこと': for instance, '人やものの紹介の仕方を知る' (*New Crown*) or 'Language Goals (...) Ask for and give telephone numbers' (*Renjiao*). The remaining Chinese textbooks are much more ambiguous about how goals are presented. At the start of each unit, they contain a pre-plans section with titles such as 'Getting Ready' (*Shangjiao*), 'Highlights' (*Shangwai*), and 'We Will Learn' (*Jijiao*) which present a brief summary of the main contents of the unit and their sequence; but within these pre-plan statements, one can find one or two basic sentences that imply the idea of goals: 'Getting Ready' has under the subtopic 'Grammar' the phrase 'Learn how to use **the simple present tense**'; 'Highlights' has under the subtopic 'Functions' the phrase 'Telling the time'; and 'We Will Learn' has under the subtopic 'Functions' the phrase 'Talking about School'. In these cases where goals can still be identified, even if in an implicit manner, it was decided to categorise these sections as both 'goals' and 'pre-plans (individual)'.

Pre-Plans (Integral): the basic concept of pre-plans is that they prepare the learner for something that will show up later in its full-fledged form. In the case of integral pre-plans, these consist of sections at the start of each textbook that present a list of main contents for each unit, so that the learner understands what he/she will be faced with later. In Chinese textbooks, almost all of them have an introduction or preface section written by the authors themselves, under the titles '前言' (*Waiyanshe, Beishida, Ren'ai*), '致同学' (*Jijiao, Yilin, Renjiao*), and '写在前面' (*Shangjiao*). These usually explain the main aspects of the textbook, and in the case of *Renji-*

ao, also include the authors' guiding principles regarding textbook compiling. Following this, comes another pre-plans section which is common to all textbooks, titled either 'Contents' (*Renjiao, Shangjiao, Jijiao, Yilin*) or 'Scope and Sequence' (remaining textbooks) which lays out the sequence of units, and for each unit presents a summary of the following aspects: titles of unit subsections and reading comprehension texts; functions and skills that will be taught; main items of vocabulary, grammar, and pronunciation.

As for the Japanese textbooks, all of them start with photos of people, foods, and places from across the world; *Sunshine* and *Columbus 21* match the photos respectively with descriptive captions of each image, or with general goals related to English communication skills, while all the others feature photos of children from different countries dressed in traditional outfits, paired with greeting expressions from each language. This focus on cultural diversity marks a clear contrast with the Chinese textbooks.

The subsequent sections are pretty much similar in all Japanese textbooks: there is a page introducing the main characters; then comes a 'Contents／目次' section that serves as an index, but can also include a listing of main sentence patterns for each unit. Following this, there is another section named either 'この教科書で[英語を]学ぶみんなさんへ' (*Columbus 21, Sunshine, One World*), 'この教科書の使い方' (*New Horizon, New Crown*) or 'この教科書を使用する前に' (*Total English*), which present the overarching structure of the textbook along with the main purposes of each section and unit; these sections include auxiliary explanations about the types of symbols featured throughout the units, and give advice on how to make the best use of the textbook for studying the language. *Columbus 21* adds to this mix a Romaji-Katakana conversion table, and *Total English* presents a list of important English expressions used in classrooms. All these

Chapter 3 / Metadiscourse Analysis in Japanese and Chinese EFL Textbooks   121

sections should be considered as integral pre-plans, because they refer to the structure of the textbook overall.

Pre-Plans (Individual): unlike integral pre-plans, individual pre-plans appear on the units themselves, but they also serve the same function of preparing the learner for things that will come later. The general category of individual pre-plans refers directly to the starting page of each unit, as it presents a very summarized list of unit contents in their proper sequence, including in some cases main sentence patterns, vocabulary items and pronunciation items. As mentioned previously in the 'goals' category, these pre-plan statements can include short sentences or 'functions' that serve as goal statements. This type of pre-plan lists at the starting page of each unit is featured in the Chinese textbooks *Jijiao*, *Shangwai* and *Shangjiao*, while the rest have either only goal statements or no individual preplans at all. Japanese textbooks do not contain this sort of pre-plans except for *Total English*, but in this case the pre-plan list is not featured in any individual unit: it is located at the starting page of each new chapter (one chapter includes three units).

Additionally, in both Chinese and Japanese textbooks we can identify other subtypes of individual pre-plan statements within the units themselves, which we have labelled as 'Context (Pre-Text)' and 'Context (Pre-Exercise)'. These respectively refer to short sentences presented right before a reading comprehension text or right before instructions for an exercise, which explain the setting in which something is taking place, or provide relevant context by preparing the learner for what comes after. Examples of such sentences include: '*Jane is from Canada. She is teaching English in China. She is writing an e-mail to her family and friends back home.*' (*Jijiao*); '*Sam and Mandy are talking about their daily lives on the internet.*'

(*Shangjiao*); '店主のブリックさんがお店の商品を紹介します。' (*Sunshine*); or '久美たちの学校に、アメリカの姉妹校のリサからメールが届きました。' (*New Crown*). These sentences are overwhelmingly written in the third person, since they are often used for character dialogues and exercises in which characters are involved.

<u>Post-Plans</u>: these refer to self-review and self-assessment sections. The main difference between Chinese and Japanese textbooks in this respect is that almost all the Chinese textbooks prefer to include some form of review or self-assessment section at the end of each individual unit, while Japanese textbooks generally place such elements as their own separate section independent from the units themselves, that simultaneously reviews the learning contents of two or three units overall. While post-plan statements are basically just a list that reviews the main contents of the unit, it is more common for them to appear in the form of a checklist (Post-Plans Checklist) or as an exercise (Post-Plans Exercise).

<u>Topicalizers</u>: of all the metadiscourse subtypes, topicalizers have proven to be the most difficult to pin down and identify within the units of both countries' textbooks. To begin with, it is tempting to assume that every single title in a unit or its subsections should be marked as a topicalizer, especially if those titles are responsible for introducing an idea to the learner for the first time. However, if we look closely at the unit and subsection titles of all textbooks, it becomes clear that they are almost always preceding a reading comprehension text or dialogue, and therefore they serve simultaneously as headings for the main texts, which do not constitute metadiscourse.

Topicalizers should be considered as a short set of words that are independent of reading comprehension materials, and that may be like key-

Chapter 3／Metadiscourse Analysis in Japanese and Chinese EFL Textbooks　123

words, or even short rhetorical questions that quickly introduce a new topic or theme, on which the learner is expected to engage with. Some examples of topicalizers are: 'Millie's school days', 'A volleyball match' (*Yilin*); and '学校行事' (*Columbus 21*).

Any question that is non-rhetorical should not be considered as a topicalizer, because instead of introducing a new topic, non-rhetorical questions act primarily as direct task instructions that require an immediate answer or action on behalf of the learner. Examples of rhetorical questions found within the textbooks that can be interpreted as topicalizers include: 'Are schools in China and Canada the same?' (*Jijiao*) or 'Are you happy?' (*Yilin*); the reason why these questions can be considered rhetorical is because of the other sentences placed around them. They encourage the learner to think about the new topic being introduced, but do not require a direct answer: they are immediately followed not just by other sentences that provide further context (individual pre-plan statements), but also by non-rhetorical questions that demand a direct response.

Another important thing to keep in mind about topicalizers is that they should not refer directly to learning task instructions, goals, vocabulary items or language contents (Examples of non-topicalizers: section/subsection titles and expressions such as 'Writing', 'Reading', 'Putting it All Together', 'Self-Evaluation', '曜日と教科', '数字' etc.).

All these categorization principles allow us to distinguish topicalizers (topics and themes) from individual pre-plan statements (namely sentences that introduce settings and contexts before exercises and reading comprehension materials). Even so, it is not rare to find ambiguous cases, and in case of doubt, it was decided not to mark them as metadiscourse. The value of topicalizers in textbooks is that they can sometimes replace the need for context sentences (i.e., 'pre-plans individual - context pre-text' / 'pre-exercise'), and serve an important role in encouraging learners to feel more interested in doing the exercises. If such learning activities are presented without any kind of theme or topic that can relate to the daily lives of 7th grade learners, they may be thought of as too 'dry' or 'boring'. Clear, unambiguous topicalizers are mainly absent from all Japanese textbooks (which include instead plenty of context sentences), and were identified more often in Chinese textbooks.

3.3.2 Attitudinal metadiscourse

Salience: this subtype demarks all elements that the authors deem to be especially relevant or important for learning. For the most part these consist of advices or strategies for learning English or for finding the solution to an exercise, but they also include optional word lists and pronunciation markers that are not directly related to learning activities, and provide additional options for language practice. In the Japanese textbooks, word list columns placed next to reading comprehension texts will often contain '□' marks that serve as a checklist, and some words which the authors deem to be especially important are marked in **bold**, including small marker arrows that indicate which syllable should be stressed when pronouncing the word. While the Chinese textbooks also contain word lists, there are no checklist marks or bolded words. These elements are categorised as 'Saliency (Word Lists/Vocabulary)'. Likewise, any separate column or subsection specifically devoted to teaching pronunciation and how to stress words adequately is defined as 'Saliency (Pronunciation)'.

In some of the textbooks there may occasionally be columns of text where it is not so easy to distinguish between lists of language practice-re-

Chapter 3／Metadiscourse Analysis in Japanese and Chinese EFL Textbooks   125

lated tips and optional learning activities. One can offer the example of a column titled 'Dig In' within Unit 3 of *Jijiao* that not only offers tips and advices on how the learner can make a positive difference in society, but also asks non-rhetorical questions to the learner about what it means to make a difference. This column appears a second time in the same unit, with advices on how to help others in need, while also including direct questions for the learner. While the tips themselves may appear at first to be metadiscourse, the inclusion of such questions strongly suggests that the column overall is intended for use as a learning activity or exercise.

The diversity of columns found outside of reading comprehension texts and exercises made it necessary to devise additional subtypes of saliency metadiscourse: columns with song lyrics for singing or humorous cartoons which indirectly present the use of certain sentence patterns are defined as 'Saliency (Humor／Fun)'; all columns with learning strategies, tips or just general advice are defined as 'Saliency (Learning Strategies)'; columns that introduce and explain sentence patterns are marked as 'Saliency (Sentence Patterns)'; and finally we can attest to small icons that ask the learner to reference other sections of the textbook for further information and practice. These last ones are defined as 'Saliency (Reference to Supplementary Materials／Other Sections)'.

A final note on saliency should be made about the occasional use of terms such as 'can' or 'may', which at first seem to suggest hedging (because they provide options for the learner and do not force him／her to execute the learning activity in a fully pre-determined manner), but after further consideration they appear to fall more closely into the subtype of saliency. Direct examples of the use of these words are: 'You can use the following questions to help you...' (*Yilin*); 'You may need these words to

help you...' (*Shangwai*); and 'The questions in 3b may help you...' (*Ren'ai*).
The point is that in practice, because learners at this stage are still beginners and do not possess a fully matured set of variant phrases, these terms
encourage learners to follow the advice, rather than ignore it. Therefore, if
these terms appear outside of fictional dialogue or reading comprehension
texts, they are to be considered as metadiscourse. Only Chinese textbooks
are affected by this, although they do not appear frequently. However, Japanese textbooks do not make any explicit use of these terms whether in
target or native language, and merely provide options implicitly using bolded and non-bolded words, and other optional columns. This marks an important difference in the ways that both countries choose to provide options for the learner, or steer them into using certain words or sentence
patterns.

Emphatics / Hedges / Evaluative: these subtypes of metadiscourse
were not positively identified in any of the analysed textbooks. There are
borderline cases where terms such as 'but', 'well' or 'I think that...' will
sometimes pop up in character dialogues or monologues, but due to the
low number of occurrences of these words, and since they are part of the
dialogue of fictional characters, and are not direct communications from
the author to the learner, it was decided not to count these terms as metadiscourse.

3.3.3 Other tags

Cultural Aspect (Native / Western): this tag is used when a certain
metadiscourse element is designed to make learners think about cultural
differences between their countries and the West. It is not *per se* an independent metadiscourse category: we find it attached to other subtypes

Chapter 3 / Metadiscourse Analysis in Japanese and Chinese EFL Textbooks 127

such as topicalizers (ex: Top+CA(N)) or saliency (ex: S+CA(W)) in the case of Chinese textbooks, and in Japanese textbooks cultural aspect markers were found to be attached to contextual individual pre-plan statements (ex: Pre-Plans Contextual Pre-Text or Pre-Exercise) and saliency (ex: Learning Strategies). In general it was found that both countries prefer to engage in cultural comparisons within reading comprehension materials and learning activities, rather than by using metadiscourse.

Use of Target-Native Language: this tag explains whether the textbooks are using native language or English (or a mix of both) to communicate with the learner. This tag was used for both metadiscourse, and for non-metadiscourse (namely, the instructions provided during exercises or learning activities).

Voice: this tag explains whether the texts and instructions are written in the first person (1P), first person inclusive plural (1PI), second person (2P), third person (3P) or non-attributable (N/A). First-person Inclusive Plural is a characteristic unique to Japanese textbooks, since they overwhelmingly use native language for almost any kind of communication with the learner: this refers to the use of verb terminations such as 'しよう／しましょう', '書こう', and so forth, which are also used in 7th grade Japanese textbooks for other disciplines. We should mark the contrast between 7th-grade textbooks that use this inclusive verb form (ex: '[Let's] do...'; '[Let's] write...'), with textbooks in later grades that resort to the use of 'なさい／ください' (ex: '[Please] do...' or simply '...do...') to address the learner. This also contrasts dramatically with Chinese textbooks, which overwhelmingly use English instead of the native language: in this case, learners are considerably exposed to second person statements written in the target language (ex: '[You] write a few sentences...'; '[You] listen to the passage...'), while Japanese learners are much more exposed to the subtle polite overtones of their own language.

The tag N/A (Non-attributable) was used when the metadiscourse column does not have any clearly identifiable voice, as is the case in word lists, formulaic sentence patterns, or pronunciation tips.

Supplementary Materials: technically, almost all the elements defined as saliency metadiscourse could be considered as extra materials: word lists, pronunciation tips, learning strategies, etc. However, applying this in practice would have made the categorisation too broad, because the metadiscourse elements appear frequently within the units themselves, especially in the case of Japanese textbooks. It was considered that this tag would be more suitable for other sections that are often placed outside the unit itself, such as vocabulary indices, language summaries, tongue-twisters, typescripts of listening activities, student workbooks, etc.

All the textbooks examined in the present study had listening practices, but typescripts were only available in the Chinese textbooks. In *Beishida*, apart from the common extra materials mentioned previously, a section titled 'Pair Work Activities' was included to reinforce the key points of each lesson through group work. A students' workbook was also included at the end of the textbook.

Unlike their Chinese counterparts, which are fairly homogeneous, Japanese textbooks tended to present more differences, although they concentrate most of the extra materials in the final pages of the textbook, in an appendix section called '付録'. All of them include song lyrics, word index, list of bonus words, summary of sentence patterns, alphabet writing samples, and pronunciation tables. Besides this, depending on the textbook, we can find some unique extra materials: a method for writing letters and postcards (*New Horizon*); a mini-dictionary (*Total English, New Crown*); a section that briefly introduces children from different countries (*Total English*); a game section (*New Crown*; *Sunshine* provides a set of 'action cards' for games); a self-assessment checklist section (*New Crown, Sunshine, One World*); additional texts for reading practice (*Columbus 21*); tips for using dictionaries and typing English on PC keyboards (*One World*); and a separate workbook with additional exercises for each unit (*One World*).

One last interesting aspect can be found in the last page of *New Horizon*, which has a column titled '保護者へ' that stresses the book's main objective as trying to develop the four skills while preparing the child for global activities in the future, and actively encourages parents and caretakers to use the textbook as an opportunity to study together with their children. A similar section can be found at the start of *Total English*, which stresses the importance of English towards international communication, and states its aim as broadening the worldview of learners.

3.4 Description of Steps Used for the Metadiscourse Analysis and Other Methodological Considerations

From each textbook, a list of units related to 'school life' were selected for analysis (Tables 3.3 and 3.4). In order to establish a new list of metadiscourse categories that would be appropriate for these textbooks, each 'school life' unit from each textbook was transcribed into an Excel spreadsheet, and annotated in detail, including the subtype of metadiscourse, the designation of target-native language (target, native or both) and voice (1st person, 2nd person, N/A, etc.) as well as comments about why each metadiscourse item was categorised as such. A sample of the Excel spreadsheet can be seen in Figure 3.1. This entire spreadsheet of 'school life' units

Table 3.3: List of Japanese textbook units analysed in this dissertation. Note: the meta-discourse analysis was conducted only on the 'school life' units.

		Japan		
Series Title	Publisher	Unit of school life	Unit of family	Unit of events
New Crown 1	Sanseido	Lesson 8: School life in the USA. Pp. 99-110	Lesson 6: My family. Pp. 70-81	Lesson 9: Four seasons. Pp. 111-122
New Horizon 1	Tokyo Shoseki	Unit 5: School cultural festival. Pp. 58-64	Unit 6: Brother in Austria. Pp. 66-72	Unit 11: Memories in a year. Pp. 116-122
Sunshine 1	Kairyudo	Program 2: Student from America. Pp. 24-29	Program 11: Grandma Baba and her friends on a sleigh. Pp. 114-119	Program 9: A New year's visit. Pp. 90-99
Total English 1	Gakko Tosho	Lesson 6: Junior high school in the U.S. Pp. 72-78	Lesson 5: Ms. Allen's family. Pp. 62-68	Lesson 7: New year. Pp. 88-95
One World 1	Kyoiku Shuppan	Lesson 6: Foreign schools and Japanese schools. Pp. 74-83	Lesson 4: Ms. King's family. Pp. 50-61	Lesson 8: different winter holidays. Pp. 98-107
Columbus 21	Mitsumura Tosho	Unit 9: Tina's school life. Pp. 107-117	Unit 7: Cheer up, Tina. Pp. 79-96	Unit 10: Happy New Year. Pp. 121-130

Table 3.4: List of Chinese textbook units analysed in this dissertation. Note: the meta-discourse analysis was conducted only on the 'school life' units.

	China		
Series Title (total units in a book)	Unit of school life	Unit of family	Unit of events
Renjiao ban 7 (9 units + 3 units)	Unit 9: My favorite subject is science. Pp. 49-54	Unit 2: This is my sister. Pp. 7-12	Unit 12:* What did you do last weekend? Pp. 67-72
Beishida ban 7 (4 units + 5 topics)	Unit 2: School life. Pp. 37-48	Unit 1: Family. Pp. 25-36	Unit 4:* Seasons and weather. Pp. 41-52
Ren'ai ban 7 (12 topics)	Topic 3:* My school life is very interesting. Pp. 17-24	Topic 8: What does your mother do? Pp. 63-70	Topic 11:* The summer holidays are coming. Pp. 89-96
Yilin ban 7 (8 units)	Unit 4: My day. Pp. 42-53	Unit 2:* Neighbours. Pp. 18-29	Unit 5: Let's celebrate. Pp. 56-67
Jijiao ban 7 (8 units)	Unit 3:* School life. Pp. 33-48	Unit 5: Family and home. Pp. 65-80	Unit 8:* Summer holiday is coming. Pp. 113-128
Waiyanshe ban 7 (10 modules+4 mod.)	Module 5: School and school life. Pp. 26-35	Module 2: My family. Pp. 8-13	Module 10: Spring festival. Pp. 60-65
Shangwai ban 7	Unit 3: Daily life. Pp. 23-33	Unit 4: People around you. Pp. 34-44	Unit 10: Enjoy your holidays. Pp. 101-112
Shangjiao ban 7 (8 units)	Unit 2: Daily life. Pp. 15-27	Unit 1:* People around us. Pp. 1-14	Unit 7: School clubs. Pp. 85-98

(which can be consulted in Appendix B) was revised and corrected two more times, during which I established the final list of metadiscourse categories, and defined a list of clear principles and rules for distinguishing between ambiguous items (this list was already discussed in the previous section).

Chapter 3 / Metadiscourse Analysis in Japanese and Chinese EFL Textbooks   131

Based on this extensive analysis, and with clear guidelines about how to identify and distinguish between different types of metadiscourse, I devised a list of code tags and a colour for each metadiscourse subtype (Table 3.5). This simplified spreadsheet was then used to generate graph charts for each unit.

It is not necessary to analyse metadiscourse elements in every single unit because within each textbook, all units follow practically the same progression structure, and resemble each other so much that from unit to unit, we frequently see the same subtypes of metadiscourse repeating in cycles, with few (if any) differences. Due to this strong homogeneity and internal consistency, even a single unit is strongly representative of the remaining units of the same textbook. If one were to point out any differences, it would be that the latter units near the end of the textbook tend to have slightly more variety of metadiscourse than the first units.

Let us look at the example of *New Crown*, namely Lessons 2 and 8, as depicted in Figures 3.2 and 3.3. Although it may appear at first sight that Lesson 8 has more diversity of metadiscourse subtypes when compared to Lesson 2, in fact it is the case that the predominant subtypes of metadiscourse have not changed. We can notice the predominance of saliency, preplan, and goal items, with at least three occurrences or more, while the newly-appearing subtypes shown in Lesson 8 are only featured at most once or twice, and are merely variants of the predominant ones (except for the topicalizer subtype). In general, the difference between units in a single textbook is even less pronounced than the New Crown example (a full list of graphs and charts for the selected units can be found at the Appendix section). Since doing a metadiscourse analysis for all units would be redundant (due to the strong homogeneity of unit structure within each text-

Exercise Number	Title	Target-Native Language (non-MD portion of text)	Voice (non-MD portion of text)	Topicalizer	Target-Native Language (topicalizer)	Voice (topicalizer)	Context Introduction / Explanation	Hint/Tip/Example
A	School life. Millie often writes to her online friend Tommy. Here is one of her emails.	Target	Third Person	School life.	Target	Third Person	Millie often writes to her online friend Tommy. Here is one of her emails.	N/A
B1	Millie's school days. Tommy wants to know what Millie and her classmates do at school. Help him match each activity with the correct time.	Target	Second Person	Millie's school days	Target	Third Person	Tommy wants to know what Millie and her classmates do at school.	N/A
B2	Read Tommy's notes about Millie's email. Write a **T** if a sentence is true or an **F** if it is false.	Target	Second Person	N/A	N/A	N/A	N/A	N/A
B3	Tommy's friend Joan is asking Tommy about Millie's school day. Complete their conversation. Use the words and phrases in Millie's email on page 44.	Target	Second Person	N/A	N/A	N/A	Tommy's friend Joan is asking Tommy about Millie's school day.	N/A
C	My day. Complete the sentences about your day.	Target	Second Person	My day.	Target	First Person	N/A	N/A

Textbook	Section	Exercise	nonMD_TNL	nonMD_Voice	Topic	TNLang	Voice	Goals	TNLang	Voice	Pr
Yilin Ban 7	Reading	A	T	3P	Top	T	3P				
Yilin Ban 7	Reading	B1	T	2P	Top	T	3P				
Yilin Ban 7	Reading	B2	T	2P							
Yilin Ban 7	Reading	B3	T	2P							
Yilin Ban 7	Reading	C	T	2P	Top	T	3P				

S(SP)	S(RSM)	S	S(LS)	S(WL)	S(SP)	S(H)	PostP(EX)	PP(Ind)CPT	PP(Ind)CPE	PP(Ind)CPE	PP(Ind)CPE	PP(Ind)CPE	PP(Ind)CPE	PP(Ind)CPE	PP(Ind)CPE	PP(Ind)CPE	PP(Ind)CPT	PP(Ind)CPE	Top	Top	Top	Top	Top	Top	Top	Top	Top	Top	Top	Top	Top	MD Category Native Language	Target-Native Language
target	target	target	target	target	target	target	target	target	target	target	target	target	target	target	target	target	target	target	target	target	target	target	target	target	target	target	target	target	target	target	target		Voice
1P	2P	2PI	N/A	N/A	N/A	1P	3P	3P	3P	3P	3P	3P	3P	3P	3P	3P	3P	2P	3P	3P	3P	3P	3P	3P	3P	3P	3P	3P	3P	3P	3P		

Figure 3.1: Samples of the Excel spreadsheet used for analysing metadiscourse items.

MD Type (#1)	MD Subtype (#1)	Reason for MD choice (#1)	Target-Native Language of MD (#1)	Voice of MD (#1)	MD Type (#2)	MD Subtype (#2)	Reason for MD choice (#2)	Target-Native Language of MD (#2)	Voice of MD (#2)
Informational	Pre-plans (individual) – Context (Pre-Text)	This sentence provides context for the task at hand; it prepares the learner for what is to come later.	Target	Third Person	N/A	N/A	N/A	N/A	N/A
Informational	Pre-plans (individual) – Context (Pre-Exercise)	This sentence provides context for the task at hand; it prepares the learner for what is to come later.	Target	Third Person	N/A	N/A	N/A	N/A	N/A
N/A	N/A	N/A	N/A	N/A	N/A	N/A	N/A	N/A	N/A
Informational	Pre-plans (individual) – Context (Pre-Exercise)	This sentence provides context for the task at hand; it prepares the learner for what is to come later.	Target	Third Person	N/A	N/A	N/A	N/A	N/A
N/A	N/A	N/A	N/A	N/A	N/A	N/A	N/A	N/A	N/A

(Int)	TNLang	Voice	PreP(Ind)	TNLang	Voice	PostP	TNLang	Voice	Sal	TNLang	Voice
			PP(Ind)CPT	T	3P						
			PP(Ind)CPE	T	3P						
			PP(Ind)CPE	T	3P						

book), and considering how the main objective of this chapter is to compare metadiscourse usage between countries, it was considered sufficient to simply analyse one 'school life' unit from each textbook.

Another point that needs to be clarified is that there are three types of graph charts for each unit: the first graph presents the types of target-native language (Chinese, Japanese and English) and voice of non-metadiscourse text (1st person, 2nd person, etc.); the second merely shows the different subtypes of metadiscourse, while the third shows the same subtypes divided by type of language and voice. The analysis of target-native language and voice for non-metadiscourse text was also only conducted on the 'school life' units, because the results overwhelmingly represent the totality of the units within each textbook, and therefore doing the same analysis for other units would be a superfluous exercise.

Figures 3.4 and 3.5 respectively show the graph charts for metadiscourse in Japanese and Chinese textbooks. These charts reveal the number of times that a certain type of metadiscourse appeared within the analysed unit. It is important to clarify that this analysis is not meant to be quantitative, but qualitative: the charts were only created for the purpose of making the research results

more accessible and easier to grasp for the reader. Metadiscourse can easily become a very abstract topic, and it is difficult to correctly visualize in one's mind the analysis results from just reading a text. Therefore, the use of a colour scheme within graph charts can help to convey the diversity and prevalence of metadiscourse subtypes within a single unit. After all, it is the balance and diversity of these subtypes that demonstrates Crismore's notion of 'stylistic variables': in other words, the decisions made by textbook compilers towards deciding which metadiscourse subtypes should

Chapter 3 / Metadiscourse Analysis in Japanese and Chinese EFL Textbooks 135

Table 3.5: Final list of metadiscourse subtypes, codes and colour scheme.

MD Code + Color	Designation
G	Goals
PP(Int)	Pre-Plans (Integral)
PP(Ind)	Pre-Plans (Individual)
PP(Ind)CPT	Pre-Plans (Individual): Context Pre-Text
PP(Ind)CPT+CA(W)	Pre-Plans (Individual): Context Pre-Text + Culture Aspect (Western)
PP(Ind)CPE	Pre-Plans (Individual): Context Pre-Exercise
PP(Ind)CPE+CA(W)	Pre-Plans (Individual): Context Pre-Exercise + Culture Aspect (Western)
PostP	Post-Plans (General)
PostP(CL)	Post-Plans (Checklist)
PostP(EX)	Post-Plans (Exercise)
Top	Topicalizer
Top+CA(N)	Topicalizer + Cultural Aspect (Native)
S	Saliency (General)
S+CA(W)	Saliency + Cultural Aspect (Western)
S(H)	Saliency (Humor/Fun/Song)
S(LS)	Saliency (Learning Strategies/Advices/Tips)
S(LS)+CA(N)	Saliency (Learning Strategies) + Culture Aspects (Native)
S(LS)+CA(W)	Saliency (Learning Strategies) + Culture Aspects (Western)
S(SP)	Saliency (Sentence Pattern)
S(WL)	Saliency (Word Lists/Vocabulary)
S(P)	Saliency (Pronunciation)
S(RSM)	Saliency (Reference to Other Sections & Supplementary Materials)

Figures 3.2 and 3.3: Graph charts of metadiscourse subtypes found in New Crown (Lessons 2/8).

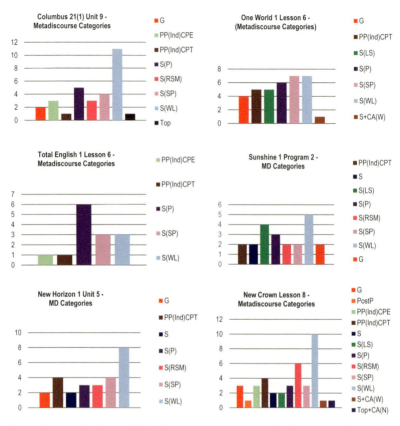

Figure 3.4: Graph charts of Metadiscourse subtypes found in Japanese textbooks (school life units).

be included ultimately reveal the 'style' of conversation that they wish to establish with the learner.

Chapter 3/ Metadiscourse Analysis in Japanese and Chinese EFL Textbooks 137

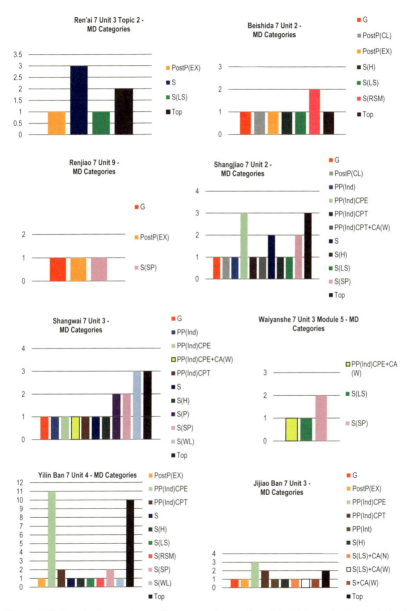

Figure 3.5: Graph charts of metadiscourse subtypes found in Chinese textbooks (school life units).

3.5 Main Findings from the Metadiscourse and Non-Metadiscourse Analysis of Japanese and Chinese EFL Textbooks

3.5.1 Voice and target-native language (non-metadiscourse)

Representative charts for non-metadiscourse text analysis in terms of target-native language use and voice are presented in Figure 3.6 (the full list of charts for 'school life' units can be found in the Appendix). The results of the target-native language use and voice use analysis show that the Chinese textbooks were all written in English, although *Renjiao* marks an exception by providing all instructions within exercises and learning activities in both Chinese and English. In the Japanese textbooks, however, besides language input, Japanese was overwhelmingly used in most sections, including instruction, interpretation, and translation of words. Even in sections where both languages can be found, the use of English is usually minimal. To some degree, this can reflect the current language use reality in classroom practice. Concerning voice use in non-metadiscourse passages, Chinese textbooks focus on the use of second-person sentences for exercise instructions, while Japanese textbooks use mainly the first-person

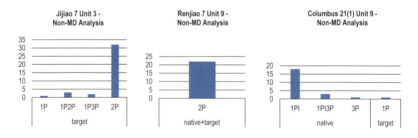

Figure 3.6: Representative graph charts of target-native language use and voice use in non-metadiscourse text sections (exercise instructions) within Chinese and Japanese textbooks.

inclusive plural when writing instructions in the native language.

3.5.2 Voice and target-native language (metadiscourse)

As for voice use in metadiscourse passages, context sentences (i.e., pre-plan statements before main texts and exercises) in both Chinese and Japanese textbooks are mostly written in the third person, because they narrate situations involving fictional characters. There are relatively few instances where learners themselves are asked to become a part of individual pre-plans context statements. Some examples of this are: 'Imagine you work for a company that helps poor children.' and 'Imagine there is a new student at your school. He is scared and nervous' (*Jijiao*). From the viewpoint of textbook compilers, they may believe that learners prefer to first practice examples of target language with story characters before applying the examples to themselves. Furthermore, it may be the case that fictional characters, who are a mix of Westerners and Asians, provide more opportunities for presenting cultural differences to the learner.

Columbus 21 can be used as a representative case for all Japanese textbooks (Figure 3.7; the charts for all the analysed units can be found in the Appendix). Pre-plan contextual sentences, goal statements and topics are mainly written as third-person, while salience-related items for the most

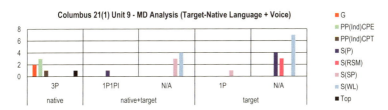

Figure 3.7: Graph chart of target-native language use and voice use in metadiscourse items within a 'school life' unit of Columbus 21.

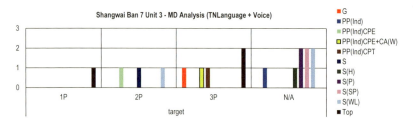

Figure 3.8: Graph chart of target-native language use and voice use in metadiscourse items within a 'school life' unit of Shangwai.

part have no clearly identifiable voice (sentence patterns, reference markers and word lists are mostly presented as incomplete sentences).

Although the Chinese textbooks are slightly less homogeneous in this respect compared to the Japanese ones, it is nevertheless correct to affirm that in general there is a stronger shift towards the second and third persons for goals, pre-plans, post-plans and topicalizers, whereas salience-related items are for the most part non-attributable just like the Japanese textbooks. The graph chart for *Shangwai* is presented here as a representative case (Figure 3.8).

Overall, it can be said that in the case of metadiscourse, exposure of different voices in the target language is relatively balanced for Chinese textbooks, although *Ren'ai* and *Jijiao* tended to neglect the first person.

3.5.3 Diversity and balance of metadiscourse subtypes

While reaffirming that this study is not intended to be purely quantitative, it is worth mentioning that units in Japanese textbooks feature noticeably more instances of metadiscourse than Chinese textbooks, especially in regards to individual pre-plan context statements (pre-text) and salience items (word lists, sentence patterns, pronunciation tips and reference mark-

Chapter 3∕Metadiscourse Analysis in Japanese and Chinese EFL Textbooks   141

ers). On the other hand, *Shangjiao, Yilin* and *Jijiao* buck the trend by featuring more pre-plan context statements (pre-exercise).

These differences are due to design decisions. In Chinese textbooks, the design and layout of learning contents is simple and straightforward, with continuous exposure to exercises being a main feature. There is a noticeable density of text, and a shortage of images, text boxes or text columns separate from the main learning content (i.e., texts, exercises, and learning activities). The Japanese textbooks are quite the opposite: they are filled with appealing images, cartoons, and separate textboxes and columns that compete for the attention of the learner and which result in relatively shorter English texts. In some cases, the high density of design elements might even become a bit confusing.

The increased use of salience items in Japanese textbooks helps to structure learning contents into degrees of importance: for example, word lists (placed next to the main texts) have some of the words written in **bold text**, which indicates to the learner that they are to be more important than the others. Additionally, we can also find in the same page lists of useful words that are not found in the text. These lists are presented as optional in terms of importance, and help the learner to experiment with variant sentences if he∕she wishes to do so. An even lower level of importance is defined by the presence of reference markers next to the separate columns, which help the learner to check other sections or supplementary materials in the book for even more variant options. Overall, we can sense a strong degree of 'handholding' across the unit, as metadiscourse is used to 'guide' learners into understanding quickly which parts of the learning contents should be apprehended first, and which parts are secondary or even tertiary. In other words, metadiscourse creates a first level of 'essential content' and a second (or even third) level of well-referenced optional content.

If we look at Chinese textbooks, they clearly tend to integrate word lists, pronunciation symbols, and sentence patterns directly into the exercises themselves, instead of presenting them as metadiscourse, so the sense of 'handholding' or 'guidance' is greatly attenuated; this means that sheer exposure to target language and drilling become important aspects of learning English when using Chinese textbooks.

3.5.4 Extra materials

In terms of extra materials, the Chinese textbooks provided in their last pages only such common things as word lists, grammar reviews and workbooks, whereas the Japanese textbooks included a wider variety of extra materials, besides additional information directly related to each lesson. The use of extra materials assists learners in obtaining a broader point of view, ranging from cross-cultural understanding to specific language skills.

As an entertainment element, the Japanese textbooks added English songs and tongue-twisters to the extra materials section (but in Chinese textbooks, songs and tongue-twisters tend to be located within the units themselves); moreover, in order to provide a better understanding of cultural diversity, they introduced not only English but also other foreign languages, and even different cultural gestures by using vivid photos. Most importantly, the Japanese textbooks displayed a truly international attitude towards communication among people, in the sense that they showed that international communication is more than just communicating in English.

3.6 Discussion and Conclusion

This section discusses the results of the textbook analysis presented above from the perspectives of *informational metadiscourse, attitudinal metadiscourse,* and *language use.* It can be said that the former two elements all provide auxiliary knowledge to learners, by contextually enriching it. Recent theory suggests that students are better at applying their own knowledge when that knowledge is contextually rich (Britton, Woodward, & Binkley, 1993); the acquisition and use of contextually rich knowledge often parallels the outcomes of 'higher-order' thinking and learning. It is argued that students should leave school not only with a meaningful understanding of academic content, but also the capacity to engage in critical thinking, problem solving, and creative efforts around that content, which are subsumed under the heading of 'higher-order' learning or thinking.

When it is said that knowledge about a topic is contextually rich, this means that it is related to a variety of situations or types of problems where such knowledge is applicable; thus, learners may have an explicit understanding about a situation, which enables them to make appropriate decisions from a few possible outcomes. This approach would be more effective regarding advanced learners, as beginning learners focus more on basic language use, rather than contextual contents. Nevertheless, this means that contextual and auxiliary information in textbooks should be viewed as an important aspect.

Informational metadiscourse: objective-oriented (CHN) vs. situational-oriented (JPN) approach

Regarding informational metadiscourse, it can be said that in general the Chinese textbooks are objective-oriented textbooks; this can be discerned from the presence of goal statements and post-plan statements within the units themselves. Only *Ren'ai, Yilin* and *Waiyanshe* failed to introduce language objectives at the very beginning of each unit. This objective-oriented tendency was further reinforced by their post-plan statements. In order to evaluate the extent to which learners had accomplished the language objectives, assessment sections were included at the end of each unit. These were designed to be manageable for both class-group check and individual check.

On the other hand, the Japanese textbooks are to some degree situational-oriented textbooks; they focused more attention on creating contexts for each lesson. This can be gathered from their pre-plan statements: a context interpretation was provided before each conversation and often just before exercise questions, to make learners aware of the situation in which something took place.

Attitudinal metadiscourse: excessive focus on saliency (CHN & JPN)

An important aspect that is common to both Chinese and Japanese textbooks is the lack of attitudinal metadiscourse, except for saliency. All subject textbooks showed an interest in using salience metadiscourse to emphasize important information featured in each lesson or unit; this information was mostly focused on grammar and words.

Regarding the remaining attitudinal subtypes (emphatics, hedges, and evaluative), they were not identified in any textbook. As mentioned previ-

Chapter 3／Metadiscourse Analysis in Japanese and Chinese EFL Textbooks 145

ously, some words that suggest hedging such as 'but' can be seen in a few dialogues, but these do not represent the 'voice of the authors', and the statements that use such words are essentially descriptive or expository instead of argumentative. It is also interesting to note that unlike the Japanese educational context, 7th graders in China have already experienced three years of English learning, and despite this previous exposure, use of attitudinal metadiscourse other than saliency continues to be unaccounted for.

As mentioned by Crismore (2000), the fact that learners continue to experience a relative shortage of exposure to attitudinal metadiscourse in textbooks may be hampering not just their own argumentative and critical abilities, but also their ability to read longer-form critical literature. These issues are especially problematic in the case of Japanese and Chinese learners, since they generally have few opportunities of engaging in daily communication with native speakers of English (or even non-native speakers), and therefore the most common purpose for learning English in these two EFL countries is to pass university-level entrance exams, and comprehend English academic texts during the undergraduate period. The overwhelming majority of such academic texts use a lot of metadiscourse, for better and for worse: in his seminal book *The Sense of Style: The Thinking Person's Guide to Writing in the 21st Century*, Steven Pinker (2014:38) has amply criticised the exaggerated use of hedging and other types of metadiscourse as a way for authors to protect themselves from accusations from their peers (especially the accusation that authors might be interpreting academic words or concepts too literally or simplistically).

Yet even despite the criticisms made by Pinker and other academics, this exaggerated use of metadiscourse by English speakers is certain to continue, and undergraduate students in EFL countries might be too ill-prepared to fully engage with such difficult argumentative texts. This leads us to question whether it may be beneficial to start providing some small amount of exposure to more forms of attitudinal metadiscourse, even at the early level of 7th grade.

Language use: excessive reliance on native language (JPN) vs. foreign language (CHN)

The Japanese textbooks overwhelmingly use native language, while the Chinese ones are almost entirely written in the target language. For non-metadiscourse exercise instructions, Japanese textbooks resort to first-person inclusive plural, and Chinese textbooks use the second person. Individual pre-plan context statements, goals and topicalizers are mostly written in the third person in both Japanese and Chinese textbooks; likewise, salience items (sentence patterns, word lists, pronunciation tips) are mostly non-attributable in terms of voice for both countries. Since this aspect has already been discussed at length on this chapter (in sections 3.5.1 and 3.5.2) it is not necessary to add any additional remarks.

Other relevant points

The following points summarize several other distinctive features of Chinese and Japanese EFL textbooks in regards to metadiscourse:

If we look at metadiscourse usage within individual textbooks rather than between textbooks, there is a considerable degree of homogeneity regarding the usage of metadiscourse from unit to unit. If we compare only between Japanese textbooks, a noticeable degree of homogeneity in terms of metadiscourse usage can be ascertained; however, when we compare only between Chinese textbooks, the situation is a bit different. In other words, Chinese textbooks use smaller amounts of metadiscourse and are less homogeneous than Japanese textbooks in terms of employed subtypes of metadiscourse: some Chinese textbooks have more diversity (Shangjiao, Shangwai, Yilin, Jijiao) while the rest generally have less diversity (Ren'ai, Beishida, Renjiao, Waiyanshe).

Japanese textbooks use mostly goals, pre-plans (especially sentences that introduce context), and saliency within the units (in order to organize learning contents by levels of importance). Post-plans usually come in separate sections that aggregate the main points of multiple units at the same time. Chinese textbooks, while being less homogeneous between themselves, do tend to focus on pre-plans and saliency as well; but in contrast to Japanese textbooks, we see more instances of post-plans (often in the form of checklists and exercises) and topicalizers included inside the unit.

While Japanese textbooks tend to present word lists, pronunciation tips and sentence patterns as metadiscourse (separately from the main learning contents), Chinese textbooks prefer to embed such aspects directly into the exercises themselves. The same goes for extra aspects such as songs and tongue-twisters that tend to appear within the units in Chinese textbooks, but are relegated to the 'extra materials' section at the end of Japanese textbooks. Textbooks from both countries use texts that are primarily expository and descriptive rather than argumentative. Attitudinal metadiscourse items, which are generally associated with argumentative and critical texts, are unaccounted for (except for saliency). Japanese textbooks are generally more representative of a 'multicultural stance' than Chinese textbooks.

Focus on accessibility/handholding (JPN) vs. sheer exposure of contents (CHN)

Based on all the points presented above, we can conclude that the primary distinction between Japanese and Chinese textbooks, besides the former being *situational-oriented* and the latter being *objective-oriented*, is the distinction between *accessibility* and *exposure*. Japanese textbooks focus on the idea that learning English should be as less of a burden or a chore as possible. This much becomes clear from the opening statements of the authors in *One World*: '主人公たちといっしょに、みんなさんが3年間英語を楽しく学習し、力を伸ばすことができるように、次のような構成になっています'. Similar statements can be found in the opening pages of *Columbus 21* ('新しい学びを楽しみながら…') and *Sunshine* ('由紀は［…］ほかのクラスメートたちと楽しい学校生活を送りながら、英語の勉強をがんばっています'). *One World*, *New Horizon*, *Columbus 21*, and *Sunshine* also feature cute animal characters that appear from time to time throughout the units to give learning advices and encouragement to learners so that they feel motivated to complete the exercises and learning activities. The appearance of cute cartoon characters in Chinese textbooks is much more limited, and consists of short humorous comic strips at the start of each unit (*Yilin*, *Shangjiao*). This focus on accessibility, guidance and 'handholding' within Japanese textbooks does recall echoes of textbook designs in the Meiji period, which had similar concerns towards accessibility (see Chapter 1).

As for Chinese textbooks, they stand out by their focus on sheer exposure to target language and drilling: that is, by carrying out several series of exercises, with less guidance by the authors as to what is crucial and what is secondary. This too recalls the case of late-Qing textbooks that tended to prefer the Direct Method, with repeated sentence drills, and shortage of vocabulary and grammar explanations (see Chapter 1).

To conclude, the metadiscourse analysis supports the notion that Japanese textbooks attempt to arouse motivation for studying within the learners by resorting to various methods of facilitation (hierarchizing learning contents, abundance of appealing images, multicultural stance, use of cute characters, etc.). In the Chinese case, it is almost the opposite: learners are asked to persevere by engaging in a continuous repetition of exercises and exposing themselves to the target language.

Chapter 4∕Rhetorical Pattern Analysis in Japanese and Chinese EFL Textbooks

4.1 Introduction

This chapter seeks to identify and analyse the types of rhetorical patterns embedded in reading comprehension texts from specially-selected units of 7th grade EFL textbooks in China and Japan. Rhetorical patterns refer to the structure of *interrelations*, or links, between sentences (or text segments) within a given text: previous studies have identified up to seven basic rhetorical patterns that can occur in general expository texts (Chambliss & Calfee, 1998). Accordingly, rhetorical patterns are an essential factor in assessing whether a text is easy to understand (i.e., to evaluate its comprehensibility).

Moreover, some empirical studies that have investigated the effects of different rhetorical patterns on text comprehensibility report that some rhetorical patterns can help readers recall the meanings of a text more accurately than other patterns. Based on the framework of rhetorical patterns, a total of forty-two units (42) were selected and analysed from government-authorized EFL textbooks. This list of 42 units (18 units from 6 Japanese textbooks and 24 units from 8 Chinese textbooks) is composed of three sub-groups, each with their own theme: 'school life', 'family life' and 'events'.

The analysis results indicate that most of the selected units employ the 'list' pattern, which is considered to incorporate the lowest level of connectivity in terms of textual structure, and that most of the selected textbooks show a clear tendency to repeat the same types of rhetorical patterns throughout their units. Additionally, this analysis of rhetorical patterns highlights the importance of aspects such as the organizing structure of textual contents and connectivity between text segments for further improving currently-established research methods on textbook design and compilation.

4.2 Main Issues Related to Text Comprehensibility and Objectives of This Analysis

In the context of teaching English reading comprehension skills, it is well-understood that English texts consist of interconnected individual sentences that are semantically related. However, scholars such as Tanabe (1991) have pointed out that there are manifest insufficiencies in the teaching of reading comprehension skills beyond the level of the individual sentence. In order to read texts and retrieve any meaningful information from them, it is crucial to grasp the connections between textual elements (Mackay, 1987).

The hierarchy of intra-textual connections consists of: connections between two sentences; between sentences in paragraphs; between two paragraphs; and between multiple paragraphs within the whole discourse. These connections or interrelations between text segments are related to the comprehensibility of texts, especially for readers who are still not fully matured in their language skills (Chambliss & Calfee, 1998: 12; Chou Hare, Rabinowits, & Schieble, 1989). In this chapter, I will seek to clarify the contents of texts within EFL textbooks, by analysing how intra-textual connections contribute to the overall comprehensibility of texts.

In previous studies concerning reading comprehension, text difficulty was viewed as one of the main aspects that influenced the overall comprehensibility of a given text (that is, if we exclude the issue of a reader already possessing background knowledge about the topic at hand). The degree of difficulty of a text is displayed as a numerical value calculated by a readability formula, which considers a few factors that make a sentence easier to read, such as the difficulty of a word and its length, or the overall length of a sentence.

However, with this formula, it is not possible to evaluate—whether in regards to *cohesion* or *coherence*—the link from one sentence to another. The existence of this mutual link helps us to identify a *coherence relation* between sentences, paragraphs, text segments, etc. From this, one can affirm that any sequence of text segments within a discourse (that is interpreted by a reader as being *interrelated* with each other) constitutes a *semantically coherent passage*.

The term 'coherence relations', popularly defined by Hobbs (1985), is also known by other names, such as *relational propositions* (Mann & Thompson, 1986). In order to comprehend a text or a discourse, readers must link together in their minds various units of information (or text segments) into a coherent representation; a 'coherence relation' is therefore a type of relationship that certain units of information mutually establish with each other. There are different types of coherence relations. For example, some types that often occur between sentences are: temporal succession, causal relation, explanation, contrast, etc.

The study of coherence relations within a text helps us to ascertain the degree of cohesion and coherence of that very text, as well as its comprehensibility and its degree of interestingness. Moreover, previous studies have indicated that it is not always easy to read texts by merely using simple words and short sentences; on the contrary, these can still lead to ambiguous and inadequate understandings of a text (Armbruster & Anderson, 1985; Pinker, 2014:139).

Experiments using historical textbooks have reported that metadiscourse affects the comprehensibility of texts, by acting as a signal that alerts the reader towards related information, and provides clues for facilitating learners' understandings of relationships between pieces of information (Fukaya, Ohkouchi, Akita, 2000). In fact, the comprehensibility of a text can be influenced not just by the relationships between individual pieces of information placed directly next to each other, but also by the system of 'coherence relations' existing within all of the text segments as a group.

When multiple sentences appear in succession, their coherence relations reveal the types of linkage or mutual relationships that exist between paragraphs (or between each sentence). And according to Iori (2007), when a chain of two or more consecutive sentences forms a semantically coherent passage, we can interpret the entire set of connections through the distinct aspects of *cohesion* (which is determined by the relations of grammatical dependency between sentences/passages) and *coherence* (which is based on inferences about general knowledge: that is, information that is shared among the sentences/passages).

Another way of explaining the definitions of cohesion and coherence would be to say that the former involves the use of grammar or lexical items to connect sentences with each other (which creates a hierarchy or network of interdependent sentences), while the latter focuses on semantic connections between words in different sentences (which allows the sentences to share a similar topic, theme or idea). In other words, in an ideal, well-written discourse, there should be a good degree of grammatical cohesion and semantic coherence within all its textual passages.

To summarize, the comprehensibility of a given text needs to be considered from the viewpoint of the web of connections (*linkages*) within the text itself; that is, the globally-linked structure of contents within semantically coherent groups.

In this analysis, I will focus on *semantically coherent paragraphs* (i.e., groups of text segments or passages based on a single theme, meaning, or idea), that as a whole, constitute the main texts of each unit in a textbook; in other words, I will study the linkages between semantically coherent paragraphs in the main texts of each unit, in order to clarify the text's overall comprehensibility, and also to investigate possible issues or problems concerning the content structure of those texts. At the same time, some suggestions will be provided for improving learners' reading comprehension skills in English, and for modifying some of the evaluation criteria for EFL textbook authorization.

4.3 Analysis Framework: Merits and Previous Experiments with Rhetorical Patterns

To analyse the linkages between semantically coherent paragraphs, the framework of *rhetorical pattern analysis* proposed by Chambliss & Calfee (1998:32) will be applied. Rhetorical patterns can express the types of relationships existing within the entire structure of a text, as well as inter-paragraph and inter-sentence relationships. To begin the introduction of the analysis framework for this part of the study, I will discuss the merits of using rhetorical patterns, and explain the main characteristics of reading comprehension texts found in the analysed EFL textbooks. Following this, in the context of reading comprehension research, I will introduce various experiments that provide a scientific basis for the relevance of rhetorical patterns towards the study of text comprehensibility.

4.3.1 Merits of rhetorical patterns

A typology of rhetorical patterns representing the possible linkages between textual passages are shown in Figure 4.1 (Table 4.1 contains a translation of the most important pattern names in Japanese). Each icon represents a type of diagram that can be used during analysis to segment and organize the various passages of a text so that its organizing structure is made visible. The use of this kind of graphic depictions to visualize the design of textual passages has been shown to be advantageous for understanding all sorts of forms of expression (Chambliss & Calfee, 1998:118). This is because diagrams can display words and descriptions in meaningful ways, and organization charts are effective for clearly conveying many interrelated contents (Tufte, 1990). By expressing the contents in a graphical way, important and non-important information are made separate, and the relationships established both before and after each textual passage can be displayed visually, rather than linguistically. In other words, it is possible to simultaneously display individual elements and show the linkages between them.

An organizational scheme that leads to a well-done design must be able to represent very complex relationships, and clarify linkage patterns between individual elements in a way that is easy to grasp for the reader. Based on this notion of graphical descriptions, Chambliss & Calfee (1998) proposed a typology of graphical rhetorical patterns that link each element of a textual passage included in expository texts within textbooks. The authors presented several demonstration cases with rhetorical patterns, in or-

Chapter 4 / Rhetorical Pattern Analysis in Japanese and Chinese EFL Textbooks   157

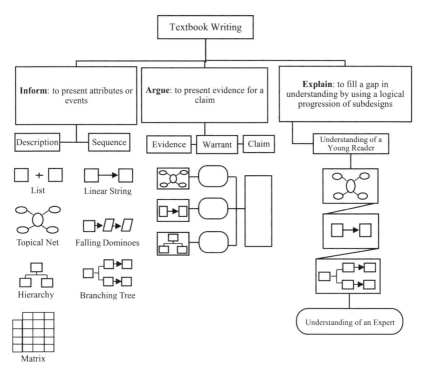

Figure 4.1: Typology of rhetorical patterns for analysing linkages within textual passages and content structure of textbook designs (Chambliss & Calfee, 1998:32).

Table 4.1: List of main rhetorical patterns and equivalent terms in Japanese.

Type of Rhetorical Pattern	Main Purpose
Matrix (マトリックス)	Compares/contrasts categories with each other.
Hierarchy (階層型)	Presents contents from most global/general to most particular.
Topical Net (放射型)	Presents subtopics around a central core theme/topic.
List (羅列)	Presents a list of mostly stand-alone statements.
Branching Tree (分枝)	Presents multiple events taking place simultaneously.
Falling Dominoes (ドミノ)	Presents cause-and-effect between actions/events.
Linear String (線形)	Presents actions taking place in temporal succession.

der to examine not just the linkages within texts, but also linkages within the organizational structure of a curriculum, and even the content structure of indexes, chapters, units, goal lists and other elements of textbook design.

The texts included inside textbooks are often descriptive texts that convey academic knowledge in order to bring insights to the reader. In other words, they are written texts intended to integrate the reader's pre-existing knowledge with the newly-read knowledge contained in the text, and as a result produce new knowledge (Miyaura, 2002). For foreign language learners such as Japanese people, reading comprehension texts in English textbooks are texts designed for acquiring foreign language expertise, especially linguistic knowledge and language skills. Conversational sentences, introduction sentences, or narrative sentences (which constitute different forms of English texts) represent the main target of language learning, because they are the preferred medium for conveying learning contents. From the viewpoint of communicating knowledge to learners, English texts within textbooks for English learning are regarded as having the same generalistic character as other typical textbook texts.

For the most part, the purpose of text writers can be divided into three aspects: conveying information (*to inform*), showing evidence (*to argue*), and clarifying a phenomenon (*to explain*).

For texts whose main objective is to inform, there are seven basic rhetorical patterns. Furthermore, depending on the characteristics of the information, each of these rhetorical patterns can be placed into one of two subcategories: to present attributes, or to describe sequences of events. In the case of presenting attributes, if there is a design where each of the subtopics is respectively matched with others that have the same characteristics, we refer to it as a *matrix* pattern; if each subtopic is linked hierarchically, it is a *hierarchy* pattern; if there are 3-5 subtopics radiating from a main topic, it is a *topical net* pattern; and if a subtopic is merely enumerated, and there are no more features in that subtopic, it is called a *list* pattern. Both the hierarchy and matrix patterns tend to show a dense linkage within subtopics, while the list pattern possesses the weakest degree of interrelationships between subtopics.

When a text is describing an event, the *branching tree* pattern is used to show one or more events progressing within the same timeline; the *falling dominoes* pattern describes relationships of cause-and-effect between events; and the *linear string* pattern is a representation of a single event developing in chronological sequence. The branching tree pattern coherently connects multiple linear events, while the linear pattern shows the lowest degree of association between stages of an event. Any of these seven basic rhetorical patterns can appear within the structure of a textbook text. Furthermore, by combining these patterns with each other, much more complicated textual structures can be created. Table 4.2 explains a set of basic principles for identifying the correct rhetorical patterns within a text.

As mentioned previously, besides giving information (*to inform*), rhetorical patterns can be used to present evidence for a claim (*to argue*) and/or clarify a phenomenon (*to explain*). Regarding arguing, one can express more complex relationships within a text by adding a rational argument (*warrant*) that provides a basis for the claim which is being argued. As for the objective of explaining a phenomenon, when we try to make a child scientifically understand a phenomenon, it is best to use methods such as metaphors and analogies. In any of these cases, the seven basic rhetorical

Table 4.2: Basic guidelines for identifying rhetorical patterns (Chambliss & Calfee, 1998:125).

Text Characteristics	Building block design (type)	
If the text presents		
attributes	then the design is	*Description*
events	then the design is	*Sequence*
Description		
If each subtopic deals with the same attributes	then the design is	*Matrix*
If subtopics present categories that are hierarchically related	then the design is	*Hierarchy*
If there are 3-5 main subtopics	then the design is	*Topical Net*
If the subtopics are none of the above	then the design is	*List*
Sequence		
If there is more than one sequence covering the same period of time	then the design is	*Branching Tree*
If there is a cause and effect relationship among events in a sequence	then the design is	*Falling Dominoes*
If the events are linked by time only	then the design is	*Linear String*

patterns are used to support the overall structure of the text.

As described above, the graphical classification method of rhetorical patterns devised by Chambliss & Calfee (1998:32) allows us to systematise the procedure of composing texts, and is often used in composition writing lectures that teach how to structure a text. This kind of graphical structure gives writers a framework that links together complicated subject matters, and plays a role in helping the reader organize the contents in his/her mind. In this sense, the rhetorical pattern framework is an effective tool for analysing the linkage within textbook texts.

4.3.2 Experiments involving easy-to-understand rhetorical patterns

An experiment was conducted to examine how rhetorical patterns in a text affect children's reading and understanding of its contents (Chou Hare, Rabinowitz, Schieble, 1989). Fourth and sixth graders were given a short text section related to knowledge about social studies, and were asked to summarize its main contents. The text was presented in four variants, each of them respectively designed using one of the following four rhetorical patterns: topical net, linear string, matrix, and falling dominoes (although the researchers used a different terminology in their study to name their patterns, which is: listing, sequence, comparison/contrast, and cause/effect). Furthermore, each rhetorical pattern was also expressed as an argumentative text, by featuring a topical sentence at the beginning that describes the main assertion or main point of the whole text. Therefore, each text starts with a topical sentence, and is followed by a few 'building blocks': namely, short sentences that develop the main idea presented in the opening sentence, but which never explicitly state the idea themselves. The building blocks are organized according to one of the four rhetorical patterns. After reading the texts (some of which featured the opening topical sentence, while others did not) the children were then asked to underline or identify the main idea of each text (if they could find it).

The results showed a significant difference in children's understanding of argumentative-style texts (which featured the topical sentence at the start explicitly stating the main idea) and the texts featuring only the 'building block' sentences (devoid of a topical sentence, and where the main idea was only implicit in the building block sentences). The average score for the argumentative-style text was 3.11, while the average score for the text composed of only building blocks organized according to one of the four rhetorical patterns was 0.63.

Having clearly understood this distinction between stating the main idea of a text implicitly and explicitly, the following question was: within the 'building block'-only texts, which of the rhetorical patterns contributed the most to children's understanding of the main ideas in a text? While the differences were not as drastic as those between implicit and explicit texts, children were most likely to understand the topical net pattern (which directly connects a single topic with a few subtopics that help to detail it and enhance it), followed by the linear string. The text comprehension rates for matrix and falling dominoes were weak, in which most fourth graders were unable to fully summarize the main idea of the texts. These experimental results were later confirmed with similar results from a separate study made by Chambliss & Calfee (1998:34). In this case, they targeted groups of fourth, fifth and sixth graders.

Also, in experiments designed for adults (Meyer & Freedle, 1984), the researchers found that the rhetorical patterns they find easier to understand are different than those of children. For adults, the ability to recall text contents was higher when using the matrix and falling dominoes patterns rather than the topical net. Whereas adults can grasp more complex linkages, children find it easier to understand the topical net type, which expresses more clearly-structured relationships between sentences. One of the reasons for this discrepancy is that many of the texts in textbooks are structured by 'topical net'-style rhetorical patterns, and the opportunities for children to regularly engage with other types of rhetorical patterns are very few. These results led Chambliss & Calfee (1998:41) to argue that although a topical net pattern is useful in some cases, it is becoming possible for children to recognize other patterns by exposing them to a wider diversity of rhetorical patterns at an early stage.

Until this point, I have looked back on several experiments that verified whether rhetorical patterns in a text can affect a reader's ability to properly grasp its main ideas. From such studies, it became clear that rhetorical patterns, which link each element within a text, are related to the comprehensibility of the text's contents, and this affects readers' development of skills for text decoding. Although these studies were conducted with learners whose native language is English, it has been argued that, based on the Linguistic Interdependent Hypothesis (LIH, 言語相互依存仮説), rhetorical patterns also influence the reading comprehension skills of Japanese learners who are studying English. According to LIH, reading in one language has much in common with reading in another language, and most of the cognitive processing related to the reading of texts is explained by an universal human ability that is independent from the features of any specific language (Horiba and Araki, 2002). The core arguments behind LIH have been verified in studies that investigate second-language reading comprehension skills.

It is clear now that in the case of English native speakers and second-language learners, regardless of the language they speak, if they can read texts in a way that integrates well the information contained in them, they will have a higher degree of understanding of the contents (Block, 1986). Fitzgerald (1995) conducted a large-scale review of studies in second-language reading comprehension, and concluded from the results that cognitive processing of second-language reading is basically like the cognitive processing of native-language reading. Also, it is now understood that, in the same way as English native speakers, Japanese high school students that study English perform top-down processing during reading, and incorporate information about the text's structure into their memory. According to the researchers that conducted the study, the readers made use of the 'structural properties of a text in order to "fill in" gaps in their mental representations' (Horiba, Van den Broek, & Fletcher, 1993). Therefore, we can assume that the same reading skills and knowledge that a Japanese learner obtains from reading Japanese texts in elementary school can be applied when they read junior high school English texts.

4.4 Method for Analysis of EFL Textbooks

4.4.1 List of textbooks whose units are to be analysed

In April 2012, junior high school English textbooks in Japan were revised as a result of the full implementation of the new curriculum guidelines (Course of Study). The main changes in the Course of Study in regards to English learning were: the increase in the number of classes; and the number of words taught under the basic policy of fostering the 'four skills' in a comprehensive manner (Ministry of Education, Culture, Sports, Science and Technology 2008).

The most recent revision of the Course of Study doubles down on these requirements, by: establishing a mandatory number of class hours for English; asking schools to define clearer language goals for learners; improve students' interest and motivation towards learning; and revise textbooks to develop learners' abilities to think, judge, express or provide explanations in English (MEXT, 2014).

As a result, each textbook publisher has made strong efforts to reflect these requirements into their textbook designs. But on the other hand, within the specialized field of textbook analysis, almost no research on the new batch of junior high school English textbooks can be found. In addition, when reviewing the preceding research on junior high school English textbook analysis over the past 10 years, I found relatively few studies focusing on the reading comprehension texts that represent the core learning content of the textbooks. By analysing the English textbooks which are currently in use, it is expected that these findings may stimulate new discussions within the various groups of teachers, students and publishing

Chapter 4 / Rhetorical Pattern Analysis in Japanese and Chinese EFL Textbooks   165

stakeholders that produce and use the textbooks; and that these findings may be incorporated into future guiding principles for textbook editing.

In total, 98 seventh-grade reading comprehension texts (23 from Japanese, and 75 from Chinese textbooks) were selected for analysis, for two main reasons: first, in the scope of school education, the main subject of English reading comprehension studies so far have been the last grades of the elementary, middle, and high school (6th grade, 9th grade and 12th grade). In the final grades, one can judge the effects of learning at the end of each stage, or verify whether a given standard was successfully achieved. On the other hand, for students at the starting grades, there has been little attention towards studying the ways by which learners are introduced to texts during the early transition period.

Secondly, seventh-graders in Japan are having their very first encounters with English textbooks, and having easy-to-understand texts is becoming an important issue. Children who had been engaging with English activities during elementary school were mostly dealing with spoken language and playing fun activities; but as they become junior high school students, English turns into a full-fledged course with textbooks and tests, and therefore this early period of exposure can be crucial for motivating students to learn English. It is expected that learners may deepen their own engagement with English by using textbooks (Torikai, 2012).

4.4.2 Brief considerations on the analysis method and list of selected texts/units

It has been argued (Holsti, 1969) in the past that the most effective 'unit of analysis' for the analysis of contents in the humanities and social sciences is the *theme*. It can be said that textbook analysis is essentially a type of textual content analysis. In the body of research conducted so far concerning the problem of 'theme', there were many discussions on the selection of themes according to categories; however, up until now there have not been any analyses that refer to the organization of textual contents, based on rhetorical patterns that operate under a specific theme. Therefore, in this part of the research, I will focus on textbook units that share the same theme or subject matter (ex: 'school life'); following this, I will then analyse the organization of contents within the main reading comprehension texts that deal with the theme, and after this, examine the current situation and issues concerning textbook design in EFL textbooks in Japan and China. From each textbook, I selected one unit that is related to the three themes of 'family life', 'school life' and 'events' (which therefore results in the study of three units from each textbook), and identified the rhetorical patterns used in the main texts of that unit.

In the Japanese textbooks, each unit generally contains approximately three or more semantically coherent passages or paragraphs that, when taken as a whole, constitute a full reading comprehension text. Therefore, each passage occurring within the same unit is semantically considered as one coherent body of text, and also as the core unit of analysis. In other words, a unit in Japanese textbooks is almost always divided into three or four 'parts', and each of them contains a portion (passage) of the whole text. I then proceed to identify a rhetorical pattern that expresses the organizational structure of its contents, and type of linkage between each part. In some rare cases, the parts may actually be fully independent texts rather than passages (ex: *New Horizon*, Unit 11), and were therefore analysed as such by attributing numbers (ex: ①, ②, ③, etc.).

Because all the Japanese textbooks exhibit a homogeneous unit design, it

Chapter 4 / Rhetorical Pattern Analysis in Japanese and Chinese EFL Textbooks   167

is easy to identify the semantically coherent passages. But in the case of the Chinese textbooks, where the unit design may vary a lot from textbook to textbook, it is slightly more challenging to select the appropriate texts. To be more specific, all of the reading passages in the units of Chinese textbooks are strongly integrated with other exercises that are unrelated with reading comprehension. For example, it is not rare to find texts that have missing words, and require the reader to fill the appropriate words in the blanks after reading the whole text, and then answer a few reading comprehension questions related to the text's contents.

Another issue is that there are many short dialogues and longer texts scattered throughout the unit, all of which have some basic relationship with the unit's theme. In sum, while Japanese textbooks mostly feature just one clear main text divided into three or four parts, the Chinese textbooks have many more texts, almost all of them longer than the ones in Japanese textbooks, and it is not always clear which of the texts is the 'main text', because they are all combined with many other exercises. Furthermore, texts in Chinese textbooks are almost never divided into multiple parts unlike the Japanese textbooks; rather, they are almost always completely independent, self-contained texts that merely depict aspects of the unit's theme. This does not change the fact that we can still identify semantically coherent paragraphs or passages within the texts, and classify them in terms of rhetorical patterns.

In order to properly select the set of semantically coherent passages from Chinese textbooks for this study, I have decided to follow a few guiding principles: 1) always include texts that belong to unit sub-sections titled as 'Reading'; and 2) include texts whose structure is clearly repeated in other units. In other words, if we look at several units within a Chinese textbook, we can realise that in each of the units' sub-sections/parts, there are always texts located in the same areas that have similar characteristics and structures. Therefore, if there are similar-looking texts consistently appearing in the same sub-sections of each unit, they are included in the analysis. The final principle is: 3) ignore texts that have no connection whatsoever with reading comprehension skills. By using the term 'reading comprehension', we mean that after reading the text, the learner will be asked to answer questions about what took place, or perhaps to summarize the main ideas contained in the text. Even after applying these principles, most of the texts featured within each unit were included in the analysis.

For this purpose, I will follow the guidelines and framework of rhetorical patterns proposed by Chambliss & Calfee (1998:32) described in Table 4.1. When identifying the rhetorical patterns, it was decided to have another person participate in the task. The other reviewer (who was formerly an Assistant Language Teacher or ALT at Japanese elementary schools for two years) conducted the task of rhetorical pattern identification independently from myself, and then both participants compared their findings in order to minimize the risk of biases. As a result of mutual discussion between both parties, we reached a consensus regarding the results and interpretation of the global structure of the texts. This strong agreement was possible since the texts themselves are simple and straightforward, and do not mix many patterns together.

4.5 Results

4.5.1 Main characteristics of rhetorical patterns in reading comprehension texts

For each of the analysed units in the EFL textbooks, the two graders

Chapter 4／Rhetorical Pattern Analysis in Japanese and Chinese EFL Textbooks   169

looked at the structure of textual contents in the main body of text, and identified five rhetorical patterns. It was found that the two main objectives of the texts were to present attributes and describe events, rather than engage in argumentative discussions, or explain phenomena to the learner. The evaluation results are summarized in a variety of ways: first, there is a graph chart for each country, showing the total occurrence of patterns for each textbook (Tables 4.3 and 4.4; Figures 4.2 and 4.3), as well as for each unit (Figures 4.4 and 4.5). Following this, a legend with the graphical icons used for the rhetorical pattern analysis is presented (Figure 4.6); and finally, detailed diagrams for each text are provided, grouped by country and by unit theme (Figures 4.7–4.12).

Regarding these detailed diagrams, the reader will notice that some of the icons have different colours (such as red, blue, etc.). These different colours are used whenever a certain text relates to a matrix, or whenever

Table 4.3: Number of rhetorical patterns in Japanese textbooks for 3 thematic units.

Textbook	Unit Theme	List	Linear String	Falling Dominoes	Matrix	Topical Net
New Crown	School	1				
	Family				1	
	Event	2	1			
New Horizon	School	1				
	Family	1				
	Event	1	1	1		
Sunshine	School	1			1	
	Family			1		
	Event			1		
Total English	School					1
	Family				1	
	Event		1			
One World	School	1				
	Family	1				
	Event		1			
Columbus 21	School	1				
	Family	1				
	Event		1			

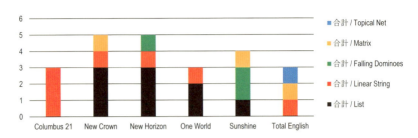

Figure 4.2: Number of rhetorical patterns in Japanese textbooks (total within the 3 units).

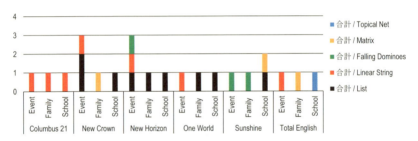

Figure 4.3: Number of rhetorical patterns in Japanese textbooks for each of the 3 thematic units.

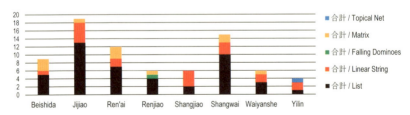

Figure 4.4: Number of rhetorical patterns in Chinese textbooks (total within the 3 units).

Chapter 4 / Rhetorical Pattern Analysis in Japanese and Chinese EFL Textbooks   171

Table 4.4: Number of rhetorical patterns in Chinese textbooks for 3 thematic units.

Textbook	Unit Theme	List	Linear String	Falling Dominoes	Matrix	Topical Net
Renjiao	School	1			1	
	Family	2				
	Event	1		1		
Beishida	School	1				
	Family	3			1	
	Event	1	1		2	
Ren'ai	School	2	1		1	
	Family	2			2	
	Event	3	1			
Yilin	School		1			
	Family	1				1
	Event		1			
Jijiao	School	5	1			
	Family	5	2			
	Event	3	2		1	
Waiyanshe	School	1	1			
	Family	1			1	
	Event	1	1			
Shangwai	School	3	2			
	Family	3			2	
	Event	4	1			
Shangjiao	School		2			
	Family	2				
	Event		2			

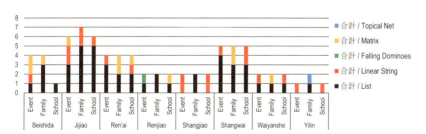

Figure 4.5: Number of rhetorical patterns in Chinese textbooks for each of the 3 thematic units.

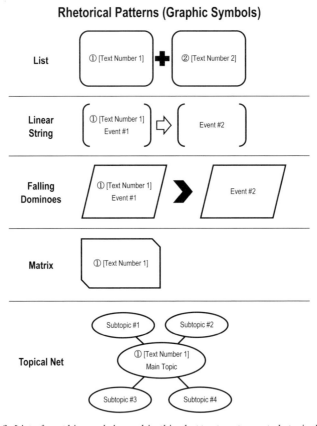

Figure 4.6: List of graphic symbols used in this chapter to represent rhetorical patterns.

the text expands into other text boxes. If a certain pattern has a colour other than black, then it is possible to check the associated matrixes or extended texts located immediately under that original pattern.

In the cases when the texts are presenting attributes, both text graders frequently found the patterns of list, matrix, and (more rarely) topical net. On the other hand, when describing events, it was more common to see the patterns of linear string and falling dominoes. In addition, if we look at

Chapter 4 / Rhetorical Pattern Analysis in Japanese and Chinese EFL Textbooks　173

both countries' textbooks, the number of texts using the list pattern accounted for more than half of the whole set. If we break it down by country, the use of list is predominant in both cases, although in Japanese textbooks it comprises a little less than half of all texts, while in the Chinese case it is clearly more than half.

In sum, the most commonly occurring patterns for both countries are (from most common to least): *list > linear string > matrix > falling dominoes > topical net*. One small difference is that matrix is given more importance in Chinese textbooks, since many of the texts directly ask the learner to compare or contrast the same categories of information with each other. We also found a noticeable tendency in most of the textbooks (especially Chinese ones), by which at least two units within each textbook share the same rhetorical patterns. Now, we will take a closer look at our findings concerning rhetorical patterns for each unit theme in Japanese and Chinese textbooks. It is worth noting that Japanese textbooks show more variety in rhetorical patterns than Chinese textbooks. If we compare Figure 4.2 and Figure 4.4, together with Table 4.3 and Table 4.4, there are 5 Chinese textbooks that share the same sequence of patterns (list-linear string-matrix) within the three units, while Japanese textbooks are not as uniform.

4.5.2　Rhetorical pattern analysis organized by unit theme

School-related units (Japanese)

Tables 4.3 and 4.4 show the rhetorical patterns of units related to school life. On the Japanese side, *New Crown, New Horizon* and *One World* only used the list pattern, while Sunshine combined list with matrix, *Columbus 21* uses a linear string, and *Total English* a topical net. There are plenty of character dialogues with question-and-reply sections, in which the list pattern is frequently used for quickly conveying the core sentence patterns that represent the goals of each unit. What can be gathered from the content of such texts is not so much the subject of the school, but the fact that the editors chose to present the usage of expressions for introducing things and people, listing favourite things, etc. Such texts usually feature a low degree of coherency between each passage.

The matrix pattern (*Sunshine*) is convenient for students to contrast their likes or dislikes, while the linear string is best suited for narrated events. But in the case of *Columbus 21*, the whole text combines a monologue passage with two dialogue passages and some manga comic panels. This text portrayed one event at a school using a linear string pattern. Tina, a student from the United States, was talking to an Australian teacher, while filming a ball game tournament in the school; in the process of explaining the game, both started talking about their feelings of living in a foreign country. Such a style of story-telling, which mixes different forms of text and images (and helps to keep things fresh for the reader) is also sometimes featured in other units of this and other Japanese textbooks; this fact marks an interesting contrast with Chinese textbooks, which are text-heavy.

As for *Total English*, the text's contents, which describe the state of an American junior high school on the Internet, are conveyed as a topical net pattern. While looking at a picture of the school's homepage, we are introduced to things such as classrooms, locker rooms, cafeteria, and lunch.

School-related units (Chinese)

Figure 4.8 shows rhetorical patterns for school units in Chinese text-

Chapter 4 / Rhetorical Pattern Analysis in Japanese and Chinese EFL Textbooks   175

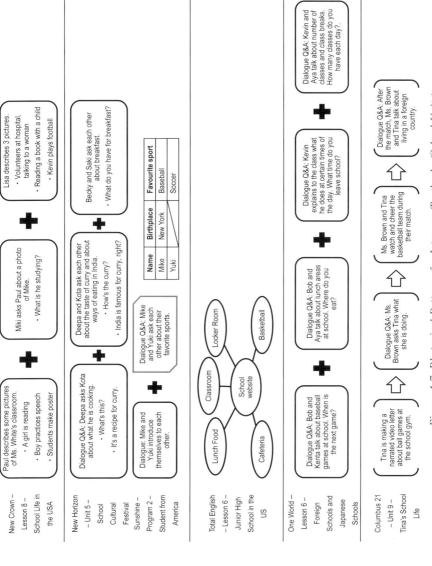

Figure 4.7: Rhetorical Patterns for Japanese Textbooks (School Units).

books. Because they feature many more texts, to some extent we should expect more variety, but the main difference is merely a larger number of matrix patterns, which encourage learners to compare bits of information with each other. However, the matrix patterns themselves are generally simplistic and contain only small amounts of comparable information.

In the same way as their Japanese counterparts, Chinese textbooks are frequently content with merely using the list pattern to present a short dialogue with question-and-answer (Q&A), in which the goal sentence pattern is made clear. Even most of the linear string texts, which should focus more on narrative aspects, tend to be very simple and over-descriptive.

Although this kind of direct, almost formulaic approach helps to keep things simple for the learner, in the long run it may also become fatiguing or monotonous, because many of the linear string texts are character monologues, which merely list the time sequence of the character's school life activities, and add only a few short extra sentences to say which activity is their favourite and why. None of the texts in Japanese textbooks attempt to list sequences of daily school activities in this level of detail.

Unit 3 in *Jijiao* (from the second semester textbook; all second-semester units are marked with an asterisk * in the tables), featured a touching story of a boy who loses his house in a fire, and is helped by the school and his classmates. This textbook is prone to feature texts that emphasize kindness towards others and mutual aid.

As mentioned previously, due to the self-contained nature of the texts, the degree of coherency is not high, both between texts and within the texts themselves. *Shangwai* features a text about an astronaut's daily schedule, which has no connection with the unit's school theme. If we take as examples the units of Ren'ai and One World (Figures 4.7 and 4.8) there

Chapter 4╱Rhetorical Pattern Analysis in Japanese and Chinese EFL Textbooks   177

is a noticeable difference in terms of continuity among parts in a unit. For instance, Ren'ai has four different parts in the unit, which differ in characters and topics within a school setting, whereas One World's four parts continue the same storyline with the same main character.

Family-related units (Japanese)

Figure 4.9 shows the rhetorical patterns of family units for each textbook. In contrast with school units, here we see more matrix patterns (*New Crown, Total English*), which aim to introduce and compare information for characters and their relatives, such as birthplace, current place of residence, occupation, special skills or hobbies, and favourite things. In the case of *Total English*, the occupation of Ms. Allen's father and mother are first introduced, and then Ms. Allen and a student named Hiro have a conversation about whether her father and mother can swim. Following this, the names and occupations of Ms. Allen's brother and sister are presented. All the three parts are composed of conversational sentences.

An interesting outlier is *Sunshine*, which has a fun story using a linear string pattern about Grandma Baba, who is sheltered in her house in the middle of falling winter snow. Gradually, several animals seek shelter and warmth in her house, but since the house is not quite warm enough, Grandma encourages the animals to jump in her bed to warm up. They do so, but accidentally break the bed's legs. Without feeling any displeasure from this incident, Grandma encourages the animals to turn the bed into a sleigh and they all go outside to play. By playing and having fun, they realised that their bodies had become very hot, which was the original objective of Grandma Baba: to not let the cold get in the way of doing things and going outside to enjoy nature. It is a well-written and humoured story,

School Life Units (Chinese)

② Friday

Time	Subjects/Activities	Time	Subjects/Activities
8:00 to 8:50	Math	12:00 to 1:00	Lunch
9:00 to 9:50	Science	1:00 to 1:50	Chinese
10:00 to 10:50	History	2:00 to 4:00	Art lesson
11:00 to 11:50	P.E.		

Renjiao – Unit 9 – My favorite subject is science.

① Dialogue Q&A: Frank and Bob ask each other about their favourite days, subjects, and teachers.

➕

② Yu Mei writes an email to Jenny talking about her daily life at school on Fridays + time of classes and favorite subjects.

Beishida – Unit 2 – School life.

Dialogue Q&A: Dad asks Jiaming about the things he carries inside his backpack, and which classes he has today.

Ren'ai – Topic 3* – My school life is very interesting.

① Dialogue Q&A: Helen and Jane ask each other about school classes (days of week, starting and ending times).

➕

② Dialogue Q&A: Zhou Yan and Maria ask each other about their favorite subjects.

Name	Subject	Like/Dislike	Reason
Zhou Yan	History	Likes	It's interesting.
	English	Dislikes	It's a little difficult.
Maria	English	Likes	It's easy and interesting.

③ Hu Bin's school life: From 8:00am, four classes in the morning and two classes in the afternoon

⇧

After school: either play basketball, or swim, or draw pictures or go to school library.

➕

③ Hu Bin introduces himself and writes a text about his daily school life and says all the things he does in one day.

➕

④ Li Mei writes a letter to introduce herself and talk about the things that she likes to read in the school newspaper.

Chapter 4 / Rhetorical Pattern Analysis in Japanese and Chinese EFL Textbooks   179

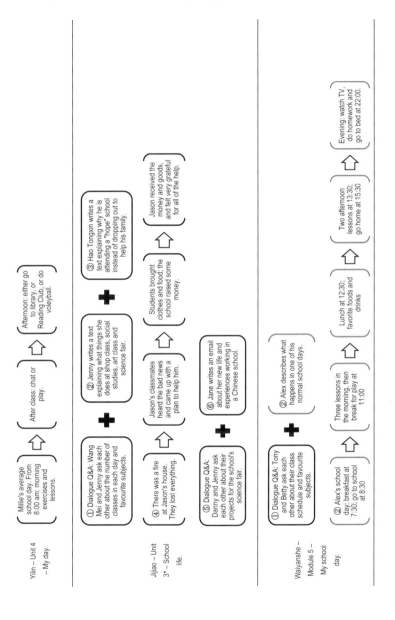

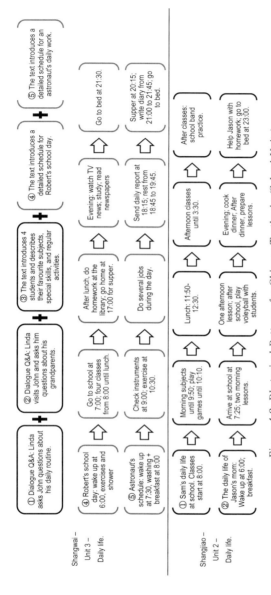

Figure 4.8: *Rhetorical Patterns for Chinese Textbooks (School Units).*

Chapter 4 / Rhetorical Pattern Analysis in Japanese and Chinese EFL Textbooks   181

featuring a narrative tone that contrasts considerably with the list pattern texts.

The list patterns of *New Horizon* and *One World* present the use of sentence patterns in conversational dialogues for Japanese characters to communicate with foreign characters, and it is often the case that foreign characters will introduce their foreign relatives (or sometimes Japanese people as well) that live abroad. For example, in *One World*, in the first part Ms. King introduces through a monologue the occupation of her father, then her mother's place of birth and special abilities; in the second part a dialogue presents the name and personal character of the younger brother, followed by the sister's name, age and personality; in the third part, the characters convey their thoughts about the brother and sister's looks and character. But in the fourth and last part, there is a talk about Ms. King's car and her mother's bike, which has little to do with the previous topic of introducing people.

As for *Columbus 21*, it features the same style of linear-string narration that we saw in its school unit.

Family-related units (Chinese)

Figure 4.10 shows family-related rhetorical patterns for Chinese textbooks. Besides the information conveyed by Japanese textbooks, the Chinese ones will often add information about looks (ex: "my father is tall and strong"; "my mom is tall and pretty", etc.) and workplace. Japanese textbooks are very much focused on the core family, sometimes adding grandparents and cousins, but Chinese textbooks feature bigger families, including brother/sister-in-law, nieces and nephews and even pets. *Beishida* adds an additional multicultural feature, which is a monologue from a girl that

Family Life Units (Japanese)

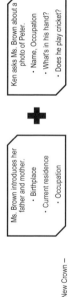

New Crown – Lesson 6 – My Family

- Ms. Brown introduces her father and mother.
  - Birthplace
  - Current residence
  - Occupation

➕

- Ken asks Ms. Brown about a photo of Peter.
  - Name, Occupation
  - What's in his hand?
  - Does he play cricket?

➕

- Kumi asks Ms. Brown about a photo of Jean.
  - Name, Occupation
  - What does she have in her hands?

Family members	Birthplace/residence	Hobbies	Occupation
Mother	Scotland · London		Art teacher
Father	Scotland · London		Taxi driver
Sister (Jean)			Musician
Brother (Peter)		Cricket player	

New Horizon – Unit 6 – Brother in Austria.

- Saki gives a speech to the class to introduce her brother Haruki.
  - Name, Residence
  - Occupation, Skills.
  - Secondary activities

➕

- Alex asks Saki more questions about her brother.
  - Does he live near a beach?
  - What does he do there?

➕

- Becky asks Saki about animals in Australia.
  - Do you know the animals of Australia?
  - Does Haruki like koalas, too?

Sunshine – Program 11 – Grandma Baba and Her Friends on a Sleigh.

Grandma lets many animals enter her house due to cold. ▶ Animals jump on bed and it brakes; then they cut its legs. ▶ They use the bed as a sleigh in the snow. ▶ They push the sleigh uphill to continue playing. ▶ They realise that by having fun together, they can stay warm.

Chapter 4 / Rhetorical Pattern Analysis in Japanese and Chinese EFL Textbooks   183

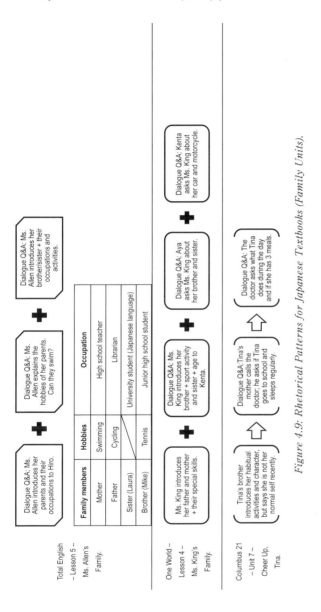

Figure 4.9: Rhetorical Patterns for Japanese Textbooks (Family Units).

Family Life Units (Chinese)

Renjiao – Unit 2 – This is my sister.

① Dialogue Q&A: Sally introduces her parents (no name given) to her friend Jane, including sister Kate and brother Paul.

➕

② Jenny writes a letter to introduce the names of her parents, brothers, sister, cousin and pet. No name is given for grandparents.

➕

④ Lisa introduces herself and her mom with their Chinese and Western names, then introduces the name of her American father.

Beishida – Unit 1 – Family.

① Four people introduce their family members; each person is presented with different attributes (either name, or hobbies or occupation).

➕

② Four people introduce one of their relatives. Different attributes are mentioned about each person (either name, hobbies, looks, likes and occupation).

➕

③ Steve's blog introduces his family members: Mom/dad (looks, likes); sisters (likes, special skills); and grandparents (likes, skills).

③ [Steve's Family]	Looks like	Likes	Is good at
Mum	Tall, pretty	Books about history, sports	
Dad	Tall, strong	Sports	
Emma		Music	
Linda	Short		Basketball
Grandma		Food	Cooking
Grandpa		Computer games	

Ren'ai – Topic 2 – What does your mother do?

① Dialogue Q&A: Maria, Kangkang, Jane and Michael ask each other about their parents' occupations.

➕

② Dialogue Q&A: Kangkang asks Maria about her parents' occupations and workplaces.

➕

③ Dialogue Q&A: Kangkang's friends ask him questions about who his family members are, based on their looks.

➕

④ Peter introduces his family: occupation and workplace for mom and dad; name and age of sister; grandparents' place of residence; and pet.

① Person	Job
Kangkang's mother	a teacher
Kangkang's father	a doctor
Michael's mother	an office worker
Michael's father	an office worker

② Person	Job	Workplace
Maria's mother	nurse	hospital
Maria's father	cook	restaurant

Chapter 4 / Rhetorical Pattern Analysis in Japanese and Chinese EFL Textbooks 185

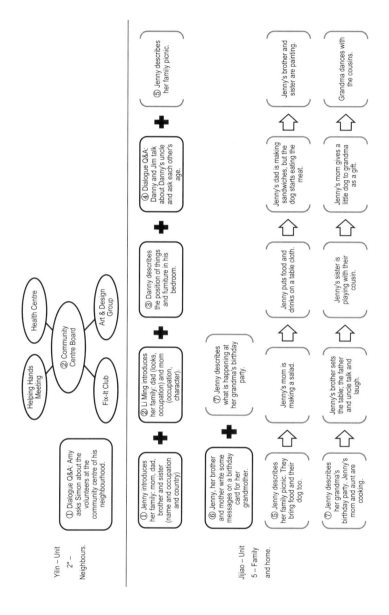

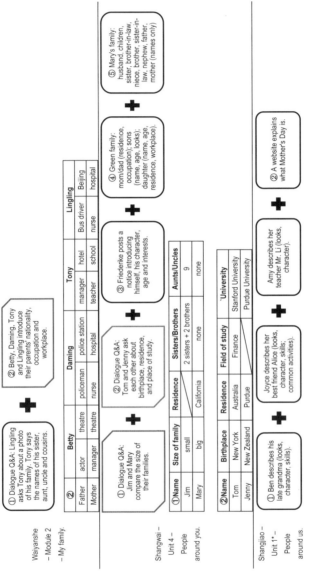

Figure 4.10: Rhetorical Patterns for Chinese Textbooks (Family Units).

Chapter 4 / Rhetorical Pattern Analysis in Japanese and Chinese EFL Textbooks   187

has an American father and a Chinese mother, and she introduces how she and her mother have Western and Chinese names.

Linear strings are used to describe family events, such as a family picnic or grandma's birthday party (*Jijiao*). But in both cases, the texts consist of short descriptive monologues associated with pictures of the events, which are organized in numbered sequence, and because of this, the sense of narrative storytelling is somewhat weakened. Yilin has an image of a neighbourhood community centre notice board, which features a number of small texts describing different services provided by the community: health support, house decoration, fixing things, and general help. This presentation style was identified as a topical net.

Matrix patterns are the preferred way of organizing descriptive information about many relatives in a single text (*Beishida, Ren'ai, Waiyanshe, Shangwai*), but list patterns that feature character dialogues with Q&A are still prevalent. Overall, the level of coherence continues to be somewhat low. Since each family member is presented through the same basic aspects, this makes it easy for the reader to predict and follow the flow of the text. However, as with previous units that use the matrix pattern, there is a shortage of elements that can draw the interest of the reader. The same can be said for texts using the list pattern, which are known to have low text cohesion and coherence. It is possible that obstacles may occur in learners' reading processes, because it is difficult to argue that each textual element and each clause are linked in a fully coherent manner.

Event-related units (Japanese)

Figure 4.11 shows the diagrams for event-related units. Finally, the dominance of list patterns is over, and linear strings (followed by falling dominoes) become the pattern of choice for describing events.

Sunshine uses the falling dominoes pattern. One event taken from the daily life of a family with 4 members is depicted. One morning, the phone started to ring, but the mother, daughter, son, and father were all occupied, and so no one could pick up the phone. And when the phone began to ring again, the son picked up the call, which came from his grandmother. At the end he reported her sayings to everyone in the house. This flow of events shows a relationship of cause-and-effect. Another instance of falling dominoes comes from *New Horizon*, which teaches the values of perseverance and continuous practice in order to succeed at the game of soccer, but which can also be extrapolated to the challenges of learning English.

Total English uses the linear string pattern, in which the use of a realistic life setting and comparison of cultural aspects helps to convey a humorous tone. During New Year, the characters Miku, Ben and Seema meet at Miku's house. When they decide to do *kakizome*, Miku writes '平和' while Seema writes 'もったいない', and then Miku asks her how to say that term in English.

At least for these two units in *Sunshine* and *Total English*, we can say that their main texts develop in the form of a continuous dialogue, in which the change of speakers and the order of speech proceeds in a smooth manner. In either case, the episodes are portrayed in a realistic manner, and we can feel the contents as being interesting or appealing.

Event-related units (Chinese)

Figure 4.12 shows the list of diagrams for event-related units in Chinese textbooks. Here we find four patterns: list, linear string, matrix and falling dominoes. Just as in Japanese textbooks, we also find a somewhat dimin-

Chapter 4／Rhetorical Pattern Analysis in Japanese and Chinese EFL Textbooks   189

ished use of the list pattern, replaced by more instances of linear string.

Most of the texts in these units deal with the topic of summer vacations, and explaining one's travel plans. Because of this, the texts are just as descriptive as those found in the school units, where characters will painstakingly list in sequence all the things they plan to do at certain dates and times (a good example is *Yilin*, that lists in sequence the various things that the character Wendy does in Halloween day and are written in a very similar way to the texts describing a character's school day). These sequences are described using the linear string pattern. If we compare figures 4.11 and 4.12, they illustrate how Chinese textbooks feature greater text length and more detailed descriptions, which constitutes a noticeable difference between countries. For instance, *New Crown* is the Japanese textbook with the longest text length, but when compared to Chinese textbooks it is merely average.

The most interesting texts using this pattern were found in *Shangjiao*, where the characters describe their fun experiences during their school's club fair, or when travelling to a beautiful island. As for the matrix pattern (*Beishida, Jijiao*) it is mostly used for interpreting travel brochures that present and compare travel plans for different popular tourist destinations in China.

Concerning the use of falling dominoes, the only example is *Renjiao*, featuring a well-written monologue by a girl that went to do camping in India with her family. In the morning, the girl saw a snake next to the campfire and became frightened, shouting to her father. The noise did not make the snake move, but when the father started jumping up and down, the snake fled. Then the father proceeds to explain to the daughter that snakes cannot hear, but only react to movements.

Event Units (Japanese)

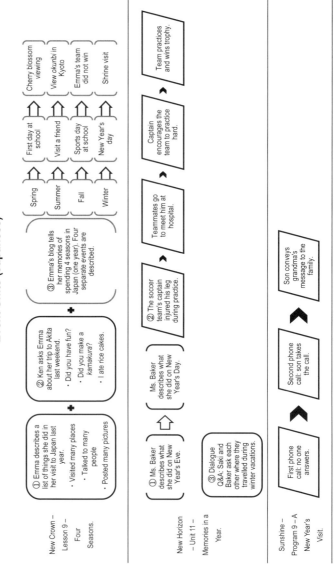

Chapter 4 / Rhetorical Pattern Analysis in Japanese and Chinese EFL Textbooks 191

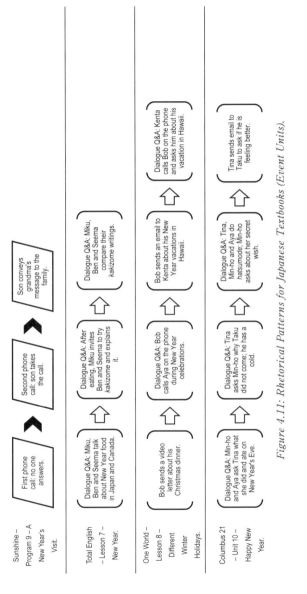

Figure 4.11: Rhetorical Patterns for Japanese Textbooks (Event Units).

Event Units (Chinese)

Renjiao – Unit 12* – What did you do last weekend?

① Dialogue Q&A: Paul and Lisa ask each other about what they did on the weekend. Lisa was a guide at the Natural History Museum. Paul: watched a soccer game.

➡ ② Lisa went with her parents and sister on a weekend camping trip to India in a small village.

➡ Long bus ride to a lake, prepare tents and campfire, tell stories to each other under the moon.

➡ The next morning, Lisa saw a big snake sleeping near the fire. She shouts out loud to her parents.

➡ Father jumps up and down, and the snake runs away. He says snakes cannot hear, but can see moving things.

Beishida – Unit 4* – Seasons and weather.

① A travel brochure gives information about weather in Beijing during the 4 seasons, and recommends clothes and sightseeing spots for each season.

①Month	Weather	Clothes
Dec-Feb.	Very cold	Overcoat, gloves, scarf
Mar.	Cool weather	
Apr.	Warm	Sweaters, light clothes
May	Hot	
Jun-Aug.	Very hot, rains hard	T-shirts, shorts, skirts
Sept.-Nov.	Cool and dry	Trainers, comfortable shoes

✚ ② A newscaster explains the weather forecast for New York, Sydney, Shanghai and London.

✚ ③ Tim writes a postcard to David describing the list of things he is going to do and places that he will visit in China.

Famous Places
The Great Wall – not many tourists
Tian'anmen Square – lots of people, windy, good for flying kites
The Summer Palace – favourite place for tourists
Fragrant Hills Park – trees with colourful leaves

③ Tim will meet his Chinese penfriend Mingming tonight and visit the Bird's Nest.

⬆ Tim's plans for summer holidays in China: first, learn Chinese at a summer camp for two weeks.

⬆ After summer camp, his parents will join him on a trip around the country: Beijing, Xi'an, Jiuzhaigou and Sanya.

④ A travel agency poster recommends a destination in China for each season of the year.

④ Place	Season	Reason	Activities
Wuyuan	Spring	Yellow flowers all over the hills	Walk in countryside, enjoy tea
Changbai Mountain	Summer	It's usually sunny	Take photos
The Great Wall	Autumn	Can see all the colours of autumn	Hiking
Sanya	Winter	You can get away from the cold	Swimming

Chapter 4 / Rhetorical Pattern Analysis in Japanese and Chinese EFL Textbooks 193

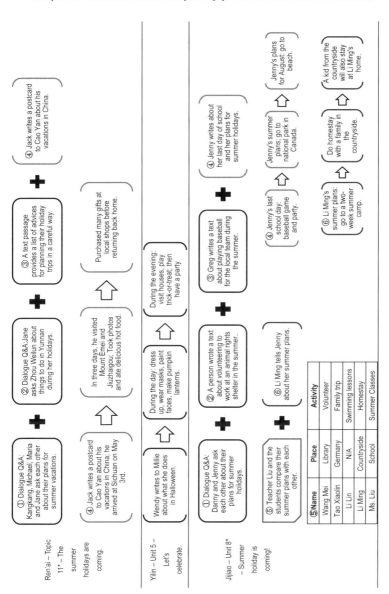

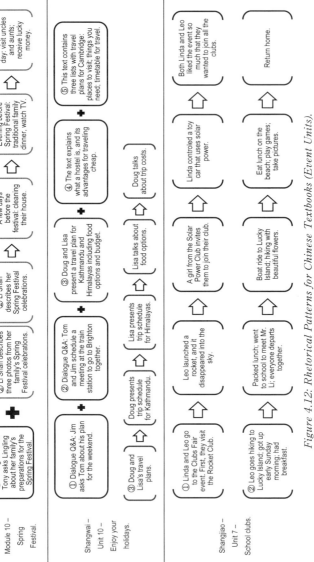

Figure 4.12: *Rhetorical Patterns for Chinese Textbooks (Event Units).*

Chapter 4 / Rhetorical Pattern Analysis in Japanese and Chinese EFL Textbooks   195

Other aspects that are presented in all these units' texts are: weather conditions (*Beishida*), describing food, homestays, and discovering tips for planning a safe trip (*Ren'ai*). Because of the focus on various types of vacation experiences, there is an exposure to a diversity of expressions, but nevertheless the degree of coherence between texts is still low.

4.6   Discussion of Results

For all EFL textbooks, the organization of contents within a selection of main texts was analysed from the viewpoint of rhetorical patterns, regarding the units related to school life, family life, and events. As a result of the analysis, the following three arguments can be made.

Excessive focus on list pattern resulting in low levels of cohesion (JPN & CHN)

By using the rhetorical pattern framework to analyse the linkage of semantically coherent paragraphs within each unit, it became clear that the use of the list pattern, featuring the least number of relevant connections between passages, generally took place in more than half of the target units. The defining characteristic of texts designed in this manner, is not that each passage relates to strong consistency or cohesiveness, but rather that these passages are a practical way of presenting the learning goals of the unit (such as using sentence patterns to portray scenes and actions). To be more specific, such texts are basically expedient tools for providing a basic context, in which a certain language function is demonstrated. In other words, they are examples of a grammar-centred design, and are merely used to embed the expressions that constitute the unit's primary learning objectives. As a result, sometimes the textual contents deviate from the unit's theme, and the sense of thematic unity within the unit is lost (ex: the community centre's notice board for *Yilin*'s family-related unit, or the astronaut's schedule in *Shangwai*'s school life unit). This has the danger of weakening the linkages between each passage, and dissipating the overall appeal of the main text itself. Therefore, if we take into consideration the ideal requirements for an English text within a unit, the level of cohesion provided here is not very high.

Description of events using linear string/falling dominoes patterns (JPN & CHN)

The texts that describe an event are generally more capable of expressing the unit's theme in an easy-to-understand manner, with a natural flow. Such texts progress sequentially using a linear string or falling dominoes pattern. Originally, linear string patterns were featured in explanatory texts that describe scientific events, as they tend to occur in a sequential manner, such as historical case studies or animal evolution; but in these textbooks we sometimes find events that represent interesting scenes based on everyday life, reproduced using lively words.

Also, when the texts that portray the events are styled in narrative form, and are organized according to the natural progression of the events, we can say that its parts are integrated into a coherent chain. These texts designed with the linear string and falling dominoes patterns were able to further increase the interest of the reader by portraying an episode with a clear progression. Therefore, even in introductory English textbooks, it is possible to devise sentences that express the unit's theme in an interesting way. Instead of arranging mostly-unrelated sentences individually with a list pattern, a set of meaningful contents can be assembled in an appealing manner (*Total English* and *Columbus 21* are generally good examples). In order to create better texts, it is not only necessary to select an appropriate rhetorical pattern, but also select contents that can attract the reader. This evokes Chambliss and Calfee's (1998:26) argument that attracting students' attention with the use of engaging passages is an important aspect of a well-written text.

Matrix pattern is not used to its full potential (JPN & CHN)

Within reading comprehension research, it is generally considered that the degree of coherency within sentences and paragraphs that directly follow each other is the highest, due to their proximity; and for most readers, the matrix pattern is the easiest to understand because it puts multiple statements in close contact with each other using a grid. However, although there were texts in both Chinese and Japanese textbooks recognized as a matrix, they were mostly short of appealing contents, in which the same categorical information about all the family members is dryly presented one by one. As a result, the readers' interest might not be fully captivated, even if ordinary things or pieces of information are assembled with a tightly-knit rhetorical pattern such as the matrix.

Additional remarks

Besides the similarities, there are differences in length, continuity, and variety between Japan and China. Chinese textbooks contain longer dialogues and passages than Japanese textbooks, and tend to provide sufficient input materials. However, this feature also leads to a repetition of sentence structures and patterns among the various parts in Chinese textbooks, which tend to lack cohesion and continuity; conversely, the unit parts in Japanese textbooks usually continue the narrative development within the same context or storyline. Furthermore, the variety of rhetorical patterns among Japanese textbooks is noticeable in comparison with Chinese textbooks.

The analysis of content structure based on rhetorical patterns can provide useful suggestions for the evaluation criteria of textbooks, and can help to improve learners' English reading comprehension skills from the perspectives of proximity (between text passages), text comprehensibility and content acquisition.

The textual contents in Japanese textbooks are for the most part assembled for the sake of learning vocabulary and grammar items under a certain theme. In the case of government-authorized textbooks in Japan, the examination of each textbook is carried out by checking items in a checklist based on predetermined requirements. In the checklist used for evaluation criteria and analysis of English textbooks, in the section that deals with textual content items, we find the items 'theme' / 'text type' / 'degree of difficulty' (Kogushi, 2011). However, these items do not refer to rhetorical patterns that express the organizational structure of the textual contents, and we have already seen in this chapter that previous research has shown this aspect to be closely related to the degree of comprehensibility of a text.

A checklist that evaluates such textbooks can determine whether certain sections match the items in the list, but cannot fully evaluate the organizational characteristics of main texts, which represent the primary learning contents of the textbook. Moreover, the results of textbook examinations are published by using the grades of 'passing' or 'failing', but the characteristics of each successful textbook are not indicated. In this sense, the analysis of rhetorical patterns that was performed in this chapter suggests that it may be beneficial to introduce a new evaluation item into the textbook evaluation checklist dealing with rhetorical patterns, which represents the linkage of text contents within reading comprehension texts.

Furthermore, it is likely that presenting the main notions and science behind the study of rhetorical patterns within guidance materials for English reading comprehension will have a positive influence on reading comprehension skills. In order to improve learners' reading comprehension of texts, it is necessary to become more aware of the relevance of each element in a text (Celce-Murcia & Olshtain, 2000). Yoshidome (2010) examined the effects of English reading comprehension guidance by focusing on the organizational structure of texts. As a result, it was confirmed that providing guidance on educational intervention policies that promoted an awareness of the importance of cohesion and coherence within texts helped Japanese learners to attain an improved understanding of English texts. Therefore, we may assume that if we emphasize the role of rhetorical patterns when conceiving the main texts of textbooks, it may lead to a meaningful improvement in the reading ability of learners.

As pointed out by Sato (2012), it is possible to realize a positive experience for learners of English through the judicious use of learning materials, even at the initial stage of junior high school. This analysis is one such attempt to achieve that goal. It is easy to judge whether an existing text is excellent, but it is a much more difficult task to produce one. As mentioned above, the difficulties in designing rhetorical patterns for textual contents can be attributed to: a lack of consideration of this aspect in the textbook evaluation process; a low awareness of the relevance and linkage of various textual elements within guidance materials and learning materials; and the challenges involved in producing good-quality texts which are suitable for various levels of learning while being able to retain the readers' interest. As one possible viewpoint among many, by investigating rhetorical patterns in texts, it is argued here that the English writing ability of learners can be improved in accordance with an increased quality in reading materials.

Chapter 5／Analysis of Practice Activities in Japanese and Chinese EFL Textbooks

5.1 Introduction

Having studied the aspects of metadiscourse and rhetorical patterns in the previous two chapters, I will now focus on the design of learning practice activities in EFL textbooks. Even though teachers spend a large amount of their time dealing with textbooks and using them in classrooms, Williams (1983) has argued that they have little or no involvement in the tasks of evaluating and interpreting textbooks. Even if these two realities seem contradictory, it is still possible in most cases for teachers to adopt supplementary materials in their classrooms, especially since there is no ideal textbook which can cater to everyone's needs (Kumaravadivelu, 2001). But how can they assess the quality of a textbook in a scientific and reliable manner? In principle, teachers should be able to evaluate, adapt and produce materials in order to put language-learning theories into practice, and to facilitate learners' learning. Because the study of learning materials development is quite relevant for the professional development of teachers, a few courses dealing with this topic have been introduced in recent years (Tomlinson, 2012).

Within this context, I will demonstrate in this chapter an operational procedure for analysing practice activities in textbooks, which teachers can then apply to the textbooks that they work with. This procedure makes use of Littlejohn's (1992, 2011) framework, which was devised to investigate English-language teaching and learning materials, and to explain the reasons why these materials turned out the way they are. Recently, this same framework was also applied in an analysis of South Korean EFL textbooks based on principles derived from second language acquisition (SLA) studies (Guilloteaux, 2012).

Firstly, I will describe in more detail Littlejohn's framework, introduce the textbooks and lessons/units which are to serve as sample materials, and methodological decisions taken prior to and during analysis. Following this, the main findings will be presented.

5.2 Overview of EFL Textbooks from the Viewpoint of Practice Activities

Considering the importance of seventh-grade textbooks, there is a need to know the real impact of textbooks on learning at such an early stage. English textbooks in Japan normally contain reading sections and passages as their primary form of language input. The intention behind these is to demonstrate to learners how target language items should be employed. Then, to support comprehension of the language in the reading sections there are practice activities. Practice activities require learners to interact, in a variety of ways, using the target language. As the language learning process is believed to take place during these activities it is essential to understand their characteristics, types, and effects. Through a critical analysis of these practice activities, the main considerations, intentions and underpinned principles of the textbooks can be revealed. In other words, by studying these aspects, one can discern the basic principles behind the design of a textbook. The contents that textbook designers choose to incorporate (or not) into a textbook can reveal a lot about what things they deem to be helpful in helping learners improve their English competencies. Practice activities of authorized EFL textbooks from Japan and China were selected for analysis through an adapted version of Littlejohn's (1992, 2012) framework to explore the above features.

Furthermore, by analysing practice activities in a descriptive manner and exposing the underlying nature of these textbooks, we can test to what extent the claims made by textbook publishers (namely, that their textbooks conform to the principles set by the national curricula) are accurate. Of particular importance is the requirement of 'balancing the four skills', mentioned in the Japanese national curriculum (also commonly referred to as 'Course of Study').

5.3 General Aspects of Littlejohn's Framework

To analyse the practice activities from each book, this study makes use of Littlejohn's framework, instead of standard textbook evaluation checklists. This framework is arguably a more objective and clear-cut way for describing and interpreting language practice activities, and for considering textbooks from a pedagogic point of view. Littlejohn (1992, 2012) suggests three levels for describing language teaching and learning materials: Level-1 is concerned with basic information and physical descriptions of the materials themselves such as the title, year of publication, number of units and supplementary materials, etc. Level-2 is designed to look closely at practice activities within the materials, focusing on what exactly they require learners to do. Finally, Level-3 sets out to discuss the underlying principles contained in the materials, as well as the overall aims of the materials, and the types of roles that teacher and learners are expected to take.

Of particular interest for this study is Level-2, because it can reveal the most information about how each textbook engages learners in the use of the four skills. It is not necessary to present here Level-1 information about the textbooks, since it was already discussed on previous chapters, and a table explaining the subdivision of units can be found in the Appendix.

Still, there is the issue of defining exactly what parts of the textbook are to be analysed, and how to label them. Littlejohn (2011) subdivides the instructions contained in the materials into *tasks*: these are defined as 'any proposal within the materials from which learners have to act upon to bring about learning of the foreign language' (p.188). In other words, they are instructions which ask the learner to do something, which should result in the improvement of his/her skill with a foreign language. However, the term 'task' is commonly taken as 'meaning-focused' classroom work, or is likely to be associated with Task-Based Language Teaching (TBLT), which is not applicable to all kinds of language materials. Even by applying a broader definition, such as 'any structured language-learning endeavour', 'task' might not be an appropriate neutral term to refer to the overall work conducted in the classroom due to its potential variety of interpretations.

At the same time, the definition of the term 'activity' has become a contentious issue revolving around its differentiation from the terms *exercise* and *task* (Nunan, 2001). Thus, for the purpose of this study, *practice activity* was the term I chose to refer to any general element—whether it is graphic, textual, or aural—within the materials upon which learners are asked to act, with the objective of facilitating language learning. This can range from a very simple and basic exercise, to a complex task which may be comprised of several actions chained together. From this definition, it becomes clear that grammar explanations and demonstrations of language rules—which are present in most of the textbooks—were not considered as practice activities in this study, because there are no instructions requiring learners to respond to them.

5.4 General Methodological Choices and Procedures

The materials sampled in this chapter are the authorized EFL textbooks that we have analysed up until now. I have mentioned in previous chapters the importance of considering a unit's *theme* in order to select the final set of units for analysis. When looking at the Japanese national curriculum, it recommends the adoption of topics that are relevant to the daily life of learners. For example, because learners spend a considerable length of time at school, they are likely to feel more involved when the topics deal with school life. Since the 'theme' is said to be the most useful aspect for conducting a general analysis of contents (Berg, 2007), I will continue looking at the same units as in the previous chapters, which are related to the themes of 'school', 'family' and 'events'.

Within each selected unit/lesson, all practice activities were identified and set apart from other contents. This begs the question of how to number (or properly identify) each type of practice activity. For this purpose, I used as a reference the same numbering system that each textbook uses to itemize each of their exercise proposals. If a practice activity exists within the textbook with a specific item number, and it is a self-contained entity, containing at least one instruction that is independent from other practice activities, then it is counted as a single practice activity, even if it contains a series of instructions (or repetitive tasks). The reason for this is to avoid dividing a comprehensive practice activity into different parts, especially as it can be difficult to set exact rules for separating interlinked instructions from each other, and this might distort our interpretation of each individual instruction, which would deviate from the original purpose of this study. Overall, my intention with this approach (and which I have followed in the previous chapters on metadiscourse and reading practices) is to emphasize the type and variety of practice activities, rather than the quantity of tasks contained within the same type of practice.

The original basic scheme for categorising learning tasks devised by Littlejohn is presented in Table 5.1. The first question posed by his scheme is, 'what is the learner expected to do?' Within the context of a classroom, the aspect of *turn-take* generally refers to the situation where a teacher starts a conversation, the pupil responds and then the teacher will provide appropriate feedback. It is also possible for the pupil to initiate the conversation instead.

During practice activities, a learner will have to *focus* on certain aspects of the learning content: their 'focus' or concentration can be directed to a

Table 5.1: Littlejohn's (1992:38) proposed basic method for initiating the analysis of learning tasks, including additional explanations by the author of this dissertation.

I – What is the learner expected to do?

A *Turn-take (initiate language, scripted response or none)*
B *Focus (meaning, form or both)*
C *Operation (list of mental operations carried out by the learner)*

II – Who with? (*participation*)

III – With what content? (*characteristics of learning contents*)

A *Form (graphics, sounds, text, speech, audio, etc.)*
→input given to learners
→output generated by learners
B *Source (from teacher, learner, textbook, dictionary, etc.)*
C *Nature (metalinguistic/linguistic items, fiction/non-fiction, etc.)*

IV – Who decides? (*parties responsible for decision-making*)

Chapter 5／Analysis of Practice Activities in Japanese and Chinese EFL Textbooks　207

certain topic (*message/meaning*), or to a certain grammatical item, sentence pattern or language function (*form/language system*), or both aspects at the same time (*relationship between meaning and form/system*).

But what is arguably the most important aspect is *operation*, because it aims to describe in a clear, unambiguous manner, what mental operations or mental processes the learner is carrying out when participating in the practice activity. To put it in simple terms, it describes *what exactly the learner is required to do*, and this data set will be useful when I later compare it with the requirements set by the national curricula of China and Japan. Examples of operations carried out by a pupil are: to compare pieces of information; repeat a sentence; hypothesize a certain grammatical rule, etc.

The second question is 'who with?' This refers to the style of student *participation* in the classroom, which can consist of individual work, pair work, group work, or various types of interactions between the teacher and the learners.

The third question is 'with what content?' Here the term *form* appears once more, but in this case, it refers to the type of input that the learner receives from the textbook, and to the type of output that the learner is expected to produce. As an example, the textbook might present an audio passage (aural form), a graphic/photograph (graphic/non-verbal form), a reading text, or words as the initial input, and based on this the learner might be asked to either talk to another learner, or draw a graphic, or write a sentence. Speaking of textual forms of input and output, it is important to distinguish between input that is comprised of a single word/sentence, and that which constitutes a full-fledged text/discourse. This distinction is crucial because, as I have mentioned in Chapter 3, many learners experience difficulties reading and interpreting text passages at a higher level than that of the individual sentence.

Another two aspects related to the issue of 'content' are the *source* of the learning contents (ex: they can come from the learners themselves, or the teacher, or the textbook, etc.) and the *nature* of the content (ex: fiction/non-fiction, general knowledge, personal information related to the learner, etc.).

The final question is 'who decides?' This describes who makes the decisions regarding the practice activities; the decision-maker can be a teacher, the learner, or a textbook.

During this study, five changes were made to Littlejohn's original framework, which are listed and explained below.

(1) **The category of *turn-take* has been modified.** Littlejohn only developed three possible sub-categories for 'turn-take', which are *initiate language, scripted response*, and *not required*. But in the case of these EFL textbooks, a learner will not be asked to initiate an unscripted conversation with a teacher or another person, and say whatever they wish, without any guidance whatsoever. Since all possible conversation options are always derived from textual examples in the textbooks, the only available choice for learners is to either engage in scripted response, or produce no response at all (*not required*). This latter option takes place, for example, when learners are only asked to silently read a text, but do nothing else. Although the textbooks were analysed under the assumption that 'initiate language' might appear, no conclusive examples of unscripted language production were found in the three sample units of each textbook.

(2) **The category *who decides* has been merged with *source*,** because in this study the textbook is the only available source of

learning contents (rather than a teacher or another learner), and all the instructions and decisions concerning the learning activities come exclusively from the textbook itself. Of course, the textbook may ask the learner to either provide some contents by themselves (ex: convey their own experiences), or reuse textbook contents to produce new language. The sources of contents for input may be different from those used during output. Accordingly, I will only consider textbook materials (T) and the learner (L) as valid sources of content during the input and output phases (audio passages in CD materials that come with the textbook are included in the category of 'textbook materials').

(3) **Addition of a *translate* sub-category.** It has already been mentioned that *operation* refers to the things that the learner is required to do, like answering a question based on things that one has already memorized, or sequencing words in order to form a sentence. In this respect, I decided to add a new sub-category called 'translate' which requires learners to translate between the target language and native tongue (this sub-category can be found in the *operation/process* section of Table 5.3). Understandably, the materials that Littlejohn originally analysed did not require any language translation at all, and therefore this feature could only possibly be found in EFL textbooks, although as we will see later, it is rarely used even in this context.

(4) **Changes in the criteria for defining *extended discourse*.** Regarding *content*, Littlejohn defined the boundary between 'extended discourse' and 'words/phrases/sentences' at 50 words, but this measuring stick is based on native English textbooks, which tend to have more text and longer sentences than EFL textbooks. While analysing the units, it was decided to lower the benchmark to 30 words, which felt more appropriate for the situation at hand, because sentences in the sampled units tend to be notoriously short.

(5) **New sub-categories: *ask-and-answer* & *unclear*.** Still within

the domain of *content*, two new sub-categories were added: 'ask-and-answer' and 'unclear'. Since our set of EFL textbooks puts much more focus on dialogues with questions and replies, it became necessary to create a specific category named *ask-and-answer*, which are basically short dialogues consisting of a question and a reply (this category is found in the *input/output contents* section of Table 5.3). In some practice activities, it may be necessary to repeat the question-and-reply pattern two or three times, in which case it is still considered as 'ask-and-answer' instead of 'extended discourse'. This sub-category occupies an intermediate space between those of 'written words/phrases/sentences' (which are isolated elements without any coherent meaning as a group) and 'extended discourse' (which are longer texts surpassing 30 words). An example of an 'unclear' practice activity can be found in *Shangwai* (Unit 4, 6 DIY Lab, Internet Surfing), in which it asks learners to study the family tree of Elizabeth II, but then provides no further guidance as to how this should be done, or even whether this study should be presented to anyone in the classroom. This kind of vague practice activities, while uncommon, is slightly more prevalent in Japanese textbooks, especially in the context of reading comprehension questions.

During the second phase of the study, and in accordance with Littlejohn's framework, all practice activities were classified on an Excel spreadsheet according to three main aspects: *operation, participation,* and *content* (namely *input* and *output content,* which also includes the sub-categories of *focus* and *nature*). For each aspect, a table is provided, showing the percentage of each sub-category, along with mean and standard deviation values. These values represent the combined totals of the three thematic units per textbook, in accordance with Littlejohn's (1992) procedures. Final-

Chapter 5 / Analysis of Practice Activities in Japanese and Chinese EFL Textbooks   211

ly, each cell in the tables was given a colour according to its percentage value. Zero percent is always displayed as white (and by using the hyphen symbol '-' instead of '0'), while the highest percentages have a darker colour such as red, orange, green, blue, or purple. By using this colour-coding scheme, the reader can quickly compare the relative intensities of various sub-categories between all textbooks, without having to individually read and memorize each percentage value.

The total number of practice activities analysed in the textbooks is shown in Table 5.2. The reason why Chinese textbooks have much more practice activities is because Japanese textbooks prefer to occupy the page space with large images and provide less workload for learners, while Chinese textbooks feature less images, using the available space to put more text and exercises.

Table 5.2: Total number of analysed practice activities, taken from three units in each textbook.

Textbook Title	Total Number of Analysed Practice Activities		
New Crown	88		
New Horizon	47		
Sunshine	49	340	
Total English	54		
One World	42		
Columbus 21	60		
Renjiao	65		967
Beishida	125		
Ren'ai	69		
Yilin	60	627	
Jijiao	103		
Waiyanshe	60		
Shangwai	72		
Shangjiao	73		

5.4.1 Guidelines for distinguishing between different sub-categories

Now I will discuss the issue of how to distinguish between different sub-categories when analysing the practice activities. To this end, a few rules and guidelines were adopted in order to have a consistent method for classifying ambiguous features.

The first issue is how to determine the distinction between 'scripted response' and 'not required' within the domain of *turn-take*. It is easy to decide when learners only must silently read or hear a piece of language, but in the sampled textbooks, many cases were found where the learner only has to draw a line between two language items, or underline a word/phrase in a text, or draw a symbol (✔, ✖), or write T or F (true of false), or write numbers to order the proper sequence of a set of images. While these actions may be considered as forms of scripted 'responses' in the broadest sense of the term, it is hard to argue that the learner is producing a coherent piece of language, or that he/she is directly engaging with the target language in the way that fluent speakers are expected to do. Therefore, to better understand how learners are engaging with the target language, it is important to mark a distinction between producing symbols, numbers, drawings, or individual letters, and writing/speaking full words, sentences, and paragraphs. Therefore, the benchmark for separating both sub-categories is the individual word. Any time that the learner must speak or write at least one full word, it is considered as scripted language. In the case of individual letters, numbers, symbols and drawings, learners are focusing more on conceptually apprehending new language items in their minds, mainly using visual mnemonics, and therefore they were marked as 'not required'. This focus on symbols, letters, and numbers in EFL textbooks reduces the unpredictability of results from learners, which

Chapter 5／Analysis of Practice Activities in Japanese and Chinese EFL Textbooks   213

is helpful for teachers in rural or less-developed areas who have much less training and proficiency in English, but may also adversely hamper the learners' ability to expand their language knowledge in the long run.

Considering the aspect of *focus*, it can often be difficult to distinguish between a focus in 'language system' or 'meaning'. As a basic rule, it was decided that doing pure pronunciation drills (i.e., merely reading and repeating individual words), completing grammar tables, and using grammar rules to fill blanks within sentences that have no semantic and structural coherence are considered as 'focus on language system／form' (ex: applying only a grammatical rule without being required to interpret any other text or audio passage). As for reading comprehension sections, or questions that ask the reader to select information from a text or audio passage, those were always coded as 'focus on meaning'. All other practice activities that did not neatly conform to these two rules were conservatively considered as focusing on 'relationship between meaning and language system／form'.

In the realm of *input* and *output content*, it was decided to define all tables, diagrams, or charts as 'graphic' items, and if they contain any letters, words, or phrases, those are also marked as 'written: letters／words／phrases／sentences'. But if the learner must draw symbols, lines, tables, charts and diagrams, those are coded as 'graphic'.

'Extended discourse' is a textual or audio passage with more than 30 words that shows a coherent meaning overall. Within one practice activity, if the individual text segments or parts show a coherent meaning and structure when properly sequenced (or they are narrated by the same fictional character), they are interpreted as one single extended discourse. However, if a passage is clearly and exclusively comprised of repetitive short questions and answers, they are marked as 'ask-and-answer' even if they cumulatively crossed the 30-word mark. In other words, the two benchmarks of '30-word limit' and 'semantic coherence between phrases' are both used to distinguish between sets of individual phrases without semantic connections between them, and coherent extended passages.

One of the trickiest issues is found in the domain of *nature*, namely in terms of how to distinguish between the sub-categories of 'linguistic items' and 'fiction/non-fiction'. In the sampled materials, it is very frequent to see 'ask-and-answer' sections or short example sentences associated with photos of real people, or illustrations of fictitious characters. It was decided that when associated with photos or illustrations of fictional or non-fictional situations, such sentences would be coded as either fiction or non-fiction. This is because the learner must interpret the fictional or non-fictional context provided by the image of a person/character in order to produce language. If the learner is only required to draw lines, symbols, individual letters, and numbers, or if the learner must fill a table with individual words or incomplete sentences taken from a textual or audio passage, they are considered as 'linguistic items'. Another common feature of these textbooks (especially the Chinese ones) is that they provide sentences with blanks that the learner must fill after reading a text, listening to audio, or after applying a language rule. In this case, I used the same benchmark that was determined for 'individual phrases' and 'extended discourse': if the individual phrases, after placed in sequence, produce a coherent discourse in terms of meaning and structure, they are considered as either 'fiction', 'non-fiction' or 'personal information'. But if learners must fill blanks in incomplete sentences, or in full sentences that do not cohere well with each other, they are coded as 'linguistic items'. Questions that are addressed directly at the learner about his/her personal situation and daily life are

Chapter 5╱Analysis of Practice Activities in Japanese and Chinese EFL Textbooks   215

marked as 'non-fiction'.

I now turn to the section of mental *operations*, which also requires various small guidelines. When a practice activity is ambiguous in the sense that it could conceivably involve two or more sub-categories, then all those sub-categories were included or marked. A simple 'ask-and-answer' activity between two learners usually does not involve negotiation. But anything beyond that, especially if it requires exchange of information or compilation of information in a table or text, was considered as 'negotiation'. 'Attend to example' is coded not only when an actual example is provided, but also in the cases when learners are directly asked to check/reference the results, contents or explanations contained in a previous practice activity or grammar section (this also includes cases where the learner is implicitly asked to pay attention to sounds, when pronouncing isolated words in pronunciation drills). As for the sub-category of 'apply knowledge about general world facts', it was decided to code it whenever learners had to discuss the contents of real-world photos, talk about climate patterns in real-world locations, speak about their vacation plans in real locations, or describe aspects of their family life or daily life to others, because they will often need to present such general facts to make themselves understood by their peers, or to justify their personal preferences for something in particular.

Another difficult decision relates to the subcategories 'retrieve information from short-term memory', 'intermediate-term memory' and 'long-term memory' because the textbooks are often very vague about this aspect. In most cases, it is hard to argue that any use of memory is involved, because practice activities frequently require the learner to merely consult another practice activity or section within the very same page or adjacent page. As a result, 'long-term memory' (LTM) is defined as remembering items from a previous lesson, or requiring the learner to remember what he/she did in the previous weekend. 'Intermediate-term memory' (ITM) refers to remembering words or phrases (that were not written down) said by another learner in a previous practice activity within the same unit, and 'short-term memory' (STM) involves remembering unwritten words or phrases expressed by oneself or another learner within the same practice activity. The last comment that needs to be made within the section of *operations* is that 'calculate' was decided to refer not just to mathematical operations, but also to the estimation of dates, time periods, or the total number of hours related to a certain fictional or non-fictional event.

Regarding the domain of *participation*, it's important to remind that it refers to the type of classroom participation and interaction between learners, such as individual work or group/pair work. Regarding the coding of some practice activities, two basic rules had to be adopted to avoid confusion and errors: the first one is that, if no clear participation style is shown in the instruction, then such a practice is to be categorized as 'individual learners execute it simultaneously' (which is the most basic form of participation possible); the second basic rule is that when more than one participation form is required, the participation structure of the final stage of that very practice is to be adopted. For example, a practice activity would be coded as 'pairs working simultaneously', if that practice asks individual learners to speak out to the class by themselves, or do preparatory work individually, before engaging in pair work. This principle allows us to focus on the core goals and objectives of learner participation, instead of dwelling on the number of times that a learner must do things individually (or as part of a group) within a single practice activity.

It should be noted that the sampled units in Japanese textbooks do not

Chapter 5 / Analysis of Practice Activities in Japanese and Chinese EFL Textbooks   217

require the learner to present something to the whole class; this kind of individual or group presentations to the whole class are handled within separate 'Project' sections found outside of the units, while Chinese textbooks do include this kind of presentation requirements within the units themselves.

5.4.2 Sequence of analysis procedures and other minor methodological considerations

Taken together, all practice activities within the selected units/lessons from the sample materials were coded according to Littlejohn's (2011) definitions of these aspects (except for the changes already mentioned in the previous paragraphs). Instead of creating a framework of categories before analysis (which may prove to be inadequate once the real analysis begins), a data-driven approach was followed, by analysing samples from the materials and using that to formulate a set of sub-categories that served as guidelines for analysis in a later phase. To improve the reliability of the results, I coded all the practice activities repeatedly, until intra-rater reliability reached 100% (meaning that the categorization and coding of all practice activities followed a set of consistent rules or principles). Additionally, another independent blind rater, who formerly served as an ALT in Japanese public schools, separately coded all practice activities as well. Periodical discussion meetings were held between both parties during the process, and in the end, an agreement was achieved on all coding results.

The final modified list of coding categories and sub-categories is presented in Table 5.3. When categorizing the practices for each textbook in spreadsheets, the letters and numbers corresponding to each sub-category were used. For instance, A*** = 'unclear', B1 = 'graphic', C9 = 'fiction', D30

= 'negotiate', and so on (see Figure 5.1).

Table 5.3: Typology of practice activities, adapted and modified from Littlejohn's (1992) research.

Elements	Definition
① Turn-Take	*do learners produce language with or without guidance?*
initiate language (unscripted)	learner(s) initiate discourse without any prompt, script or guidance.
scripted response	learner(s) produce language under guidance by the textbook.
not required	textbook does not require direct production of language items / unclear.
② Focus	*where do learners need to concentrate/focus their attention?*
language system (form)	focus on grammar, pronunciation, sentence patterns, linguistic items.
meaning	focus on semantic aspects (ex: reading comprehension).
relationship of system and meaning	focus on the connections between meaning and language form.
A: Input to learners	*the form of content that is provided to the learner by the textbook*
1. graphic	pictures, illustrations, photographs, diagrams/tables, symbols, etc.
2. word/phrases/sentences: written	written letters/numbers/words/phrases/sentences without coherence.
3. word/phrases/sentences: audio/oral	spoken letters/numbers/words/phrases/sentences without coherence.
4. extended discourse: written	texts composed of more than one sentence/pattern which cohere (>30 words).
5. extended discourse: audio/oral	texts composed of more than one sentence/pattern which cohere (>30 words).
*. ask-and-answer: written	short dialogue with one question and one reply (can be repeated).
**. ask-and-answer: audio/oral	short dialogue with one question and one reply (can be repeated).
***. unclear	the form of input is not clearly specified in the practice instructions.
B: Expected output	*the form of content that is to be produced by the learner as a result*
1. graphic	pictures, illustrations, photographs, diagrams/tables, symbols, etc.
2. word/phrases/sentences: written	written letters/numbers/words/phrases/sentences without coherence.
3. word/phrases/sentences: oral	spoken letters/numbers/words/phrases/sentences without coherence.
4. extended discourse: written	texts composed of more than one sentence/pattern which cohere (>30 words).
5. extended discourse: oral	texts composed of more than one sentence/pattern which cohere (>30 words).
*. ask-and-answer: written	short dialogue with one question and one reply (can be repeated).
**. ask-and-answer: oral	short dialogue with one question and one reply (can be repeated).
***. unclear	the form of output is not clearly specified in the practice instructions.
C: Nature	*what is the nature of the content provided/created by learners?*
6. metalinguistic comment	comments on language use, structure, form or meaning.
7. linguistic items	words/phrases/sentences/symbols devoid of any global message.
8. non-fiction	factual sentences/texts/photos/graphics/audio with coherent meaning
9. fiction	fictional sentences/texts/photos/graphics/audio with coherent meaning
10. personal information/opinion	personal information about learner(s) or their own opinion(s).
D: Operation / Process	*which mental processes are involved while the activity is performed?*
11. repeat identically	the learner is to reproduce exactly what is presented.
12. repeat selectively	the learner is to choose before repeating the given language.
13. repeat with substitution	the learner is to repeat the basic pattern of the given language, but replace certain items with other given items.
14. repeat with transformation	the learner is to apply a (conscious or unconscious) rule to given language and to transform it accordingly.
15. repeat with expansion	the learner is given an outline and is to use that outline as a frame within which to produce further language.

Chapter 5 / Analysis of Practice Activities in Japanese and Chinese EFL Textbooks   219

16. retrieve from STM	the learner is to recall items of language from short-term memory, that is, within a matter of seconds.
17. retrieve from ITM	the learner is to recall items from intermediate-term memory, that is, within a matter of minutes.
18. retrieve from LTM	the learner is to recall items from a prior lesson (long-term memory).
19. formulate items into larger unit	the learner is to combine recalled items in a way that requires the application of consciously or unconsciously held language rules.
20. decode semantic/propositional meaning	the learner is to decode the 'surface' meaning of the given language.
21. select information	the learner is to extract information from a given text/graphic/audio/talk.
22. calculate	the learner is to perform mathematical operations.
23. categorise selected information	the learner is to analyse, classify or organise selected information.
24. hypothesise	the learner is to hypothesise an explanation, description or the meaning of something.
25. compare samples of language	the learner is to compare two or more sets of language data on the basis of meaning or form.
26. analyse language form	the learner is to examine the component parts of a piece of language.
27. formulate language rule	the learner is to hypothesise a language rule.
28. apply stated language rule	the learner is to use a given language rule in order to transform or produce language.
29. apply general knowledge	the learner is to draw on knowledge of 'general facts' about the world.
30. negotiate	the learner is to discuss, decide or collaborate with others in order to accomplish something.
31. review own English output	the learner is to check his/her own foreign language production for its intended meaning or form.
32. attend to example/explanation	the learner is to 'take notice' of something.
*. translate	the learner is to translate between target language and mother tongue.
E: Participation	***who are learners expected to interact with during the activity?***
33. teacher and learner(s), whole class observing	the teacher and selected learner(s) are to interact together.
34. learner(s) to the whole class	selected learner(s) are to interact with the whole class, including the teacher.
35. learners with the whole class simultaneously	learners are to perform an operation in concert with the whole class.
36. learners individually simultaneously	learners are to perform an operation in the company of others but without immediate regard to the manner/pace with which others perform the same operation.
37. learners in pairs/groups; class observing	learners in pairs or small groups are to interact with each other while the rest of the class listens.
38. learners in pairs/groups, simultaneously	learners are to interact with each other in pairs/groups in the company of other pairs/groups.

Name	Unit	Pg	Num	IL	SR	NR	LS	M	M+LS	A1	A2	A3	A4	A5	A*	A**	A***	Ti	Li	C6i	C7i	C8i	C9i	C10i	B1	B2	B3	B4	B5	B*	B**	B***	To	Lo	C6o	C7o	C8o	C9o	C10o
				Turn-Take			**Focus**			**Input**								**Source**		**Nature (Input)**					**Output**								**Source**		**Nature (Output)**				
Beshida	2	37	1			1		1		1	1							1		1										1		1	1		1				1
Beshida	2	37	2		1				1		1							1					1		1	1					1	1	1	1				1
Beshida	2	38	1	1				1		1	1							1		1					1							1	1		1				
Beshida	2	38	2			1		1			1		1					1					1							1	1	1	1				1
Beshida	2	38	3			1		1			1		1					1					1		1					1	1	1	1		1		
Beshida	2	38	4	1					1	1	1							1		1						1					1	1	1				1
Beshida	2	39	5	1					1	1	1							1		1					1					1	1		1				
Beshida	2	39	6			1	1			1	1							1		1					1	1					1	1		1				1
Beshida	2	39	7			1	1				1							1		1					1	1					1	1		1				1
Beshida	2	39	8		1			1						1				1		1										1	1	1	1				
Beshida	2	39	9		1			1						1				1		1										1	1	1	1				
Beshida	2	39	10		1		1			1	1	1	1					1			1				1						1	1				1	
Beshida	2	39	11		1		1			1	1	1	1					1			1									1	1		1				
Beshida	2	40	1	1				1		1	1							1			1				1								1				1
Beshida	2	40	2			1		1			1							1			1					1					1	1		1				1
Beshida	2	40	3	1				1		1	1							1			1				1						1	1		1				
Beshida	2	41	4	1				1		1	1			1				1			1							1			1	1		1				
Beshida	2	41	5	1				1			1			1				1		1					1	1					1	1		1				
Beshida	2	41	6			1			1		1							1		1							1					1	1		1				
Beshida	2	41	7	1					1		1							1		1										1	1	1	1				
Beshida	2	41	8		1			1		1	1	1						1			1				1						1	1		1				1
Beshida	2	41	9			1		1		1	1	1						1			1										1	1		1				
Beshida	2	42	1		1			1		1	1							1		1	1				1						1	1		1				
Beshida	2	42	2		1			1		1	1							1		1	1				1						1	1		1				
Beshida	2	42	3		1			1		1	1			1				1			1					1					1	1		1				
Beshida	2	43	4	1				1		1	1							1		1						1					1	1		1		1		
Beshida	2	43	5			1	1			1	1							1		1						1					1	1		1				
Beshida	2	43	6	1				1		1	1							1		1						1					1	1		1				

Figure 5.1: Excerpt from the spreadsheet used for cataloguing the characteristics of practice activities found within the three selected sample units from each EFL textbook (see Appendix C).

5.5　Results

5.5.1　Learners' roles in regards to turn-taking

In response to the role of learners when engaging in practice activities, all practice activities were labelled as either 'make learners respond with scripted language' or 'response not required' (see Tables 5.4 and 5.5). As mentioned above, although I still included the 'initiate language (unscripted)' sub-category during the analysis procedure, no conclusive results were found in the sampled units of both Japanese and Chinese textbooks. It's important to mention in this regard that even when a specific practice activity only asks two learners to talk about a specific topic without providing any further explicit instructions, if one looks at the position of the activity within the other neighbouring activities in the same page, it becomes very clear that both learners will have to reference or reproduce the contents and results of previous practice activities if they are to be successful. Therefore, when deciding if a practice activity refers to unscripted or scripted responses, it is crucial to investigate the general context in which the practice activity exists, and how it relates to previous practice activities.

Overall, it is not surprising in any way to see that 'scripted response' (JP-M=60%; CH-M=75%) dominates consistently across all textbooks, whereas 'not required' (JP-M=40%; CH-M=25%) has a more modest presence. The reasons for a higher prevalence of 'not required' in the Japanese textbooks is that there are less practice activities in general (when compared to Chinese textbooks), and in many cases, such practice activities only ask the learner to passively observe an image, read or listen to a passage (or sentence pattern ∕ pronunciation rule), or they ask reading comprehension

Table 5.4: Percentages of practice activities in terms of learners' roles (Japanese textbooks).

Code	Turn-take	New Crown	New Horizon	Sunshine	Total English	One World	Columbus 21	Mean
IL	initiate language (unscripted)	-	-	-	-	-	-	0%
SR	scripted response	59%	60%	57%	61%	67%	57%	60%
NR	not required	41%	40%	43%	39%	33%	43%	40%

Table 5.5: Percentages of practice activities in terms of learners' roles (Chinese textbooks).

Code	Turn-take	Renjiao	Beishida	Ren'ai	Yilin	Jijiao	Waiyanshe	Shangwai	Shangjiao	Mean
IL	initiate language (unscripted)	-	-	-	-	-	-	-	-	0%
SR	scripted response	65%	72%	83%	85%	84%	72%	63%	74%	75%
NR	not required	35%	28%	17%	15%	16%	28%	38%	26%	25%

Chapter 5 / Analysis of Practice Activities in Japanese and Chinese EFL Textbooks   223

questions without clarifying in any way how the learner is supposed to respond (or even whether the learner has to respond at all).

These results resonate with those of two other studies: an analysis of English language teaching textbooks produced by UK publishers for 12 to 13-year-old learners (Littlejohn, 1992); and a study of authorized English textbooks for 7th graders used in South Korea (Guilloteaux, 2012). This strongly indicates that, at least in terms of encouraging students to be more flexible in their use of a foreign language, English teaching and learning materials have not changed significantly in recent decades. It also shows that, on this aspect, there does not seem to be any major differences between ESL and EFL materials.

For English beginners, this scenario is likely to provide them with an accumulation of words and grammar points to facilitate future language learning. However, opportunities for learners to initiate language or attempt to use language in their own way might be more indispensable for beginners than we have realized. It has been pointed out by Ellis (2005) that when learners have to use their own words (i.e., communicate their own thoughts, opinions and feelings in an unscripted way, as opposed to reproducing pre-defined speech), it allows them the chance to produce a sustained output in the form of extended talk.

5.5.2 Focus of practice activities

Tables 5.6 and 5.7 present the percentages related to the *focus* category. To investigate what learners need to focus on, practice activities were coded under three categories: *language system (form)*, *meaning*, and *relationship between meaning and language system*. To remind the reader of what these terms mean, one can say that a practice activity may ask learners to

Table 5.6: Percentages of practice activities in terms of focus (Japan textbooks).

Code	Focus	New Crown	New Horizon	Sunshine	Total English	One World	Columbus 21	Mean
LS	language system (form)	11%	-	-	17%	-	3%	5%
M	meaning	41%	38%	45%	37%	50%	47%	43%
M+LS	relationship of meaning and system	48%	62%	55%	46%	50%	50%	52%

Table 5.7: Percentages of practice activities in terms of focus (China textbooks).

Code	Focus	Renjiao	Beishida	Ren'ai	Yilin	Jijiao	Waiyanshe	Shangwai	Shangjiao	Mean
LS	language system (form)	2%	14%	16%	20%	11%	10%	21%	11%	13%
M	meaning	38%	41%	54%	47%	35%	30%	24%	30%	37%
M+LS	relationship of meaning and system	57%	45%	30%	33%	54%	58%	56%	59%	49%

focus their attention on a specific element of the target language: namely, the semantic contents of a word/expression, or a group of words (*meaning*); or the linguistic aspects of a text or sentence (*language system*). In the latter case, learners must look more closely at the rules that allow them to organize words and compose sentences, rather than understanding the meaning of the words or sentences themselves. Finally, some practice activities might place their focus at the connection between form and meaning (*relationship between system+meaning*). In this case, learners must realize that by altering or applying a rule, the meaning of a sentence is also affected in a certain way, and vice-versa.

The results show that nearly half of all practice activities (JP-M=43%; CH-M=37%) require learners to 'focus on meaning', while the rest can be divided into 'focus on language system' (JP-M=5%; CH-M=13%) and 'meaning-system relationship' (JP-M=52%; CH-M=49%), which is slightly prevalent. However, due to the slight ambiguities involved in determining if a practice activity focuses more on form or meaning, it is more accurate to say that throughout the sampled units, 'meaning' and 'relationship of system and meaning' are present in roughly similar numbers. Having said this, if we consider that the notion of 'meaning' is present in both sub-categories, it is undeniable that it constitutes a dominant feature of these EFL textbooks.

This shows that meaning-focused practice activities are predominantly favoured in all textbooks. Practice activities that focus on meaning are mostly comprised of listening and reading questions that ask learners to extract information from a given audio track or a written text. This kind of meaning is what Ellis (2005) called 'pragmatic meaning', which is crucial to language learning. Requiring a learner to organize images and photos in a correct sequence after reading or listening to a passage is another common case of a 'meaning-centred' activity found in all textbooks.

Practice activities that focus on the 'relationship between language forms and meaning' usually require learners to apply basic language rules to incomplete sentences, so that they can convey the correct meanings provided by illustrations or other textual/audio passages.

Regarding 'focus on language system', its frequency of usage within the textbooks is relatively low. For the most part, these are speaking or writing activities that ask learners to repeat given sentence patterns or individual words, which do not possess any clearly coherent structure or meaning. It seems that system-focused (or form-focused) practice activities are not considered as essential as they used to be for beginners. The recent prevalence of new trends in the fields of English teaching and learning, such as CLT (communicative language teaching) and TBI (task-based instruction) might have pushed textbook designers to limit the number of drills and other form-based practice activities in order to avoid accusations of lagging behind the times, or causing feelings of excessive monotony among learners. To be clear, Japanese textbooks do have sections within each unit that explain sentence patterns and grammatical rules; it just so happens that for the most part, these sections clearly do not contain any practice activity and are included only for reference purposes. Having said this, we can see that Chinese textbooks tend to include more 'language system-focused activities' than the Japanese ones.

5.5.3 Mental operations in practice activities

As explained in the methodological procedures section, the aspect of *operation/process* includes a list of mental operations that are put into effect during practice activities. It should be stated once again that a single practice activity often involves more than one operation. Based on a modified version of Littlejohn's (2011) framework, twenty-three types of operations in total were identified within the sampled units of the textbooks; their percentage values are represented in Tables 5.8 and 5.9.

The results can be organized into three groups in accordance with their frequency of occurrence. These are: 'prominent' results (high percentage values), 'less-prominent' results (with percentages around the 10-40% mark) and 'poorly-featured/inexistent' results (percentage values from 0-10%).

Regarding the strongest results, it is to be expected that 'decode meaning' and 'select information' are highly featured in all textbooks, regardless of the country. In most cases, it is impractical or almost impossible to carry out a practice activity successfully without understanding the basic meanings of text passages and illustrations, and without extracting relevant data from them. In fact, the overwhelming majority of activities require learners to look at a piece of data (text, audio, image), understand its basic meaning, extract pieces of information from it, and then either organize the extracted pieces of data in a coherent way, or use them to produce language such as reading comprehension sentences, conversations, and so forth.

In the second category of 'less-prominent' results, we start to notice differences between the Japanese and Chinese textbooks: in the former case, one can point out the sub-categories of 'attend to example/explanation' (JP-M=37%), 'repeat with substitution' (JP-M=22%) and 'repeat identically' (JP-M=11%); and in the latter case, those of 'compare samples of language' (CH-M=34%), 'attend to example' (CH-M=33%), 'categorise selected information' (CH-M=22%), 'formulate items into larger unit' (CH-M=16%), 'apply general knowledge' (CH-M=14%), 'repeat identically' (CH-M=13%), 'repeat

Table 5.8: Percentages of practice activities in terms of mental operations (JPN).

Code	Operation/Process	New Crown	New Horizon	Sunshine	Total English	One World	Columbus 21	Mean
D11	repeat identically	16%	4%	-	28%	10%	7%	11%
D12	repeat selectively	1%	4%	10%	7%	-	12%	6%
D13	repeat with substitution	15%	36%	18%	17%	40%	8%	22%
D14	repeat with transformation	10%	17%	14%	-	-	15%	9%
D15	repeat with expansion	7%	2%	2%	-	5%	3%	3%
D16	retrieve from STM	15%	4%	-	-	10%	22%	8%
D17	retrieve from ITM	-	-	-	-	2%	-	0%
D18	retrieve from LTM	-	-	-	-	-	13%	2%
D19	formulate items into larger unit	8%	2%	2%	9%	10%	3%	6%
D20	decode semantic/propositional meaning	23%	45%	67%	54%	57%	53%	50%
D21	select information	61%	51%	55%	59%	81%	77%	64%
D22	calculate	-	-	-	-	2%	-	0%
D23	categorise selected information	23%	4%	12%	-	2%	17%	10%
D24	hypothesise	1%	-	10%	-	-	10%	4%
D25	compare samples of language	2%	2%	16%	6%	2%	2%	5%
D26	analyse language form	5%	-	-	6%	2%	-	2%
D27	formulate language rule	2%	-	-	-	-	-	0%
D28	apply stated language rule	1%	-	-	6%	-	7%	2%
D29	apply general knowledge	11%	4%	14%	2%	7%	5%	7%
D30	negotiate	1%	-	8%	11%	5%	10%	6%
D31	review own English output	-	-	-	-	-	-	-
D32	attend to example/explanation	30%	55%	37%	37%	43%	22%	37%
D*	translate	3%	2%	2%	6%	5%	8%	4%

Table 5.9: Percentages of practice activities in terms of mental operations (CHN).

Code	Operation/Process	Renjiao	Beishida	Ren'ai	Yilin	Jijiao	Waiyanshe	Shangwai	Shangjiao	Mean
D11	repeat identically	8%	9%	26%	18%	3%	8%	28%	5%	13%
D12	repeat selectively	15%	14%	-	-	10%	15%	4%	10%	8%
D13	repeat with substitution	18%	13%	14%	12%	7%	13%	10%	8%	12%
D14	repeat with transformation	2%	4%	-	-	14%	7%	7%	12%	6%
D15	repeat with expansion	8%	13%	16%	8%	12%	10%	8%	8%	10%
D16	retrieve from STM	8%	2%	-	-	-	2%	-	-	1%
D17	retrieve from ITM	-	2%	1%	-	2%	-	-	1%	1%
D18	retrieve from LTM	5%	1%	-	-	2%	-	1%	-	1%
D19	formulate items into larger unit	23%	14%	9%	5%	17%	25%	21%	12%	16%
D20	decode semantic/propositional meaning	74%	55%	71%	77%	92%	90%	81%	92%	79%
D21	select information	60%	54%	74%	72%	71%	52%	69%	81%	67%
D22	calculate	-	-	-	-	1%	-	4%	1%	1%
D23	categorise selected information	31%	4%	26%	15%	26%	32%	31%	15%	22%
D24	hypothesise	2%	1%	9%	-	4%	2%	1%	-	2%
D25	compare samples of language	-	18%	29%	68%	37%	60%	26%	30%	34%
D26	analyse language form	-	13%	3%	27%	4%	5%	17%	11%	10%
D27	formulate language rule	-	-	-	-	-	-	-	5%	1%
D28	apply stated language rule	-	1%	1%	12%	2%	10%	-	4%	4%
D29	apply general knowledge	17%	18%	20%	7%	17%	2%	15%	15%	14%
D30	negotiate	-	8%	14%	2%	15%	8%	7%	10%	8%
D31	review own English output	-	-	-	-	-	-	1%	-	0%
D32	attend to example/explanation	40%	31%	35%	32%	21%	45%	26%	36%	33%
D*	translate	-	-	-	-	-	-	-	1%	0%

with substitution' (CH-M=12%), 'repeat with expansion' (CH-M=10%) and 'analyse language form' (CH-M=10%).

The wider diversity of operations in the Chinese textbooks is easily explained by the fact that they contain much more practice activities than Japanese textbooks, and this forces textbook designers to diversify the instructions in each practice, to reduce the number of repetitive tasks.

The 'prominent results' section describes how learners have to absorb and extract information from the textbooks, but in the case of 'less-prominent' results, we begin to understand how the textbooks from each country expect learners to process or produce language as an output. In the Japanese textbooks, there is a stronger sense of explicit guidance, since learners usually need to follow examples or repeat a given sentence pattern in some form or another (repeating with substitution is a strong feature of *New Horizon* and *One World*). 'Repeat identically' appears more often in instructions for stress and intonation, by asking learners to repeat sentences identically after an audio demonstration; this is the only practice that is directly related to phonology and is employed in a similar way in the textbooks of both countries.

It seems that the more complex forms of language processing operations in Japanese textbooks are reserved for the 'Project' sections located outside of the units (which generally involve group activities), but since these sections are relatively short, and usually do not appear more than three or four times within any given textbook, one must question whether this is sufficient for proper language acquisition and development of advanced language skills.

As for the Chinese textbooks, while there is more diversity of operations, it can be said that the main two requirements placed upon learners are: to

Chapter 5 / Analysis of Practice Activities in Japanese and Chinese EFL Textbooks 231

organize words, sentences and pictures in a summarized form (ex: produce a table with the daily schedule of a fictional character); and to ask learners to produce language corresponding to extended discourse ('repeat with expansion' and 'formulate recalled items into larger unit'), although in most cases, not that much guidance is provided beyond one or two example sentences.

'Apply general knowledge' often occurs in cases where learners need to figure out the names of cities or countries in different maps, and write their names accordingly. It requires the application of general knowledge in domestic and world geography, because the names of places and countries are not directly provided. There are also many cases in Chinese textbooks where learners need to talk about famous people, weather patterns, or general knowledge related to the learner's province.

We now reach the third category, which is that of 'poorly-featured results': this is where the differences between Japanese and Chinese textbooks become more diffuse and difficult to describe. There are still some commonalities: 'repeat selectively' (JP-M=6%; CH-M=8%) 'repeat with transformation' (JP-M=9%; CH-M=6%), 'negotiate' (JP-M=6%; CH-M=8%) and 'hypothesise' (JP-M=4%; CH-M=2%) have similar prevalence rates in both countries. Likewise, operations that require the use of memory (short, intermediate, and long-term) are relatively rare.

'Hypothesize' is mostly present within some reading comprehension questions, asking learners to look at a text, and without any explicit hints, to write their assumptions about a given situation (a possible example would be: 'After reading the text, what do you think this fictional person was feeling? Elaborate an answer'). There is one major difference: Chinese textbooks often require the learner to hypothesize the meaning or significance of a text/audio passage in English, while every instance found in the Japanese textbooks asked the learner to do so using the native language. Although this operation encourages learners to think creatively and develop a greater degree of attachment to fictional characters and events, in the Japanese case it is of limited value, because there is no active production of target language.

As for other notable differences between both countries, we can see that Japanese textbooks in general barely feature any operations that involve a strong focus on grammar rules and language system, such as 'analyse language form', 'formulate language rule', 'apply stated language rule' and 'review own English output'. It is true that Chinese textbooks are not focused on this aspect either, but it is nevertheless less neglected. 'Analyse language form' asks learners to look at a given language item and study it in terms of its language form, rather than its meaning: this appeared most frequently when learners had to analyse phonetic differences in the sounds of words within pronunciation activities. 'Formulate language rule' occurs whenever the learner must look at a language item and guess what language rule was used to produce it. 'Apply stated language rule' requires learners to produce language, by applying a sentence pattern or grammar rule explicitly stated in the practice activity using examples or instructions: these were mainly found within speaking and writing practice activities.

Another difference is the presence of the category 'translate' only in the Chinese textbook *Shangjiao*, and in all the Japanese textbooks, although it is a minor feature. In most cases, 'translate' consists of a translation practice that provides Japanese sentences as dialogues (or sometimes individual words), with corresponding disordered English words, offering an opportunity to connect target language and mother tongue; the task is to put English words into their correct order.

5.5.4　General considerations about mental operations: diversity & frequency

Looking at the overall picture, most of the 23 types of mental operations are relatively scattered across all textbooks. In terms of diversity of operation types, *New Crown, Beishida, Jijiao* and *Shangjiao* are the most varied. We can assume that the types of operations featured within each textbook reflect the designers' values as to what elements are best for developing language competency. From this viewpoint, a wider variety of operations might offer more opportunities for learners to interact closely with a language, and become more flexible in their use of it.

As for frequency of operations, the ones who appear the most often involve those related to: decoding the meaning of language items and pictures; selecting and extracting information from textbook materials or other learners; repeating language items with substitution; combining isolated language items into larger units through the application of language rules; and finally, following the examples provided along with the practice activities. Since only these occur in all textbooks, we can see that common operations among the authorized textbooks of both countries are not that many.

But just as important as describing the operations that were identified, is to list the ones missing or poorly featured in the sample materials: namely high-cognitive operations, related to categorizing, analysing, negotiating, and researching. Even while since these operations may appear in group project sections outside of the units, it is debatable as to whether this is sufficient or not. It is not the purpose of this study to argue that these operations should invariably be introduced or not, but it does suggest a topic that is worthy of further discussion in the future.

5.5.5 Modes of participation in practice activities

'Participation mode' describes the entity with whom learners are required to work with during practice activities. The results in Tables 5.10 and 5.11 reveal that almost all practice activities require learners to complete tasks simultaneously either by themselves (JP-M=76%; CH-M=81%), or in pairs (JP-M=23%; CH-M=17%).

Listening and reading comprehension questions are mostly conducted in the form of 'learners individually' while speaking practice activities are almost always expected to be completed in pair mode. If we consider that most of these speaking practice activities are restricted to the mere repetition of sentence examples provided by the textbooks, on one hand this makes it easier for less-trained teachers to evaluate and correct the results produced by learners, but on the other hand it is hard to imagine that the proper communication requisites are met during pair or group work. Despite this shortcoming, group activities have been found to be particularly suitable for EFL learners, because the sense of belonging to a group is heavily valued in collectivist cultures (Tomlinson, 2005).

As a distant third place, I regularly found in the sampled units of five Chinese textbooks practice activities where a learner must talk either individually or as part of a group to the whole classroom. This was not the case in the sampled units of Japanese textbooks, although as previously said, external 'Project'-style sections sometimes ask for group presentations in front of the whole classroom.

Table 5.10: Percentages of practice activities in terms of participation (JPN).

Code	Participation	New Crown	New Horizon	Sunshine	Total English	One World	Columbus 21	Mean
E33	teacher and learner(s), whole class observing	-	-	-	-	-	-	-
E34	learner(s) to the whole class	-	-	-	-	-	-	-
E35	learners with the whole class simultaneously	-	-	-	-	-	-	-
E36	learners individually simultaneously	82%	60%	73%	81%	81%	82%	76%
E37	learners in pairs/groups; class observing	-	-	-	-	-	-	-
E38	learners in pairs/groups, simultaneously	18%	40%	27%	17%	19%	18%	23%

Table 5.11: Percentages of practice activities in terms of participation (CHN).

Code	Participation	Renjiao	Beishida	Ren'ai	Yilin	Jijiao	Waiyanshe	Shangwai	Shangjiao	Mean
E33	teacher and learner(s), whole class observing	-	-	-	-	-	-	-	-	0%
E34	learner(s) to the whole class	2%	4%	1%	-	2%	2%	-	-	1%
E35	learners with the whole class simultaneously	-	-	-	-	-	-	-	-	0%
E36	learners individually simultaneously	75%	78%	74%	88%	79%	83%	86%	86%	81%
E37	learners in pairs/groups; class observing	-	-	-	-	-	-	-	-	0%
E38	learners in pairs/groups, simultaneously	23%	18%	25%	12%	18%	15%	14%	14%	17%

5.5.6 Input contents

The percentage values related to *input contents* are summarized in Tables 5.12 and 5.13. The main form of input (i.e., language content presented to learners) is graphics in Japanese textbooks (JP-M=50%) and written words/phrases/sentences in Chinese textbooks (CH-M=65%). Most graphics are pictures or photos, either accompanied by 'extended discourse' texts to assist learners' understanding, or presented in practice activities to provide terms for use in 'repeat with substitution'. Unsurprisingly, the widespread use of graphics is a typical feature of textbooks for beginners, although in Chinese textbooks one tends to see more tables and diagrams than illustrations or photos, and it is clear in the case of Japanese textbooks that they strive to look more aesthetically pleasing to young learners, using large-size, appealing images and manga-style characters. Since Chinese texts prefer to use tables and diagrams, with a higher density of text per page, this contributes to a noticeable increase in the number of 'written words/phrases/sentences'.

Written 'extended discourse' texts mainly appear in association with reading comprehension practice activities, and are especially prominent in *Sunshine* (61%) and *Ren'ai* (48%).

'Written: ask-and-answer' is mostly provided in the form of examples within speaking practice activities, which means that, for the most part, speaking activities consist of a single question with a short reply; in some cases, isolated written words or phrases are provided as items for learners to substitute while repeating the given example. Moreover, isolated written words also occur in incomplete forms with blanks that learners must fill as part of listening activities. It should be noted that in Japanese materials, some of these forms are written in Japanese, although the corresponding

Table 5.12: Percentages of practice activities in terms of input contents (JPN).

Code	Form of Input Contents	New Crown	New Horizon	Sunshine	Total English	One World	Columbus 21	Mean
A1	graphic	53%	51%	14%	52%	71%	58%	50%
A2	words/phrases/sentences: written	41%	23%	29%	31%	33%	30%	31%
A3	words/phrases/sentences: audio/oral	15%	13%	10%	-	-	10%	8%
A4	extended discourse: written	23%	32%	61%	22%	21%	23%	30%
A5	extended discourse: audio/oral	22%	13%	2%	22%	29%	38%	21%
A*	ask-and-answer: written	6%	23%	8%	17%	24%	3%	14%
A**	ask-and-answer: audio/oral	7%	2%	2%	17%	2%	2%	5%
A***	unclear/unspecified	-	-	-	-	-	-	-
	Source of Input Contents							
Ti	teaching materials	89%	100%	96%	93%	95%	95%	95%
Li	learner(s)	11%	-	4%	11%	10%	13%	8%
	Nature of Input Contents							
C6i	metalinguistic comment	8%	-	-	-	-	5%	2%
C7i	linguistic items	17%	-	-	-	2%	7%	4%
C8i	non-fiction	5%	-	-	-	-	2%	1%
C9i	fiction	72%	100%	98%	94%	93%	85%	90%
C10i	personal information/opinion	8%	-	2%	6%	10%	12%	6%

Table 5.13: Percentages of practice activities in terms of input contents (CHN).

Code	Form of Input Contents	Renjiao	Beishida	Ren'ai	Yilin	Jijiao	Waiyanshe	Shangwai	Shangjiao	Mean
A1	graphic	48%	38%	32%	43%	43%	37%	38%	62%	42%
A2	words/phrases/sentences: written	54%	68%	55%	73%	69%	75%	61%	67%	65%
A3	words/phrases/sentences: audio/oral	11%	13%	1%	7%	4%	10%	17%	3%	8%
A4	extended discourse: written	22%	26%	48%	43%	35%	28%	42%	26%	34%
A5	extended discourse: audio/oral	8%	8%	35%	17%	20%	13%	29%	5%	17%
A*	ask-and-answer: written	20%	6%	6%	2%	7%	10%	10%	10%	9%
A**	ask-and-answer: audio/oral	3%	-	-	7%	-	-	10%	1%	3%
A***	unclear/unspecified	2%	-	-	-	1%	2%	7%	11%	3%
	Source of Input Contents									
Ti	teaching materials	100%	98%	93%	100%	98%	97%	99%	97%	98%
Li	learner(s)	2%	2%	7%	-	2%	3%	1%	3%	3%
	Nature of Input Contents									
C6i	metalinguistic comment	-	-	-	-	1%	5%	7%	18%	4%
C7i	linguistic items	23%	33%	17%	30%	30%	40%	14%	12%	25%
C8i	non-fiction	5%	16%	14%	7%	12%	5%	15%	14%	11%
C9i	fiction	71%	50%	62%	73%	56%	50%	63%	62%	61%
C10i	personal information/opinion	2%	2%	7%	-	2%	3%	1%	3%	3%

Chapter 5 / Analysis of Practice Activities in Japanese and Chinese EFL Textbooks   239

aural materials are in English. As for these aural materials, there is not much to say, other than mention their predominant usage as input contents within listening practice activities.

In sum, isolated written words/phrases/sentences (w/p/s) and extended audio passages are the main forms of input, which means that learners are obliged to *read* and *listen* to them. In other words, the main forms of input come in the following order: *read* (w/p/s + extended discourse + ask-and-answer) > *watch* (graphics) > *listen* (extended discourse + w/p/s + ask-and-answer).

Concerning the source of input contents, it is obvious that the textbook provides the bulk of learning contents: the few exceptions happen when learners must bring to the classroom a photo of their family and talk about it, or list their personal interests and favourite places as a basis for further language production.

Having understood these different forms of input, it is also necessary to look at the nature of these inputs to investigate, for instance, whether the contents are based on real facts or fiction. It turns out that fictional contents overwhelmingly predominate in Japanese textbooks (JP-M=90%) while less so in the Chinese ones (CH-M=61%). Fictional contents refer to texts or dialogues taking place in imaginary contexts or between imaginary characters, most of which are extended discourse texts. All the input found in the sampled units of *New Horizon* was fictional.

Non-fictional contents refer to dialogues based on true or real information. If learners are required to answer according to given photos of real objects or representations of universally-held concepts (such as for example time differences across the globe), these practice activities were coded as non-fiction, because the input represents objects and information existing in the real world.

The main difference between both countries is the greater importance of 'non-fiction' (CH-M=25%), and 'linguistic items' (CH-M=11%) in Chinese textbooks, and their near-inexistence in the Japanese ones (respectively, JP-M=4% and 1%). This reinforces what I have previously said about 'language system' being given slightly more importance in China than in Japan, although both remain heavily focused on 'meaning'.

Although it is common to provide examples alongside practice activities, and these examples are likely to be fictional, this does not mean that such practice activities do not encourage learners to express personal information or their ideas and opinions. In order to clarify this aspect, the nature of the output needs to be examined as well.

5.5.7 Output contents

Here we find some differences from what was previously seen in the case of inputs. The most frequently required output is 'written: words, phrases or sentences' (JP-M=36%; CH-M=55%), followed by graphic output such as symbols or drawings (JP-M=19%; CH-M=18%) and in third place we find in proximity spoken language items in the form of 'oral: words/ phrases/sentences' (JP-M=16%; CH-M=10%) and 'oral: ask-and-answer' (JP-M=15%; CH-M=12%). Especially in the Japanese textbooks, their reading comprehension questions are asked without giving any instructions as to their output forms; consequently, they can be answered in both oral and written forms, and were categorized as 'unclear' (JP-M=17%; CH-M=4%).

Although written words, phrases or sentences are bundled into a single category, in reality several of the practice activities in both countries merely consist of isolated names, numbers or multiple choice letters such as "A/

Table 5.14: Percentages of practice activities in terms of output contents (JPN).

Code	Form of Output Contents	New Crown	New Horizon	Sunshine	Total English	One World	Columbus 21	Mean
B1	graphic	18%	21%	24%	13%	10%	30%	19%
B2	words/phrases/sentences: written	39%	13%	37%	35%	40%	53%	36%
B3	words/phrases/sentences: audio/oral	22%	19%	10%	20%	14%	12%	16%
B4	extended discourse: written	1%	2%	2%	-	-	-	1%
B5	extended discourse: audio/oral	-	9%	-	-	-	2%	2%
B*	ask-and-answer: written	2%	13%	4%	11%	14%	2%	8%
B**	ask-and-answer: audio/oral	13%	21%	12%	17%	19%	8%	15%
B***	unclear/unspecified	20%	21%	16%	17%	14%	13%	17%
	Source of Output Contents							
To	teaching materials	77%	81%	76%	78%	83%	68%	77%
Lo	learner(s)	23%	19%	24%	24%	21%	32%	24%
	Nature of Output Contents							
C6o	metalinguistic comment	1%	-	-	-	-	-	0%
C7o	linguistic items	23%	15%	37%	22%	19%	35%	25%
C8o	non-fiction	2%	-	2%	-	-	-	1%
C9o	fiction	58%	68%	43%	65%	71%	45%	58%
C10o	personal information/opinion	17%	17%	18%	15%	14%	22%	17%

Table 5.15: Percentages of practice activities in terms of output contents (CHN).

Code	Form of Output Contents	Renjiao	Beishida	Ren'ai	Yilin	Jijiao	Waiyanshe	Shangwai	Shangjiao	Mean
B1	graphic	23%	17%	26%	5%	23%	20%	7%	22%	18%
B2	words/phrases/sentences: written	57%	60%	43%	55%	71%	52%	44%	56%	55%
B3	words/phrases/sentences: audio/oral	3%	6%	13%	18%	7%	13%	15%	4%	10%
B4	extended discourse: written	5%	2%	9%	5%	10%	3%	8%	7%	6%
B5	extended discourse: audio/oral	5%	3%	20%	-	4%	5%	18%	3%	7%
B*	ask-and-answer: written	-	1%	-	-	-	3%	1%	1%	1%
B**	ask-and-answer: audio/oral	17%	11%	10%	12%	12%	12%	8%	14%	12%
B***	unclear/unspecified	-	7%	1%	8%	-	-	6%	5%	4%
	Source of Output Contents									
To	teaching materials	71%	77%	77%	80%	75%	77%	81%	73%	76%
Lo	learner(s)	31%	24%	26%	20%	26%	23%	21%	27%	25%
	Nature of Output Contents									
C6o	metalinguistic comment	-	-	-	-	-	-	-	-	0%
C7o	linguistic items	42%	50%	35%	42%	52%	50%	43%	38%	44%
C8o	non-fiction	-	2%	3%	-	-	-	4%	1%	1%
C9o	fiction	34%	24%	39%	38%	24%	27%	36%	29%	31%
C10o	personal information/opinion	26%	26%	28%	20%	22%	23%	18%	33%	25%

Chapter 5 / Analysis of Practice Activities in Japanese and Chinese EFL Textbooks   243

B/C/D" or "T/F". Likewise, in the case of graphics, it is symbols and lines that are often produced (ex: ✔ and ✖) rather than actual drawings. The fact is that there is not as much production of full sentences as one would expect. In any case, it is the Chinese textbooks that tend to encourage more production of actual sentences.

Furthermore, the category of 'written: extended discourse text' is practically inexistent in the sampled units of Japanese textbooks (JP-M=1%), which makes it hard to say that seventh-grade Japanese learners are being challenged to produce long-form texts (only *New Crown*, *New Horizon* and *Sunshine* included such practices). While the situation is not much better in the Chinese textbooks (CH-M=6%), at least all textbooks had practice activities that required 'extended discourse' as written output, and the same is valid for spoken extended discourse (CH-M=7%; only *Yilin* had no such activities).

To summarize, the prevalence of *writing* (w/p/s + ask-and-answer + extended discourse) > *speech* (w/p/s + ask-and-answer + extended discourse) > *drawing* is a common feature in both countries.

The source of output contents is practically identical for Japan and China: 'teaching materials' (JP-M=77%; CH-M=76%) followed by 'learner' (JP-M=24%; CH-M=25%). In the former case, the learner must make use of the contents provided by the textbook in order to produce language; but in the latter, all contents come from the personal opinions, information and facts related to the learners themselves.

Regarding the nature of these output contents, three categories were identified: fiction, non-fiction, and personal opinion. 'Fictional output' remains strong (JP-M=58%; CH-M=44%), whereas 'non-fiction' (JP-M=1%; CH-M=1%) and 'personal opinion/information' occur in similar amounts (JP-

244

M=17%; CH-M=25%).

Regarding the latter category, all the textbooks make a reasonable effort to engage learners in expressing their own ideas and opinions about themselves or certain topics of their choosing.

5.6 Discussion of Results and Conclusion

In total, 18 units/lessons/programs (Japan) and 24 units/modules/topics (China) were analysed from the full batch of authorized EFL textbooks for seventh-grade learners. The results were presented in Tables 5.4 to 5.15, each of them describing a particular aspect: *learners' roles, focus, mental operations, participation modes,* and *input/output.*

Although a more comprehensive review of the textbooks will take place in the next chapter, for now it is important to summarize the main results

Table 5.16: Summary of percentage values related to the 'four skills' (JPN).

JP input	reading	w/p/s	31%
		extended	30%
		ask+answer	14%
	listening	w/p/s	8%
		extended	21%
		ask+answer	5%
JP output	writing	w/p/s	36%
		extended	1%
		ask+answer	8%
	speaking	w/p/s	16%
		extended	2%
		ask+answer	15%

Table 5.17: Summary of percentage values related to the 'four skills' (CHN).

CH input	reading	w/p/s	65%
		extended	34%
		ask+answer	9%
	listening	w/p/s	8%
		extended	17%
		ask+answer	3%
CH output	writing	w/p/s	55%
		extended	6%
		ask+answer	1%
	speaking	w/p/s	10%
		extended	7%
		ask+answer	12%

Chapter 5 / Analysis of Practice Activities in Japanese and Chinese EFL Textbooks   245

of 'input' and 'output' contents, which are especially relevant for under-standing whether the 'four skills' are balanced throughout the textbooks (the aspect of 'graphics' will be ignored here.). The results are displayed in Tables 5.16 and 5.17.

5.6.1   Output: writing and speaking

If one combines the output contents of textbooks in both countries, it can be said that 'written: words / phrases / sentences', 'oral: ask-and-answer' and 'oral: words / phrases / sentences' are the main targets of practice activities.

By looking at the results more closely, we find that most of the output within 'written: words/sentences/phrases' is information that is merely copied from reading and listening activities (not to mention the notable amount of times that only single letters and numbers are required as output). Since learners do not have many opportunities to produce completely novel pieces of language, it cannot be concluded that the outcome of this output can be fully associated to the improvement of writing skills. As for 'oral: one ask and answer' and 'oral: words/phrases/sentences', these are indeed related to speech skills, but the majority of its occurrences are 'substitution and repetition' exercises that are placed at a lower level of development of speech competency. In these two cases, it turns out that neither writing nor speaking is required in a way that equips learners with flexible tools for language use. Along with writing, reading practices in Japanese textbooks were also found in a previous study to be relatively lacking in terms of equipping learners with communicative competency (Wang, 2012b).

5.6.2 Input: reading and listening

Once again looking at the combined results from both countries, 'written: words / phrases / sentences', and 'written: extended discourse texts' comprise most of the reading input while 'oral: extended texts' constitutes most of the listening input. The main issue here is that I could only find a strong correlation between 'read input / written output' and 'heard input / spoken output' in the case of isolated words, phrases and sentences (i.e., there is not much difference between the amount of input and output). But in the case of 'extended discourse' and 'ask-and-answer', there is a much greater imbalance between the amount of content that learners receive and the amount of content that learners are expected to produce. Since the output demands placed on learners are of a lower level of complexity ('w/p/s' and 'ask+answer'), the difference between the realities of *input* (read/listen) and *output* (write/speak) is striking.

Still regarding the category of 'written: extended discourse' as input, I found that the extended texts themselves are of limited length in the case of Japanese textbooks, and do not provide learners with sufficient exposure to everyday language usage. Thus, learners are expected to continue experiencing difficulties when reading passages longer than a single sentence. This leads us to the issue of implicit vs. explicit learning. Masuhara (2003) has presented theoretical evidence asserting that it is generally preferable for learners to acquire language in an implicit way, by reading texts that are meaningful and motivating, rather than reading 'distilled' or 'simplified' texts in which the main points are conveyed explicitly. Furthermore, Tomlinson (2005) suggests that the most effective way of acquiring language implicitly (within a context of 'meaningful and motivated exposure') is through extensive reading. It might be argued that it is unrealistic to intro-

Chapter 5 / Analysis of Practice Activities in Japanese and Chinese EFL Textbooks   247

duce extensive reading to beginners; however, altered, or simplified reading materials (without going to the same lengths of simplification that the materials analysed in this study display) can pave the way towards a more significant exposure to language in use. Chinese textbooks certainly do provide longer texts than the Japanese ones, but looking at the overall picture, the contents offered by the sample materials do not seem to constitute sufficient input to prepare for further language use and learning. Also, it is hard to say that the four skills are fully well-balanced among the totality of practice activities.

As for other findings common to both countries, the most striking ones are: a focus on individual participation, followed by pair work; few attempts to improve learners' presentation skills in English in front of the whole class; and the dominance of mental operations that request learners to decode meanings, select information, repeat with substitution, and follow the given examples.

The results of this study illustrated the characteristics of practice activities in EFL authorized textbooks and pointed out the lack of real and learner-initiated language use. However, this study did not examine how practice activities are applied in real classrooms and should be considered in any future studies.

In the next chapter, I will compare the main findings from Chapters 3-5, and discuss them in regard to the requirements stated by the national curricula of both countries.

Chapter 6／Results of EFL Textbook Comparisons with the English Language Curricula of Japan & China

6.1　Introduction

To briefly recap the contents and overall structure of this dissertation, I first provided a brief history of textbook development in China and Japan, and an analysis of the English national curricula in both countries (Chapter 1), followed by a presentation of the methodological framework for textbook analysis at the micro-scale of the individual unit (Chapter 2). In Chapters 3, 4 and 5, a few sample units from each textbook were analysed in terms of metadiscourse, rhetorical patterns and practice activities.

In this chapter, I will seek to discuss the main findings from each chapter, and argue to what extent the currently-authorised textbooks are truly reflective of the objectives and methods stated in the curricula. In response to the shared issues pervading these two sets of EFL textbooks, I will propose a new approach for EFL material development and introduce an action research case study to verify its validity. Finally, I will suggest possible avenues for further research.

6.2　Main Objectives of Textbook Contents According to the Curricula

To begin with, let us overview the main points espoused in the English curricula of both countries, to be clear about which requisites the textbooks should satisfy. These crucial curriculum requisites are summarised in Table 6.1. Both curricula share many similarities regarding their overall

Table 6.1: Requisites for textbook contents in the curricula of Japan and China.

	Japan EFL Curriculum	China EFL Curriculum
Overall Objectives	To develop students' basic communication abilities (listening, speaking, reading and writing), deepen their understanding of language and culture, and foster a positive attitude toward communication through foreign languages.	To develop students' comprehensive language competence, promote their cognitive and mental development, and improve their humanistic qualities. Comprehensive language competence is achieved through five general objectives including language skills, language knowledge, attitude to learning, learning strategy, and cultural awareness.
Language Activities	> Listening: to enable students to understand the speaker's intentions when listening to their English. > Speaking: to enable students to talk about their own thoughts using English. > Reading: to accustom and familiarize students with reading English and to enable them to understand the writer's intentions when reading English. > Writing: to accustom and familiarize students with writing in English, and to enable them to write about their own thoughts using English.	> Listening: to understand and participate in statements and discussions about familiar topics. > Speaking: to exchange information and express opinions about various topics in daily life. > Reading: to understand texts such as those of newspapers at each corresponding level, overcome the barrier of unknown words in order to grasp key ideas, and use appropriate reading strategies according to reading purpose. > Writing: to draft and edit short compositions. > Attitude: to have clear motivation, active learning attitude and confidence, to cooperate with others towards completing tasks, solve problems and report results. > Learning strategy: to assess one's own learning and summarize one's own learning style, by making use of a wide variety of learning resources. > Culture: to further increase one's understanding and awareness of cultural differences.
Treatment of Language Activities	> Students should use language to share their thoughts and feelings with each other in actual situations. > Students should be able to perform language activities in which they have to think about how to express themselves in a way that is appropriate to a specific situation and condition. > Teachers should focus on the indicated language-use situations and functions of language.	*Suggestions for teaching:* > Provide English learning groundwork for all students. > Focus on using English to do things in order to develop language competence. > Provide guidance regarding learning strategies in order to cultivate students' autonomous learning. > Raise cross cultural awareness to promote cross cultural competence. > Use teaching materials creatively in order to adjust them to real-world teaching needs. > Integrate various teaching resources in order to improve learning efficiency. > Organize lively and active extracurricular activities in order to expand learning channels.
		> Teachers should improve their own professional level in order to meet the requirements of the curriculum.
Language Elements	Speech sounds; letters and symbols; words, collocations and common expressions; grammatical items.	Speech sounds; grammatical items; words; functions; topics; cases of classroom teaching; cases of evaluation; teaching suggestions for language skills; classroom English.
	> Both the writing of letters and their corresponding pronunciation should be adequately taught. > Language activities should be conducted in such a way that grammar is effectively utilized for communication, based on the idea that grammar underpins communication.	> Pronunciation teaching should focus on meaning, context, intonation and speech flow, rather than on pursuing accuracy of one single sound. It should be done by imitation mainly for beginners. Teachers should provide various opportunities for students to listen, to imitate repetitively, and to practice so as to form good pronunciation habits.

Treatment of Language Elements	> Consideration should be given so that instruction does not centre on issues like explaining grammatical terms or differentiating between usage, but rather focusing on the actual use of grammatical items. Instruction should be provided for the awareness of the differences between English and Japanese in terms of word order, modification, and other aspects. > Effective instruction should be devised in order to have students understand the unique features of English, such as organizing mutually-related grammatical items in a cohesive manner.	> Words should be learnt and used through activities that represent relevant contexts and situations. > When teaching language skills, teachers should clarify the teaching objectives, set specific skill objectives, design and implement effective activities, optimize all sorts of teaching resources, and fulfil their duty to provide teaching guidance. > Assessment should be focused not only on the final results, but also the process of learning. Formative and summative assessment should be integrated in order to guide teaching and learning. Assessment methods should be variable and flexible.
Lesson Plan Design	Language elements should be taught in a stepwise fashion from easy to difficult, according to the respective learning stage. > **Pronunciation**: continuous instruction should be given, through activities such as pronunciation practice while taking heed of the differences between English and Japanese. Instruction using phonetic notation can also be provided as a supplement to pronunciation instruction, if the need arises. > **Alphabet writing**: it is possible to teach cursive writing, while giving consideration to the students' capabilities, so that they are not overburdened. > **Lexical teaching**: for instruction of words, collocations and common expressions, frequently-used items should be chosen so that they take root in students' minds through their actual usage. > **Dictionary**: students should familiarize themselves with how to consult dictionaries in order to make good use of them. > **Learning style**: teachers should innovate through various learning formats, such as by incorporating pair work, group work, and so on as appropriate.	> **Pronunciation**: to enable students to understand the significance of phonetics in language learning, to speak with basically accurate, natural and fluent pronunciation and intonation in daily conversations, to understand and express different intentions by altering stress and intonation appropriately, to spell words and phrases according to phonics rules. > **Lexical teaching**: to enable students to understand words, phrases, accustomed expressions and collocations, to understand and distinguish basic and expanded meanings of words, to use vocabulary to describe things, behaviours, characteristics, statements, to learn to use 1500-1600 words and 200-300 expressions and collocations. > **Grammar**: to enable students to understand and use the grammatical items found in the appendix, to understand and apply structures and functions of language forms in daily use, to use appropriate language forms to describe people, objects, things, process of happenings, time, position, and place. > **Functions and Topics**: to enable students to understand and apply the functions and topics found in the appendix.
Treatment of Teaching Materials	With regard to teaching materials, teachers should give sufficient consideration to actual language-use situations and functions of language, in order to comprehensively cultivate communication abilities such as listening, speaking, reading and writing. > **A.** The materials should be useful for enhancing the understanding of various ways of viewing and thinking, while fostering the ability to make impartial judgments and cultivate a rich sensibility. > **B.** The materials should be useful for deepening the understanding of the ways of life and cultures of foreign countries as well as Japan, while helping to raise interest in language and culture and develop respectful attitudes toward these. > **C.** The materials should be useful for deepening the students' international understanding from a broad perspective, by heightening their awareness as Japanese citizens living in a global community, and cultivating in them a spirit of international cooperation.	*Suggestions for the Elaboration of Teaching Materials:* > **A:** The materials should help students to know the essence of foreign cultures, as well as develop their critical thinking skills in regard to different cultures, in order to form a correct view of life and values. An appropriate ratio of Chinese culture should be imbedded in the materials. > **B:** The materials should follow language learning principles suitable for students' needs at different levels. Typical authentic language materials should be selected so as to benefit students' long-term language development. > **C.** The materials should consider students' interests, hobbies and other needs so that they relate closely to their real lives and enrichen their expressions in a modern way. > **D.** The materials should be flexible so as to cater to urban-rural differences while reflecting the requirements of the curriculum.

requirements, yet they differ in terms of smaller aspects which are particularly emphasised by one curriculum, but not the other. This type of comparative examination provides an insightful perspective from which to interpret the previously-obtained textbook analysis results.

Regarding the overall objectives, both Japan and China aim to address the improvement of *language abilities, attitude to learning,* and *cultural awareness.* In addition to devising a learning strategy, China stresses the benefits of English learning towards promoting cognitive and mental development, as well as improving one's humanistic qualities. This reflects the unique character of English as a school subject, which integrates both practical and humanistic features. In other words, English learning is not merely a process for students to achieve language knowledge and skills, but also a process for which to widen their visions, enrich their life experiences, develop thinking skills, and improve comprehensive humanistic qualities.

Concerning the value of learning a foreign language, Rivers (1981) mentions that one can attain a deeper understanding of one's mother tongue by acquiring general language knowledge. This aspect is neglected in the current national curricula, showing that some values can be either stressed or omitted depending on the social dynamics of the time.

Regarding language activities and the treatment of the four skills, both countries present a list of expected learning outcomes, which appear to be very similar due to the use of vague expressions. Besides the four skills, extra attention is devoted to attitude, learning strategies and culture in the Chinese curriculum. In terms of how to organize language activities, Japan gives importance to the use of language for expressing students' thoughts and feelings according to specific situations and functions of language.

Like Japan, China also focuses on using English to carry out tasks or do various sorts of things. Additionally, China makes a few suggestions regarding teaching methods and scenarios, stressing the importance of learning strategy guidance and promotion of cultural awareness. In addition, further suggestions for teachers to be more creative, resourceful, and professional are proposed. The need for extracurricular activities is addressed as well.

As for language elements, treatment, and lesson plan design, both countries list the types of contents which should be covered in the textbook. Besides this, in the appendices, China includes case examples of classroom teaching, evaluation of exercises and suggestions for teaching language skills, which are a response to teachers' feedback during the curriculum revision process. Like its treatment of language activities, Japan continues to focus on teaching grammar through communication activities, rather than by explaining grammatical items. It is considered important for teachers to single out the differences between English and Japanese for close attention, to help learners better understand the unique features of English. This aspect is worth noting, since it provides a potential anchor point for engaging the mother tongue towards the learning of English.

Regarding teaching materials, a few general principles are provided for consideration. In terms of common principles, the materials should be useful for deepening learners' understanding of foreign lives and cultures, as well as heightening their respective awareness of Japanese or Chinese identity. Moreover, the significance of fostering critical thinking and sensibility skills through various perspectives and ways of thinking is stressed in both curricula.

6.3 Summary of EFL Textbook Characteristics

By using the work of Littlejohn (1992, 2011) as a reference, I will now produce a summary of the main findings of Chapters 3 to 5, in the form of a comparative table (Table 6.2), which allows us to get a broader understanding of the underlying nature of the analysed materials, both in terms of their similarities and differences.

Table 6.2: Summary of the main characteristics of Japanese and Chinese EFL textbooks.

Japanese textbooks	Chinese textbooks
① *Aims and Objectives*	
1st aim: to develop the linguistic skills of learners, with meaningful content related to their lives and interests	
2nd aim: *motivate learners* to study English in a fun way	2nd aim: provide *strong exposure to target language*
Slight emphasis on reading and writing	Strong emphasis on reading and writing
Main features: *accessibility*, encouragement, handholding	Main features: *drilling*, grammar-focused
Predominance of *native language*	Predominance of *target language*
Focus on communication with *many world cultures*	Stronger focus on *Anglophone cultures*
Songs, tongue-twisters, etc. usually appear as extra materials	Songs, tongue-twisters, etc. usually appear inside the units
② *Metadiscourse Analysis*	
Tendency to be *situational-oriented* (description of context)	Tendency to be *objective-oriented* (clear language objectives)
Stronger use of metadiscourse (uses native language)	Weaker use of metadiscourse (uses target language)
Lack of attitudinal metadiscourse (except saliency): possible negative influence on development of critical/argumentative skills	
Almost all metadiscourse is found outside of practice activities	
High homogeneity in terms of diversity of metadiscourse types; Focus: *goals, pre-plans (context), saliency*	*Low homogeneity* in terms of diversity of metadiscourse types; Focus: *pre-plans (context), saliency* > post-plans, topicalizers
	Most diverse: Shangjiao, Shangwai, Yilin, Jijiao
	Less diverse: Ren'ai, Beishida, Renjiao, Waiyanshe
Hierarchy of language items: essential vs. optional content	Tendency to present all language content as equally important
③ *Rhetorical Pattern Analysis*	
Mostly *descriptive and expository texts* (lack of argumentative texts; texts in narrative form are poorly represented)	
Lower quantity of texts; they tend to be *relatively short*	More quantity of texts; they tend to be *relatively long*
Texts are *simple and straightforward* (they avoid mixing many rhetorical patterns together)	
Text passages are usually used for conveying language elements: vocabulary & grammar items, etc. (*grammar-centred design*)	
Heavy use of list pattern (*low degree of coherence/connectivity* between textual passages, phrases & sentences)	
'Event' units: focus on linear string and falling dominoes (temporal sequence of events / cause-and-effect)	
Matrix pattern is not used to its full advantage due to shortage of appealing contents (fails to captivate the interest of readers)	
Most appealing/engaging texts: *Total English, Columbus 21*	Most appealing/engaging texts: *Shangjiao*
④ *Principles of Selection & Sequencing of Language Contents*	
Practice activities: *written output > oral output*; written input > aural input;	
Main types of linguistic elements: sentence patterns & semantic meanings, vocabulary items, pronunciation sections	
Units generally progress from reading comprehension texts → practice activities → self-assessment / review sections	
Linguistic elements and practice activities *organized by level of difficulty*: simple to complex	
⑤ *Subject Matter and Focus of Subject Matter*	
Textbooks prefer to *use fictional stories/characters to present language contents* to learners	

Chapter 6 / Results of EFL Textbook Comparisons with the English Language Curricula of Japan & China   255

Use of *personal information/opinion in practice activities is quite limited* and mostly restricted to the output phase	
Input: mostly graphics, followed by text and audio; (*extended discourse ≃ words/phrases/sentences* > ask-answer)	Input: mostly text, followed by graphics and audio; (*extended discourse* > words/phrases/sentences > ask-answer)
Output: mostly individual *graphics/letters/symbols/words/phrases/sentences* + ask-and-answer	
Low complexity of output; strong neglect of extended discourse; possible difficulties in language ability beyond sentence level	
Predominant source of contents: textbook/teaching materials	
⑥ *Types of Practice Activities*	
Heavy focus on *meaning + relationship of meaning & language system* (shift away from language system/form)	
Learners are mostly expected to engage in *scripted response* (they do not initiate unscripted language)	
Learner *response is not required for 25-40%* of practice activities (mostly reading comprehension/listening practices)	
Strong emphasis on *repetition/reproduction* of scripted language, *decoding meaning* and *extracting pieces of information*	
Lower diversity of mental operations: follow given examples (guidance for producing language); combine language items into larger units (i.e., produce language corresponding to extended discourse).	*Greater diversity of mental operations:* follow examples; compare and categorise pieces of language; organize words/sentences/pictures into a summarised form; produce language corresponding to extended discourse; apply general knowledge.
Strong *neglect of higher-level mental operations* such as analysing, hypothesising, memory recall, researching, etc.	
Little demand for translation of language items between L1 & L2 (shift away from grammar-translation approaches)	
Little demand for negotiation between learners; pair/group work is predominantly *focused on reproduction + ask-and-answer*	
Prevalence of content (**input**): *heavy focus on fiction* (fiction > personal info/opinion > linguistic items > metalinguistic comment > non-fiction)	Prevalence of content (**input**): *fiction and linguistic items* (fiction > linguistic items > non-fiction > metalinguistic comment > personal info/opinion)
Prevalence of content (**output**): *fiction and linguistic items* (fiction > linguistic items > personal info/opinion > non-fiction)	Prevalence of content (**output**): *ling. items, fiction, personal* (linguistic items > fiction > personal info/opinion > non-fiction)
Relatively *low number of mental operations* within each practice activity; most practices involve only *low cognitive skills*	
Mental operations (most diverse): *New Crown, Columbus 21* Mental operations (least diverse): *Total English*	Mental operations (most diverse): *Beishida, Jijiao, Shangjiao* Mental operations (least diverse): *Renjiao, Yilin*
⑦ *Participation: who does what with whom?*	
Main mode of classroom participation: *Learners are asked to work individually* (76%-81%)	
Learners in pairs/groups simultaneously (23%)	Learners in pairs/groups simultaneously (17%); Learners to the whole class (approx. 1%)
⑧ *Classroom Roles of Teachers and Learners*	
In general, *learners are passive absorbers of knowledge*, while teachers remain as figures of authority	
Most of the curriculum's decisions and contents are conveyed by the textbook rather than the teacher	
Textbook *contents are heavily scripted so as to reduce unpredictability* in student evaluation (less burden for teachers)	
Textbook serves mostly as a foundation from which the teacher can create lesson plans and activities	
Instructions in practice activities imply a slightly collectivist stance (native language; use of inclusive plural)	Instructions in practice activities imply a slightly individualist stance (target language; use of second-person)
⑨ *Learner Roles in Learning*	
Learners expect to be taught; they must follow textbook instructions, under the guidance of the teacher	
Learning usually involves the *acquisition of language elements by repetition or reproduction* of sentences found in textbooks	
Textbooks try to make learning 'fun' or less burdensome	Textbooks treat learning as 'work' with some 'fun' elements
⑩ *Role of Textbook Materials as a Whole*	
Textbook units provide a *basic structure for teaching and learning* English, as well as managing classroom time and interaction	
Textbooks should function as a 'package' in which the curriculum's determinations and decisions are embedded	

In the following section (6.4), I will proceed to compare the contents of Tables 6.1 (curricula) and 6.2 (EFL textbooks) in regards to the four skills and other relevant aspects. But before that, it is worthwhile to compare the main aspects of Table 6.2 with a previous study by (Wang, 2015) concerning practice activities in Japanese EFL textbooks. The batch of six officially-approved textbooks (for 7th grade students) featured in the 2015 study was the first to be published after the 2012 curriculum revision, and directly precedes the new batch of textbooks that is under analysis in this doctoral dissertation. In each textbook, practice activities within units related to 'school life', 'family life', and 'events' were analysed (total: 18 thematic units).

The main conclusions of the 2015 study of Japanese EFL textbooks are as follows:

① The balance of practice activities (related to each of the four skills) was biased towards writing and reading, at the expense of listening and speaking;

② Language input is mainly focused on meaning and language system. There is also a strong reliance on non-verbal information, such as photographs and illustrations;

③ In terms of language output, there is too much focus on replacement drills, which require learners to repeat a given sentence or discourse while substituting some words or applying a certain language rule;

④ Most of the written language output does not go beyond the level of the single sentence (words/phrases/sentences). There are relatively few practice activities that ask learners to write more than two sentences. Reading comprehension activities mostly only ask learners to verify if a statement is true or false, or fill in the blanks of sentences with single words;

⑤ In listening activities, either most of the produced output is non-verbal, or there is no requirement for the learner to respond at all;

⑥ As for speaking activities, learners were frequently asked to repeat the contents they heard (with some form of substitution) and take memos during conversations, but it was also not rare to see an integration of multiple activities;

⑦ Regarding the *nature* of the language contents in practice activities, most of them are based on fiction and language items;

⑧ The number of practice activities that ask for the personal opinion, experiences and information of learners is relatively low;

⑨ Metadiscourse and metalanguage is barely present within the instructions of practice activities; these elements could be helpful in conveying useful information about language principles and the structural organization of texts. Metadiscourse was found in exercises that asked learners to compare the pronunciation of similar words, or to summarize pronunciation rules of different phonemes, or ask them to pay particular attention to a certain aspect of a language element.

The textbooks analysed in the 2015 study had several differences in terms of unit contents and overall organization of units, when compared to the current batch of textbooks. However, if we compare the above ten points to the contents of Table 6.2, we can see that there are no significant changes to the underlying nature of the language contents and mental operations found in practice activities. Furthermore, there was a noticeable gap between the requirements for skill balance espoused by the 2012 Japanese EFL curriculum, and the types of language skills stimulated by practice activities in the previous batch of EFL textbooks.

6.4 Adequacy of EFL Textbooks to the English Curricula of Japan and China

I will now discuss the adequacy of the currently-authorised textbooks in terms of how they teach each of the four skills, as well as some additional important aspects.

6.4.1 Reading

Some aspects of reading comprehension were already mentioned in previous paragraphs, but just to recap, I have quoted several studies arguing that: learners should be exposed to content relevant to their lives and interests; reading passages should be coherent and well-structured with interesting narratives; and there should be more exposure to longer texts, because many learners struggle to read beyond the level of individual sentences.

The objectives of both curricula regarding the skill of reading are not overtly ambitious, which is understandable, considering the many challenges experienced by learners in EFL countries. Even in this study, it was decided to define *extended discourse* texts as those that have in total more than 30 words (as opposed to Littlejohn, who set the mark at 50 words when analysing ESL textbooks). Both Japanese and Chinese textbooks have extended discourse texts as input, but the Chinese ones have not just more texts, but longer texts overall. Thus, there is a meaningful difference in terms of exposure to target language between both countries.

The curricula of Japan and China agree that learners should be able to grasp the general outline, ideas and intentions expressed by short stories and descriptive texts. The Chinese curriculum is more demanding, in the sense that instructions in practice activities should be understood by learners, and it also sets a target for extracurricular reading. It is natural for Chinese textbooks to incorporate these demands, since learners already had in theory four years of exposure to the language. But in practice, after comparing the reading comprehension texts of textbooks in both countries, it was found that except for text length and overall number of texts, there is not that much difference in the internal structure of the texts. Most texts/dialogues are clearly tailored to convey a sentence pattern or a grammatical item, and tend to lack the natural flow and narrative character of normal English texts. And despite the differences in years of official English teaching, there is a clear similarity in the types of sentence patterns that are presented in the textbooks of both countries. These issues tend to make the texts and conversations less appealing for learners, and this may hamper their ability to deal with more argumentative and complex texts in the future.

Having said this, if we consider that the curricula prefer to teach an international form of English that focuses on basic communication, such as providing basic services to foreign customers and tourists, and conveying basic ideas in a clear manner, then it cannot be said that the provided texts are completely inadequate. The main issues going forward are: how to improve the retention of language elements in the minds of learners; and how to provide a quick entry point into the world of argumentative texts. Firstly, there is a lot that can be done in terms of improving text composition and structure, by incorporating our knowledge of rhetorical patterns to make them more coherent; we can also provide more exposure to the attitudinal metadiscourse elements known as *hedges, emphatics* and *evaluative*. These are elements used not just to express uncertainty and doubt, but they also play a big role in making the texts feel less rigid and more natural. As Ken Hyland argues in his work *Metadiscourse: Exploring Interaction in Writing* (2005), it is important not to overuse metadiscourse within texts for foreign learners, as that can have counterproductive effects, but at the very least it should be desirable to find a healthy balance between overtly-dry texts and overwrought texts.

Metadiscourse is primarily used in the analysed textbooks to provide guidance to the learner, mostly by introducing the context in which a story or dialogue takes place, or by informing the student which language elements are more important to learn first, or by giving commentaries and helpful information about the content of the texts. As such, we find that Japanese textbooks use a lot more metadiscourse than Chinese ones. Even though in the former case such metadiscourse is entirely written in Japanese, it can be said to be a positive feature, since it provides useful guidance to learners, and may even help them to cover a lot of linguistic ground faster and more efficiently than the drill-based approach of Chinese textbooks. Perhaps the latter could benefit as well from introducing some more metadiscourse guidance in Chinese language, especially in terms of creating a hierarchy of contents (ex: to specify which contents are essential for learning and which ones are secondary, just like in the case of Japanese textbooks).

On the other hand, in order to read longer texts in English, learners must train themselves to develop longer attention spans and become able to memorise a larger amount of language contents, so that they can interpret long paragraphs. So, there is something to be said about asking learners to push themselves, by engaging with larger amounts of text (if the contents of the text are meaningful and compelling). However, too many texts in both countries' textbooks are heavily based on the *list* pattern, which means that there is a low degree of linkage and coherence between phrases, sentences, and paragraphs. This study found that the best textbooks in terms of having engaging and coherent texts are *Total English*,

Columbus 21 and *Shangjiao*, although it is certainly possible to achieve further improvements; these textbooks could be used as a starting point for developing better reading comprehension texts.

On a positive note, I found relatively few exercises that ask learners to translate language items; and for the most part, translations are only present in vocabulary lists (mostly in the Japanese textbooks). This means that, at least in this aspect, textbooks are making some effort to distance themselves from the grammar-translation approach, even if in practice many senior classroom teachers are still reliant on this method.

6.4.2 Writing

Unlike reading, writing is a form of output, even though such output is heavily dependent on reading examples. The Japanese curriculum states the importance of being able to take notes and convey one's impressions, thoughts, and feelings, while paying attention to the way that sentences connect with each other. The Chinese curriculum is more utilitarian, and merely asks the learner to be able to write short stories and simple descriptions of pictures, convey information through posters and charts, and consult examples in order to reply to greeting / invitation cards.

These statements imply that at the very least, learners must master the ability of writing individual sentences, and even chain sentences together in a coherent manner, regardless of whether they are expressing their own thoughts, or taking notes from a book or a speech. But this study has found that an excessive portion of the exercises in both countries' textbooks merely requires the learner to draw lines, or individual letters and numbers, or individual words. In comparison, there are comparatively few exercises that require learners to write whole sentences and texts. It can

also be said that there is an excessive dependence on repetition and reproduction of scripted language, a lot of which is conversational in nature (ask-
and-answer).

While the use of examples is certainly crucial for understanding a sentence pattern for the first time, it appears that learners find themselves
unable to escape from the boundaries of the examples. Considering the
many problems that most EFL teachers face in adequately rating the diverse language production of learners in communicative language activities, it is perhaps unwise for textbooks to deviate too much from the current approach. All that can be said in terms of possible improvements is to
feature more written practice activities where students can express their
personal opinions, information, and ideas. Currently, only one quarter of all
practice activities in both Japanese and Chinese textbooks require learners
to output language that features their own experiences, while almost ev-
erything else is related to fictional contents (this figure of 24–25% includes
both writing and speaking-related practice activities). Although it is understandable that some learners feel anxious or hesitant to express their own
opinions, and that fictional settings allow learners to deal with a greater diversity of social contexts, it is still advisable to slightly increase the number of exercises that involve the personal experiences of learners, as well
as introduce more practices where learners must write full sentences. If
such exercises can allow learners to explore humorous situations, or topics
that they are personally interested in, it may be feasible to increase their
number.

6.4.3 Listening

The curricula of both countries stress two major objectives: (1) to be able

Chapter 6╱Results of EFL Textbook Comparisons with the English Language Curricula of Japan & China   263

to detect nuances in pronunciation, intonation and accent; and (2) to grasp the basic outline and ideas from audio passages and dialogues. In regards to the first aspect, both Japanese and Chinese textbooks provide pronunciation sections with ample guidance and information by way of metadiscourse. On the other hand, there are relatively few practices where learners talk to each other, which are mostly ask-and-answer exercises. While it is true that learners do not get full exposure to native pronunciation from practising with each other, it is nevertheless an important practice activity, because most English communication in Asia takes place between non-native speakers.

Regarding the second aspect, because most listening practices are merely aural versions of reading comprehension texts, they are generally subject to the same issues that I already referred to in the 'Writing' section. The textbooks in both countries usually feature some practices that are not linked to texts, but in most cases, they merely ask learners to look at images, or extract some simple information such as individual words. One difference between both countries is that in terms of *extended discourse*, Japanese materials have more listening practice activities than the Chinese ones. In any case, the proportion of listening activities is not that well-balanced, when compared to other skills such as reading.

6.4.4 Speaking

In general, both curricula approach the skill of speaking as a synthesis of the previous three skills, but expressed in spoken form, with proper intonation and accent. It requires learners to grasp and comprehend information conveyed by others (listening/reading), and to formulate one's thoughts in a coherent manner (which is also an aspect of writing). There are some aspects unique to speaking: the Japanese curriculum asks for learners to conduct short oral presentations to the entire classroom, and to pay close attention to the ways in which words link together when spoken aloud. The Chinese curriculum does not explicitly mention presentations, but it does state that learners should feel comfortable providing short descriptions of pictures and slides, communicate easily about familiar topics, tell short stories, recite poems and sing simple songs.

As I have mentioned in the 'Listening' section, all textbooks provide enough content and practices related to pronunciation, most of which require learners to repeat things out loud. All Japanese textbooks provide metadiscourse that explains how the pronunciation and accent of certain words change when they appear together in a sentence taken from a reading comprehension text. In the Chinese textbooks, only *Shangwai* had this kind of metadiscourse related to pronunciation.

Regarding speaking activities, these are subject to the same limitations and issues that I have mentioned in the previous sections: there is an excessive dependency on repetition and reproduction of scripted dialogue; the contents of ask-and-answer dialogues are usually low on coherence and are merely designed to present a basic sentence pattern; there are relatively few exercises requiring learner-to-learner conversations; and the sample texts tend to be too short, even if they barely match the definition of 'extended discourse'.

Another issue is that of oral presentations to the entire classroom. The Japanese textbooks prefer to assign group presentations onto special sections (which are often titled as 'Project' sections) which exist outside of the units themselves, while some Chinese textbooks do include individual presentations inside the units. But because the total number of such 'project' activities usually does not surpass two or three in Japanese textbooks, it is questionable whether that is sufficient. Furthermore, group presentations can play out in a very different way than individual presentations, because in the former case, the workload and amount of speech is distributed among various members, while in the latter case one learner must handle all aspects of preparing the presentation and speaking for a longer period.

There is also more anxiety involved in individual presentations, since the learner cannot rely on the support of others in case something goes wrong. However, developing one's presentation skills is crucial for success in job interviews, school applications, work meetings, and many other real-life situations. So, it may be necessary for Japanese textbooks to focus more closely on this issue, either by asking learners to see on the Internet examples of successful presentations in English, or by providing metadiscourse that helps learners to deal adequately with nervousness and anxiety. Later in this chapter, I will present some classroom experiments that attempt to coordinate the learning of English together with that of Japanese language, which involves conversation and language games between learners, among other activities.

6.4.5 Other aspects: moral education, cultural awareness, learning strategies, and mental operations

Looking at the summary of curricula characteristics in Table 6.1, there are some relevant aspects that have not been addressed yet: *moral education, cultural awareness, learning strategies* and *mental operations.*

Most textbooks have a somewhat narrow approach to the aspect of moral education: for the most part, they just include implicit and explicit messages about how it is important to keep studying, and working hard in order to be successful. Although the dialogues and texts sometimes mention negative emotions such as boredom or lack of interest, there is a strong focus on uplifting messages and positive emotions. As expected, none of the textbooks discusses politics or religious issues, or present a preference for any ideology. One example of a textbook that tries to address the issue of moral education in a more explicit manner is *Jijiao*: its school unit asks learners to read texts about helping others in need, including abandoned animals, and it also asks learners to talk with each other and offer ideas on how they can help others and contribute to society in a positive manner. It would be interesting to see other textbooks follow this example, including discussing ways to improve relationships among students in school.

As for cultural awareness, Japanese textbooks exhibit a broader range of exposure to aspects of different cultures, since they consistently show dialogues with characters of non-Anglophone countries and present interesting pictures and facts about those countries in a balanced manner. In contrast, Chinese textbooks are strictly focused on Anglophone countries, especially the U.S., U.K., and Australia. In both countries, the contrasting of cultural differences is essentially done in terms of daily habits, traditional cuisine, major festivals, sightseeing spots, weather patterns and seasons. There is no discussion of political issues, conflicts, disasters, or anything that could be framed in a negative light. In terms of metadiscourse, we find that it is not used often for communicating aspects of cultural awareness. Only *One World*, *New Crown*, *Shangjiao*, *Shangwai*, and *Waiyanshe* had this kind of metadiscourse. Most instances of cultural comparison occur within reading comprehension texts, and usually present the situation in foreign countries, after which the learner is asked to write a short text presenting the situation in his or her country.

As for the issue of learning strategies, some textbooks feature this kind of information more explicitly than others. In *One World*, *Sunshine*, *New Crown*, *Ren'ai*, *Beishida*, *Shangjiao*, *Waiyanshe* and *Yilin*, I found metadiscourse within the sample units that specifically provides useful learning strategies. For example, they explain how to quickly identify important information in a reading comprehension text, or how to find information on a dictionary or on the Internet, etc. As for the remaining textbooks, this kind of information is conveyed more implicitly in sections outside of the units, such as review sections, extra materials, project sections, or even practice activities (when they ask learners to come up with learning strategies themselves and share with colleagues). But in any case, it can be said that all textbooks provide learning strategies in one form or another.

To summarise, looking at these first three aspects, it appears that all textbooks attempt to incorporate the requirements of the curricula. One possible suggestion would be for Chinese textbooks to expand their cultural outlook towards non-Anglophone nations in the same way as Japanese textbooks.

One final word can be said about the problem of mental operations. All textbooks in general tend to feature only a small number of low-level cognitive operations in any given exercise. It is rare to see exercises that require high-level operations such as hypothesizing, analysing, and categorizing language items, negotiating with other learners, acquiring metalinguistic knowledge, etc. As mentioned in Chapter 5, when 'hypothesize' appears in Japanese and Chinese textbooks, it usually comes after reading comprehension sections, where learners are asked to imagine what a character is feeling. But while in the Chinese textbooks all linguistic output must be done in English, in the Japanese ones it is always done in the native language, which means such practices have limited linguistic value. It is true that there should not be too many difficult exercises, but it is advisable to aim for a better balance of low-level and high-level mental operations.

6.5 Final Verdict: Balance of the Four Skills & the Role of L1 in EFL Education

6.5.1 Balance of the four skills

In practice, it might be impossible to produce a textbook that perfectly balances all four skills, since textbooks are physical objects that tend to focus on written/visual elements. Furthermore, teachers can choose to focus on certain skills to the detriment of others during classes. And there are still debates as to whether it is even desirable to have an exact balance of the four skills, because not enough scientific evidence has been accumulated to fully validate Nation's theory. So, in this respect, we are still facing the question of overall reliability regarding the 'balanced skills' approach.

In any case, looking at the results in Chapter 5, we can see that the four skills are not well-balanced in Japanese and Chinese textbooks, all of which focus more on reading and writing. It is true that on average, Japanese textbooks stand closer to achieving that balance than the Chinese ones, but it is important to state that 'balance' should not be measured only in terms of skills: the type of language that is produced matters just as much. And regardless of country, all the textbooks focus too heavily in the production of individual letters, words, and sentences, to the detriment of extended discourse. The advantage of applying Littlejohn's framework is that it allows us to identify this clear imbalance between individual words and longer dialogues/texts. There is also a need to increase the number of practice activities that involve student interaction, class presentations, and the personal experiences of learners, to properly achieve the objectives stated in the curricula of both countries, which reflect the ideologies of communicative learning and learner-based teaching. Additional recommendations are to increase the diversity of types of metadiscourse, improve the coherence and structure of reading comprehension texts, increase the diversity of mental operations, and achieve a better balance of high- and low-level mental operations.

It is difficult to judge whether the focus of Japanese textbooks on accessibility and that of Chinese textbooks on exposure and drilling is misguided or not; these distinct approaches seem to reflect historical developments in both nations (see Chapter 1). In any case, the fact that Japanese textbooks have devised several interesting design elements (ex: cute characters that provide encouraging messages; large, visually-appealing images, etc.) to maintain the interest of learners should be a net positive; therefore, it may be of interest for Chinese textbook compilers to consider adopting some of these ideas.

Given that each textbook has a variety of different strengths and weaknesses, it is not possible here to identify one that perfectly satisfies the requirements of its respective national curriculum, but it would be beneficial for textbook compilers to look at each chapter in this study to learn more about the respective strengths and weaknesses of each textbook.

6.5.2 Role of native language in the teaching of foreign languages

Having tacked the issue of the four skills, there is one last crucial question that needs to be addressed. How does each country interpret the role of mother tongue (L1) in teaching a foreign language? As we have seen,

Japanese textbooks feature a lot of L1 while Chinese textbooks have almost completely embraced English, but it can be fully said that neither country values the importance of L1 in learning a foreign language.

Japan does use L1 to do things such as translating instructions for practice activities, providing pre-plan (context) statements, and explaining grammar rules in sentence patterns, but it cannot be said that Japanese textbooks treat L1 as a valuable language resource for doing comparisons with English, or that L1 can be used to understand English at a metalinguistic level. As for China, its textbooks avoid using L1 because of an over-reliance on the communicative learning approach, which is predominantly used in ESL learning. This excessive trust in CLT and strong connections with ESL teaching might be explained by the fact that all Chinese EFL textbooks were either developed through a partnership with textbook publishers in the Anglophone world, or are adaptations of foreign English textbooks, or were developed by Chinese scholars with the aid of foreign scholars as consultants (see Chapter 1). And although the Chinese curriculum is attempting to minimize the role and importance of grammar-based instruction, we find that there is a clear conflict with the results in this study, since the Chinese textbooks are still very much reliant on grammatical drills, and this situation is expected to continue for now.

If we look at the new Japanese EFL curriculum guidelines for 2020, they state the importance of 'knowing the differences between English and Japanese, and noticing the fun and richness of language', and 'noticing the differences in word order between Japanese and English'. And in the curriculum's section for national language at the elementary school level, it is written: 'from the viewpoint of improving linguistic competence, learners should actively engage in relationships with other subjects, such as foreign language activities and foreign language departments, and so on, so as to increase the effectiveness of the [teachers'] guidance'. This aspect of language comparison, which I had already stated in Table 6.1, could be explored in a more meaningful and effective manner, and makes for a compelling case for current and future research, which I will explain in more detail in section 6.7.

6.6 Applicability of the Analytical Framework of This Study

As one may guess from looking at this extensive study, it must be acknowledged that it is labour-intensive and time-consuming. However, the best application of this methodology is not necessarily for analysing textbooks that have already been compiled: ideally, textbook publishers could apply these methods during the process of designing the contents of a textbook from the very start. By having a small team dedicated to cataloguing and registering the characteristics of each textbook element (practice activities, texts, meta discourse, etc.), they can gradually create detailed spreadsheets that they could then submit to the national textbook review committees; the committees could use software to check the contents of the spreadsheets and randomly choose one or two units for more detailed inspection, to verify the publishers' claims. One could even envision the creation of software with specific features that would facilitate and speed up the elaboration of such spreadsheets.

Since there is no clear provision for specific language practice activities in the guidelines of the national curriculum, the selection of practice activities and tasks used in textbooks is entrusted to each publisher. Likewise, the current process for authorizing textbooks by the national textbook evaluation committee is likely to continue relying on checklists. Regarding this situation, I argue that the methodological framework employed in this entire study suggests several points that could be incorporated as evaluation criteria for the process of authorizing textbooks:

- Verify whether there is a reasonable diversity of types of metadiscourse;
- Verify whether there is a high degree of coherence in reading comprehension texts;
- Verify whether practice activities employ a reasonable diversity of mental operations, and feature a good balance between low-level cognitive skills and high-level cognitive skills (especially in regards to the development of metalinguistic knowledge);
- Verify that there is a reasonable balance between the number of times that learners must do practice activities individually, or in pairs/groups, or/by presenting to the entire classroom.
- Verify whether the required four language skills are proportionately balanced in terms of language inputs and outputs within practice activities;
- Verify that the types of required language output (graphics/symbols; w/p/s; extended discourse; ask-and-answer) are reasonably well-balanced across each unit, and that learners can practice the necessary skills for producing coherent texts with more than two sentences.

It is also important to recognize that the world of textbooks is gradually facing a digital revolution. For many years, we have been promised a new dawn of educational software, but it appears that such promises are finally starting to materialise with the help of artificial intelligence and machine learning. For example, there is significant advantage in having an app that continuously monitors improvements in the language skills of a learner (especially speech and pronunciation), and whenever it finds an obstacle, the app can immediately suggest areas of improvement to both the student and the teacher in real time, so that they can improve their learning methods before any exams take place.

But regardless of whether students will learn from traditional textbooks or digital applications, the methods and analytical framework presented in this study can be applied in all contexts: it can be used by teachers to devise new teaching materials or lesson plans; it can be used by textbook publishers and application designers to evaluate the detailed characteristics of teaching materials; and national committees can also use this framework to evaluate the suitability of textbooks for the educational milieu, and compare textbook contents with the requirements of the national curriculum.

Chapter 7 / Towards an Approach for Enriching Learners' Metalinguistic Awareness

7.1 A Collaborative Approach for Enriching Metalinguistic Awareness

Asmentioned in chapter 1, the distinctions between EFL and ESL started to become clearer during the 1960s (Okihara, 2011). Different terms were used to make these distinctions, in accordance with the growing prevalence of English teaching in a worldwide context. For instance, Kachru (1982, 1992) classified 'world Englishes' into three concentric circles to demonstrate different socio-cultural environments where English is used and taught. Similarly, Holliday (1994a, b) used the two terms BANA and TESEP to make a distinction between two types of educational contexts in various countries. BANA refers to Britain, Australia and North America, where English language teaching is mostly of a private nature much like a daily commodity product, which is similar to Kachru's concept of 'inner circle' within his 'world Englishes' framework. TESEP refers to state education, either in tertiary institutions, or secondary and elementary schools in countries where English teaching is associated with national public education, which relates to Kachru's definitions of 'outer circle' and 'expanding circle'.

In East Asian EFL countries, there is a growing tendency to reinforce the distinction between ESL and EFL teaching and learning, and thus the applicability of formerly preferred ESL teaching methods is being reconsidered. As an imperative rule, the 'English-only' policy has come under question, while the essential role that mother tongue plays in developing language awareness tends to be underestimated. While relating target language to learners' mother tongue, Cook (2010) pointed out the value of translation for most language learners by reviewing best practices from the last 100 years of language teaching. Given the results of his comparative studies involving various methods, he argued that translation provided learners with an academic metalanguage and a deeper understanding of the nature of language and language use. Subsequently, Wang (2012, 2018) examined how mother tongues were dealt with in EFL textbooks in South Korea, Japan and China, and showed that mother tongue is not fully used as a language learning resource, other than in instruction and explanation.

The significance, however, of incorporating mother tongue and foreign language has been acknowledged in national language policy. The Japanese EFL curriculum guidelines for 2020 assert the importance of 'knowing the differences between English and Japanese, and noticing the fun and richness of language', as well as 'noticing the differences in word order between Japanese and English' (MEXT, 2018). This resonates with the mother tongue language curriculum, which suggests that 'from the viewpoint of improving one's linguistic competence, learners should actively engage in making connexions with other subjects, such as foreign language activities and foreign language departments, and so forth, so as to increase the effectiveness of the guidance'. This aspect of active collaboration between mother tongue and foreign language provides a compelling case for conducting the action research detailed in this chapter.

Foreign language learning (EFL) can benefit native language learning (L1). In contexts where English is taught as a second language (ESL), especially in the case of immigrants living in English-speaking countries, more exposure to English means less exposure to one's first language (L1). High

Chapter 7／Towards an Approach for Enriching Learners' Metalinguistic Awareness   277

proficiency in ESL is necessarily attained by sacrificing exposure to L1, which is called the *balance effect* (Macnamara, 1966). However, this is not the case in the context of individuals that learn English as a foreign language (EFL) within L1 speaking countries. Studies in behavioural sciences since the 1980s have shown that foreign language learning can benefit L1 learning. Most of these studies collected data from outcome-driven exams to prove that there was a positive transfer of linguistic skills within learners' minds. It is important to mention that most case studies involved English-speaking students learning another European language as a foreign language. Due to similarities between English and other European languages, it is easier for positive transfers to occur; but such transfers are not likely to occur if there are few similarities between the two languages.

In contrast, the *deep structure hypothesis* (Hill, 1970) states that learning a foreign language can have positive effects on L1 skills, since learning can occur at a more abstract and deeper level beyond that of superficial linguistic similarities. If we compare Japanese and English, they are said to be drastically different languages: apart from clear differences in word order and phonemes, Japanese language is agglutinative, whereas English is relatively independent (and therefore is said to be an analytic language). In the same way as Chinese, Japanese Kanji characters are ideograms, whereas English alphabet letters represent phonograms. Although on the surface there are no immediate similarities between Japanese and English, Chomsky's (1981) *generative grammar* theories claim that common syntax structures exist in all-natural languages. Hence it is possible that EFL learning would have positive effects on the learning of Japanese as L1, especially at the more abstract and deeper levels of the mind.

To test this hypothesis, Ojima, Nagai, Taya & Otsu (2011) designed an experiment based on the *event-related potential* (ERP) technique. This technique involves measuring electrical activity in the brains of learners by using special equipment. The researchers compared Japanese adults who had either high or low proficiency in English, by monitoring their brain reactions to linguistic stimuli. These stimuli consisted of spoken sentences in Japanese which contained syntactic violations. The results show that Japanese individuals with high English proficiency had a stronger response to syntactic violations in Japanese than those who had low proficiency in English.

Metalinguistic awareness can boost language competence in both L1 and EFL learning. Otsu & Torikai (2002) state that the cultivation of English communication ability should not be the true purpose of English education in school. Instead, they argue that the real purpose is to enhance one's communication ability by emphasising their level of cross-cultural understanding and developing their metalinguistic ability. Moreover, Otsu (1998) proposes that the priority of English education is to enable students to notice that this language is interesting and rich, while referencing their learning experiences with their mother tongue. In doing so, language can be learnt in an objective manner. Since English is studied in relation to the mother tongue, both languages are treated as having equal status. A reasonable amount of linguistic and cultural relativity can lead to a common acknowledgment of the diversity and richness of multiple languages.

The 'language awareness movement' that started in the 1980s was a defining moment that placed an emphasis on the intellectual value of learning a foreign language. To solve important problems such as ESL's unpopularity, the overall decline of English ability, and discrimination against minority languages in the U.K., a new holistic language program titled 'language awareness education' was introduced in order to connect mother tongue and foreign language education as a 'new language' subject (Hawkins, 1984). It is an educational program that focuses on raising language awareness of linguistic topics, for the sake of understanding linguistic universality and variability in multi-ethnic and multicultural contexts. Cook (2001) adds that promoting language awareness helps to enhance one's sense of language.

As James & Garrett (1991) stated, textbooks or materials can have a heavy impact on how to raise language awareness in the classroom. In practice, concrete materials or activities must be designed in order to enhance learners' sense of language. Saito (2000) suggests a range of activities such as turning English texts into *haiku* poems, which altogether aim to enhance literature comprehension and language awareness, thus leading to an improved understanding of close relationships between language, literature, and culture.

Furthermore, Otsu (2009; 2010; 2011) conducted some classroom experiments that aimed to provide learners with improved metalinguistic awareness by directly comparing aspects of Japanese and English. Otsu (2011) defends that one of the main reasons why the teaching of EFL has not succeeded in Japan is because Japanese learners lack a proper understanding of metalinguistic aspects of Japanese at the time that they start to learn English at school. Crucial metalinguistic concepts such as 'subject', 'object', 'case', 'person', 'hierarchical phrase structure' and 'gender' are only implicitly present in the minds of elementary school learners, and they often have only a deficient understanding of such concepts. The reason why these concepts are relatively unknown at the elementary school level is because the discipline of *kokugo* (Japanese language) at the elementary level focuses on the appreciation of poems and literary works, rather than teaching grammar or metalinguistic aspects. The pairing of both Japanese and English can therefore help learners to fully grasp these concepts in a clearer way, which should then have a positive effect on their linguistic skills.

This approach is primarily intended to help learners improve their knowledge of the Japanese language, but it can also help learners to become better prepared for tackling the learning of English if they so choose. In Otsu's method, both L1 and English are included in a framework labelled as 'language teaching' and are taught together in a systematic manner. In fact, Otsu goes as far as affirming that the teaching of English at the elementary school level has few chances of succeeding unless Japanese learners have a better understanding of metalinguistic knowledge.

Otsu's method has six main stages. In Stage 1, learners must explore their own knowledge of Japanese to form an initial grasp of crucial metalinguistic concepts; then in Stage 2 they further explore such concepts while learning English, which also helps to introduce new metalinguistic concepts; in Stage 3 these new concepts are then brought back into the study of Japanese language. In Stage 4, learners begin to directly compare and experiment with aspects of English and Japanese, by avoiding the use of ambiguous expressions. In Stage 5, learners make efforts to use L1 and English to further enrich their metalinguistic awareness, and finally in Stage 6 they complete the cycle by gaining a greater understanding of L1.

One of his experiments (Otsu, 2010) was to provide students with an incomplete sentence that only lacked the final word. By asking students to provide suggestions for the missing word, and exploring what kind of ambiguous interpretations could result from their choices, students were able to better understand how slight changes in hierarchical phrase structure can greatly affect the meaning of the phrase. Another experiment (Otsu,

Chapter 7 / Towards an Approach for Enriching Learners' Metalinguistic Awareness   281

2011) asked students to participate in a game of *shiritori*, in which participants provide nouns beginning with the final part of a noun that was just
previously spoken. In the first play session, the game is played in its normal fashion. But in the second session, the teachers deliberately introduced
adjectives, adjectival nouns, and verbs instead of nouns to see if children
were able to tell that something was not right. If a child sensed that something was strange, the teacher asked him or her why they thought so. By
using this method, the teachers sought to help children intuitively grasp a
clear understanding of these syntactic categories.

If we are to summarise Otsu's (1989; 2008) main argument, it is that both
mother tongue and foreign languages can be cultivated synergistically and
effectively, by encouraging learners to become aware of linguistic commonalities and the unique characteristics and mechanisms of each language. He
specifically labels his approach as that of developing an 'awareness towards
language' within learners. In addition, Candelier (2007) has also argued that
the multilingual and multiculturalist education that is being increasingly
cultivated in Europe can be applied to foreign language activities in Japanese elementary schools (Oyama, 2016); this type of education consists of
'activities for promoting language awareness' that encourage learners to
observe, analyse and infer about their mother tongue as well as other languages.

7.2   Rationale Behind these Case Studies

The experiments and evidence that I have just presented are part of an
ongoing attempt to deal with an old issue, which is the tendency of traditional English language education to discourage the use of native languages as much as possible (especially in the case of China). In the West, schol-

ars are increasingly questioning the validity of this traditional stance (Cook, 2010). According to an international survey targeting 120,000 learners in 18 countries, it was found that the more they talk about their mother tongue together with their target language, the better their academic abilities at school will be (Agirdag & Vanlaar, 2016). Also, when mastering a foreign language, Ortega (2018) has pointed out that we should place more importance on the value of the native language.

Compared with other East Asian countries such as China, Japan has taken a relatively cautious stance toward introducing English into elementary schools, due to various discussions about the ideal stages for linguistic development in children, and issues concerning the implementation of a system for training classroom teachers. But now that the implementation of the curriculum is undergoing at the elementary school level, we must find ways to mobilize teachers effectively and make the best use of the teaching knowledge that they already possess. In other words, in order to develop an English language curriculum that makes full use of the unique strengths of classroom teachers, it is important to consider the potentials of articulating between foreign language education and native language education (see Figure 7.1). By doing so, we can expect to devise an innovative model for integrating L1 in EFL teaching materials development. This approach has not attracted much attention in multilingual education so far, and even though it is starting as a pilot initiative, it has the potential to exert a positive impact in the study of foreign language education around the world.

Positive transfers between foreign language and mother tongue involve metalinguistic awareness, which is considered a fundamental linguistic competence for learning all languages. The 'learning language awareness' texts.

Based on this practice, a practical research project focusing on the development of meta-grammatical competence was conducted in collaboration with teachers of Japanese and English departments and university researchers (Saito et al., 2012; Akita et al., 2012; Saito et al., 2013; Akita et al., 2013; Akita et al., 2014; Akita, Saito, and Fujie, 2019). Meta-grammatical competence is a grammar-specific concept of metalinguistic competence, which is defined as the ability to make people aware of the mechanisms and rules of language (Saito et al., 2012). In order to develop meta-grammar skills that work across languages, we designed meta-grammar classes for both English and Japanese language classes, analysed the class development process, the students' pre- and post-work assignments, along with the comments written on students' worksheets during the class, and conducted a class research conference with the class teacher and the subject teacher in charge. The results suggest that meta-grammar skills cannot be fostered without an incorporation of activities designed to intentionally bring one's attention to the mechanisms of language. The results also show that cross-linguistic lessons designed to promote awareness of language mechanisms are effective.

The need to shift from English-only foreign language education to multilingualism is an ongoing concern. According to historical documents, there was a time when Japan interacted with a variety of languages and different cultures. From a historical perspective, Erikawa (2017) examined why Japan shifted from a diverse foreign language education to the current English language mainstream system. Political and ideological factors, as well as low education budgets, were cited as the key reasons. In regards to English education in Japan, Torikai, Otsu, Erikawa, and Saito (2017) are con-

Chapter 7 / Towards an Approach for Enriching Learners' Metalinguistic Awareness   285

and Morizumi, 1982; Otsu, 1982, 1989; Okada, 1998). Most notably, a proposal for 'metalinguistic ability' was brought up, thus suggesting the possibility of collaboration on this domain.

Metalinguistic ability is defined as 'the ability to objectify and use the grammatical knowledge built into one's brain' (Otsu, 1989). The idea behind this proposal is to promote foreign language education by making students become aware of the existence of a common foundation that supports all individual languages and the nature of language, such as its mechanisms and functions. Otsu and Kubozono (2008) argue that promoting the development of this metalinguistic competence is a core goal that Japanese language education and foreign language education should have. Later, they proposed 'awareness of language' as a concept that includes metalinguistic ability.

Since 2000, some practical cases of cross-linguistic collaboration have been reported. The practice of collaboration between Japanese language education and foreign language education was seen in classes at junior high schools, high schools, and universities (Akita et al., 2014). Specifically, the following activities were conducted in Japanese and English departments with the common goal of fostering logical thinking skills: (1) common activities related to cohesion and coherence of sentences and paragraphs in Japanese and English departments, (2) providing instruction in Japanese for enhancing one's logical thinking and expressive skills in cooperation with English departments, and (3) providing instruction for establishing basic English skills in cooperation with Japanese departments (Saito et al., 2013). Cross-linguistic practices are becoming a point of focus within high schools. The reason for this is that high school students are expected to have the ability to think logically and express themselves in relation to Chinese ma, 2016). This involves 'activities promoting language awareness' that encourage learners to observe, analyze and infer about their mother tongue and other languages.

From a historical perspective, Masaki (2012, 2015, 2016a, 2016b) organized the prehistory and history of collaborations between Japanese and English education by dividing them into periods. First, he found that from the Meiji period to the 1950s, descriptions of cross-linguistic grammar instructions were used as a method of 'liaison', indicating a close relationship between Japanese, Chinese, and foreign languages. Okakura (1894) pointed out that one of the shortcomings of the foreign language teaching method was the lack of 'liaison' or 'communication' with the national language and Chinese literature, as well as their respective grammars. 'Communication' in this case means to create an interrelated knowledge system by comparing the known grammar from the Japanese and Chinese languages with the grammar of the new foreign language.

Furthermore, in the 1960s and 1970s, the concept of 'language education' (Nishio and Ishibashi, 1967) was proposed as a common philosophy for both Japanese and foreign language education. It stated that the essence and purpose of language education is to achieve a 'complementary relationship' between foreign language education (by using the knowledge of Japanese acquired through Japanese language education), and deepening one's awareness of Japanese through foreign language education. However, in the 1980's and 90's, due to the popularity of the 'communicative approach' teaching method, there was a strong tendency to eliminate the use of the native language as much as possible. As a counterpart to that period, we can find some discussions regarding the importance of promoting further cooperation between Japanese and foreign language education (Miyakoshi

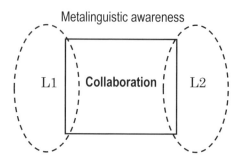

Figure 7.1: Basic diagram for the current research project based on L1+FL collaboration.

movement in European countries from the 1980s is one of the defining moments that placed an emphasis on the intellectual value of learning a foreign language. To solve the problems of the unpopularity of ESL, decline in English ability, and discrimination against minority languages in the U.K., a new holistic language program titled 'language awareness education' was introduced to connect mother tongue and foreign language education as a 'new language' subject (Hawkins, 1984). This is an educational program that focuses on raising language awareness of linguistic topics for the sake of understanding linguistic universality and variability in multi-ethnic and multicultural contexts. Tunmer, Herriman and Nesdale (1988) defined metalinguistic awareness as an awareness of the underlying linguistic nature of language use by objectifying and reflecting on features of the language system. Tunmer and Bowey (1984) divided metalinguistic awareness into four categories: phonological awareness, word awareness, form awareness and pragmatic awareness. Cook (2001) states that promoting language awareness helps to enhance one's language sense. In addition, it is argued that the plurilingual and multiculturalist education that is being increasingly cultivated in Europe can be applied to foreign language activities (Oya-

Chapter 7／Towards an Approach for Enriching Learners' Metalinguistic Awareness   287

cerned that English-only foreign language education will eventually fail, and therefore they recommend a possible return to multilingualism. It has been proposed that the multilingual and multicultural education taking place in Europe—in other words, 'language awareness activities' in which students observe, analyse, and reason about their mother tongue along with multiple languages—can be applied to elementary school foreign language activities in Japan (Iwasaka and Yoshimura, 2015; Oyama, 2016).

Wang (2017, 2019a, 2019b) analysed a set of elementary school Japanese language textbooks and proposed a number of subjects that can be connected to foreign language learning. Regarding the development of metalinguistic ability, Otsu points out that 'when two or more language systems are available, it becomes possible to compare and contrast them, and meta-linguistic ability is more likely to develop' (1989: p. 30). From this point of view, two or more languages can provide useful suggestions for developing one's metalinguistic ability. Wang (2018a, 2018b, 2018c, 2019a, 2019b, 2019c) conducted three comparative classroom practices involving English teaching linked with the national language (with the addition of Chinese as a control language), and examined their effects.

Cummins (1979, 1984), a linguistic psychologist who has studied bilingualism and language education for immigrant children, criticized second language education that excludes the mother tongue and proposed the 'bilingual interdependence hypothesis' in which the mother tongue and the second language share a common base (central base language ability and central operating system). Sato, Uchida, and Otsu (2011) interpreted the deep common ground between languages as the ability to think in abstract terms, by engaging in logical analysis, by making analogies, comparisons, and summaries, and having the metalinguistic ability to grasp the structure and flow of sentences.

Therefore, they argue that in order to acquire two languages, one must build on the foundation of the native language. They argue that there is a common foundation for all languages, and that it is important to develop awareness and consciousness of the various properties of language, or in other words, to develop one's awareness of language. They also posit that awareness of language is advantageous for the effective use of both mother tongue and foreign language.

By referencing these studies, I have shown that the primary significance of learning English as a foreign language in Japan is to obtain the means for making connections with one's mother tongue, and to enrich one's awareness of language. Thus, we can expect to achieve an effective command of mother tongue and foreign language, by organically linking Japanese and multiple foreign languages in educational activities.

7.3 Action Research Initiatives Towards Metalinguistic Awareness Development

The early seeds of this case study came from action research studies that were carried out through a collaboration between teachers from Japanese language departments and English departments in an innovative curriculum design project (Saito et al., 2013; Akita et al., 2013; Saito et al., 2014; Akita et al., 2014; Akita et al., 2015; Akita, Saito, Fujie, 2019). Together, they designed metalinguistic lessons focusing on language structures for senior-high school students, which were aimed at nurturing their metalinguistic ability during language classes dealing with English, Ancient Japanese and Modern Japanese. Besides engaging with the process of classroom teaching and learning, they analysed multiple factors such as

Chapter 7／Towards an Approach for Enriching Learners' Metalinguistic Awareness 289

students' pre- and post-task tests, students' work written during classes, and worksheet comments, while also engaging with lesson study meetings in order to verify the potentials and effectiveness of these metalinguistic awareness activities. As a result, it was proved that students' metalinguistic awareness of specific language forms had increased by means of the designed collaborative lessons.

7.4 Case Study of an English Class for Grade-7

This case study seeks to highlight the necessity and significance of inter-relating mother tongue with foreign languages, specifically within English as a Foreign Language (EFL) classrooms, and in the process illustrate a new approach for EFL education by elaborating upon recent action research initiatives. The goal is to provide learners with different viewpoints on language structure and function, so as to be aware of the richness and power of language.

The case study, which involved analysing a poem in Chinese and Japanese in EFL classrooms, was carried out as an action research with three Grade 7 English teachers in a Japanese junior high school. The lesson was conducted in two classes on 18 January, 2019, and in three classes—in which two classes joined together for one lesson—on the 16 December of the same year. In total, this case study consists of four lessons.

I was asked to serve as a guest teacher to introduce Chinese culture to students in a unit called 'Let's go to Chinatown', derived from a currently-adopted EFL textbook. While preparing for this task, a Chinese Kanji quiz (Figure 7.2) featured in the textbook inspired me to design a metalinguistic-oriented lesson drawing on the fascinating potential of Kanji characters. I decided to design a lesson that would help students think deeply about the characteristics of Japanese language by exploring similarities and differences between Japanese and Chinese in an English class. While searching through Japanese language textbooks, I found a poem titled 'Chunxiao' (spring dawn), first introduced in the 5th grade Japanese textbook and in more detailed form in the 8th grade Japanese textbook; coincidentally, this poem is included in the Chinese language textbook for elementary schools (Figure 7.3). This poem was selected because it is

1.机	□desk	□airplane
2.湯	□shower	□soup
3.汽車	□bus	□car
4.作業	□practice	□homework
5.去英国	□come from the U.K. □go to the U.K.	

Figure 7.2: Chinese-English quiz.

春暁
春眠暁を覚えず、
処処啼鳥を聞く。
夜来風雨の声、
花落つること知る多少。
孟浩然

chūn xiǎo
春 晓
mèng hào rán
孟 浩 然
chūn mián bù jué xiǎo
春 眠 不 觉 晓 ，
chù chù wén tí niǎo
处 处 闻 啼 鸟 。
yè lái fēng yǔ shēng
夜 来 风 雨 声 ，
huā luò zhī duō shǎo
花 落 知 多 少 。

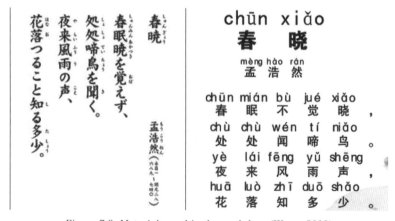

Figure 7.3: Materials used in the worksheet (Wang, 2019).

Chapter 7 / Towards an Approach for Enriching Learners' Metalinguistic Awareness   291

common and familiar to Japanese learners.

7.4.1 Lesson Implementation Process

School starts in April in Japan, so the lessons conducted in December of 2020 were partially revised based on my reflections regarding the ones carried out in January of 2020. Four lessons were recorded, transcribed and categorized in terms of a four-stage-structured lesson analysis (Sarkar Arani, 2014). The flow of the lessons can be seen in Table 7.1.

Regardless of revisions, there are four activities in common among these four classes. The first activity is to present the selected poem in Japanese from the Japanese textbook, then present the Chinese version. Students are encouraged to read it in Chinese with the guest teacher, followed by a discussion in groups of four, focused on identifying any noticeable similarities and differences by comparing the Japanese and Chinese poems. Given the fact that students have already learned this poem in the Japanese language, they are likely to focus on the language itself.

The second activity is a Chinese Kanji quiz. Quizzes differing from the textbook examples are prepared in advance, and students are engaged in a warm-up activity that builds a sense of achievement, as they realise they actually know some Chinese already, without having learned it previously. The purpose of the Chinese Kanji-English quiz is to provide students with a comparative perspective that links the three languages.

The *karuta* game is the third common activity in this case study. Students play *karuta* card games with a selection of Chinese words sharing the same Kanji, same meaning and similar pronunciation as the corresponding Japanese words. This activity aims to stimulate students' sense for distinguishing *onyomi* in Japanese and *pinyin* in Chinese. The last ac-

292

Table 7.1: Lesson flow throughout the case study.

Category	Lesson Segments in January: Class 7A (32 students), Class 7C (35 stud.)	Lesson Segments in December: Class 7A' (34 stud.) + 7C' (31 stud.)*, Class 7B (27 stud.)
Introduction	> Several students are invited to write and pronounce their names in Chinese after the guest teacher's self-introduction. > Students are asked to point out cities where the guest teacher has lived, by looking at a Chinese map in their hand as they hear city names in Chinese. > Students are asked to shout out what Chinese words they know. (15 minutes)	> Students shout out what Chinese words they know as a warm-up activity, after the guest teacher is introduced. > Students are asked to answer Chinese-English quizzes by guessing the meanings of words. Students sit if their answers are wrong, until only three students are left standing up, whose names are then taught by using Chinese pronunciation. (15 minutes)
Development	> The poem is presented and read in Japanese first, followed by its Chinese version. > Students are asked to form groups and write down similarities and disparities in individual worksheets where they draw underlines and write notes. (10 minutes)	> *Karuta* game is played in groups of 4. Chinese cards are given to each group. Students are asked to choose the correct Chinese word cards when they hear the corresponding Chinese term. > The poem in Japanese is shown to Students. It is read and interpreted through students' discussions. Then the poem in Chinese is presented and read together with students under the guidance of the guest teacher. Worksheets are handed out, as students are asked to write down any similarities and disparities they have noticed, both individually and in groups. (25 minutes)
Turn	> Several students are called to speak out their opinions to the whole class. > Students are asked to choose the correct Chinese word cards when they hear Chinese in groups during a *karuta* game. > Students answer a Chinese quiz as a whole in order to choose the correct pictures as they see Chinese Kanji words. > Self-introduction through a sentence pattern of S+V+O is shown in Chinese, English and Japanese. > Several students are invited to do a self-introduction in Chinese. (15 minutes)	> Students are free to share their opinions in groups, while two teachers walk around to facilitate. (5 minutes)
Conclusion	Students are asked to write their insights, discoveries, questions or comments on the worksheet as reflections. (5 minutes)	There is no time during the lesson, so students are asked to write their insights, discoveries, questions or comments on the worksheet as reflections after the lesson is finished.

*Note that classes 7A' and 7C' are different from 7A and 7C, which were in Grade 8 at the time.

tivity is to ask students which Chinese words they know, and interact with them based on their answers. This activity not only introduces an unfamiliar language in a familiar way, but also builds up the relationship between guest teacher and students.

7.4.2 Analysis of Worksheet Answers and Reflective Writings

67 worksheets were collected from the two classes in January, and 92 worksheets were gathered from the three December classes. The students' remarks concerning the similarities and differences of the poem in Chinese and Japanese as well as their reflective writings about what they had learned of Chinese, Japanese, and English from this lesson were analysed in comparison to the four categories proposed by Tunmer and Bowey (1984): *phonological awareness, word awareness, form awareness* and *pragmatic awareness*. 'Phonological awareness' refers to phoneme segmentation, appreciation of rhyming and acoustic signals. 'Word awareness' relates to word segmentation, word-referent differentiation, and appreciation of words and their meanings. 'Form awareness' refers to the structural representation of parsing items, linguistic items or literal meaning. 'Pragmatic awareness' indicates an awareness to pragmatic and inferential rules, inconsistent communication failures, macrostructure, and intended meaning.

In addition, one extra category, *emotional awareness*, emerged from the analysis of students' reflections. In particular, 'emotional awareness' refers to any personal emotions felt toward language or language learning in general beyond specific linguistic items, involving both interest and motivation. These categories provided the basis for classifying the various manifestations of metalinguistic awareness. Each entry was coded under a single main category, even when there was more than one category mentioned. Therefore, the frequency of responses equals the students' numbers in total. A blank category was created to designate worksheets where both answers and reflections were absent (no fully blank worksheets were collected). The main reasons for the incomplete worksheets were that the teacher instructed students to write only a portion, or due to time limits.

7.4.3 Results & Discussion

As can be seen from Table 7.2, students' answers to the similarities and differences in the Chinese and Japanese versions of the poem took place primarily within the category of word awareness (44%) and 16% of the reflective writings can be included in the same category. In total, one-third of the students' answers and reflective writings were included in the word awareness category, which can be attributed to the fact that Kanji is a common factor in both languages. Students identified Kanji meanings, Kanji writing, and poetic style/language components. The majority of the students noticed differences between simplified Chinese characters and traditional ones, between horizontal writing and vertical writing, and between Kanji numbers and space segmentation. They also noticed that the Japanese language includes Kanji from Chinese, *katakana* words from English and other foreign languages, and of course the original *hiragana*. Some students commented that Japanese was more receptive and enriched, in contrast with the alphabet-only English and Kanji-only Chinese.

The phonological awareness category was identified in 23% of student answers and 27% in the reflection writings. Similarities between Japanese *onyomi* and Chinese *pinyin* were noticed, as well as differences in the phonics system which were addressed through specific symbols. It can be assumed that students are able to notice and analyse sound with phonemes in detail when they are given appropriate materials. Given their prior knowledge about Kanji, some students listed different pronunciations of the same Kanji in Japanese, although it seemed to have a single pronunciation in Chinese. The students' assumptions reveal that they applied what they learned from the Japanese language and other subjects in order to question the phonetic rules of a different language.

Chapter 7 / Towards an Approach for Enriching Learners' Metalinguistic Awareness   295

Table 7.2: Frequency of categories and examples taken from students' writings.

Category	Answers	Reflection
① **Phonological awareness**	37 (23%)	43 (27%)

Examples:
> Chinese has many sounds like [sha], [sho], [h] and [o]. There are also similar sounds like [yelai].
> [春] sounds like [shun] in Japanese, but [chun] in Chinese. Pronunciations of [g] and [z] are different.
> Chinese has more vowels and sounds rhythmical; Japanese sounds clearer.
> Each word has different tones in Chinese. There are symbols similar to musical notes [-] and [ˋ].
Japanese Kanji has more than one sound, like:
(あかとき, あかつき, きょう) 暁 = xiǎo;
(お, こ, しょう) 小 = xiǎo;
(ふう, かぜ, かざ) 風 = fēng;
(ほう, ほこ, ほこさき) 鋒 = fēng.
> Unlike Japanese, Chinese uses English alphabet symbols on top of it to show pronunciation.

Category	Answers	Reflection
② **Word awareness**	70 (44%)	26 (16%)

Examples:
> Some Kanji are the same, but some are different in writing. Numbers of Kanji and spaces are different.
> The Chinese poem has 5 kanji only, with comma and periods in horizontal writing; the Japanese poem has kanji, hiragana, and okurigana in vertical writing. The segmentations of the sentences are different.
> There are identical Kanji with the same meaning in Chinese and Japanese, but identical Kanji with different meanings also exist.
> Different Kanji: [暁—晓, 暁を覚えず—不觉晓, 処—处, 閧—闻, 鳥—鸟, 風—风];
  Same Kanji: [春眠, 雨, 知, 帝, 声, 多少, 夜来, 花落, 孟浩然]
> Some Kanji are repeated in pairs (処处 = chu chu). There are both English and Chinese words in Japanese.

Category	Answers	Reflection
③ **Form awareness**	7 (4%)	9 (6%)

Examples:
> Chinese put [不] in front of verbs to express the negative form; Japanese add [ず] after the verb instead.
> The verb comes first in Chinese and English, like [暁を覚えず→不覚 (おぼえず) 暁 (あかつき)].
> Japanese is like [S + ~ + V]; Chinese and English are like [S + V + ~].
> How to structure a sentence is handled differently. The sequence of words is different.
> There are no connecting words in Chinese or English, like [の], and [を].

Category	Answers	Reflection
④ **Pragmatic awareness**	25 (16%)	35 (22%)

Examples:
> We have different languages in East Asia, but we were able to communicate using Kanji and gestures.
> I found connections between Japanese and Chinese. We have similar Kanji, but different sentence structures, writing style and intonation. It might not be a problem to go to China.
> I've noticed the characteristics of Chinese and Japanese languages.
> I've learnt that the meanings of Kanji differ due to cultural differences in a social study lesson, but now I felt so different by comparing cultures from the viewpoint of Kanji.
> Japanese sounds soft and uses both Kanji and Hiragana; Chinese sounds angular and uses only Kanji.

Category	Answers	Reflection
⑤ **Emotional awareness**	0 (0%)	29 (18%)

Examples:
> I'd like to learn more English so as to look at other languages from the perspective of 'English'.
> Japanese originated from Chinese, but I am surprised how they turned out to be totally different now.
> I'd like to research how to say my name in Chinese and know more Chinese word meanings and their sound.
> It's important to respect other cultures and differences. I want to learn another country's culture and differences more.
> It's a lesson for me to see a long-time relationship between China and Japan.

Category	Answers	Reflection
⑥ **N/A**	20 (13%)	17 (11%)
Total	159 (100%)	159 (100%)

Answers and reflections categorized as pragmatic awareness were more diverse, as they included a mix of descriptions of each category with a focus on macrostructure. Linguistic distance between Chinese, Japanese and English and the relationship of language and culture were mentioned, by showcasing the unique characteristics of each language. Most of the comments stated that their mental images and pre-assumptions of Chinese and Japanese had changed throughout the lesson. This shows that providing opportunities for realising and understanding features of a different language can motivate students to reconsider their previous understandings of mother tongue and foreign languages.

Some students were able to deduce several unique characteristics of Japanese language from their comparisons. Some of them wondered how *katakana* developed as a part of Japanese language writing after Kanji was introduced in Japan. With English and Chinese being provided as reference languages for examining Japanese in an objective manner, not only did students pay attention to the unique features of Japanese language, but also felt inspired to inquire and deduce certain language rules based on the stimulus provided by the materials.

Form awareness showed up the least in both answers (4%) and reflections (6%), which could be attributed to the lack of specific instructions or guidance about structures during the lesson. It might be the case that some students were engaged in form awareness by thinking and inferring by themselves, when they were given the two poems. Sentence patterns, verb position and negative form were mainly discussed in this category among the three languages. Besides these, some students noted that there were connecting particles in Japanese, like 'は', 'が', 'を', 'の', 'く', but none of them was used in English (purely alphabet) or Chinese (purely Kanji). This

Chapter 7 / Towards an Approach for Enriching Learners' Metalinguistic Awareness   297

pointed out a unique characteristic of Japanese as an agglutinative language.

Emotion awareness (18%) was identified only in reflections because students were asked to write anything they felt or noticed in general. Most of the comments in this category expressed their interest and motivation to learn other languages, their respect for and questions about different languages and cultures, and their views concerning history and the relationship between Japan and China. It can be said that this lesson opened a door for students' potential thinking and learning without being restricted to linguistic features. Regarding the important role of motivation in human self-development, this kind of emotional awareness is more likely to lead to students' further learning in the future.

7.4.4 Summary

This case study examined the impact of newly-designed lessons articulating Japanese with Chinese during four English classes. These lessons were designed to provide students with opportunities to compare, analyse, categorize, and discover the similarities and differences between different languages for the purpose of developing metalinguistic awareness. These lessons, which incorporated a poem in Chinese and Japanese, were carried out in Grade 7 English classes in a Japanese junior high school. The students' worksheet answers and reflective writings during the lessons were collected and analysed so as to clarify their level of metalinguistic awareness.

It can be inferred from the writings that students felt attracted to the richness of language, felt engaged in the exploration of language systems, and were able to recognize the importance of various languages for participating in global communication. The results also show that the designed lessons awakened students' metalinguistic awareness in various potential aspects, not only on linguistic features but also on cultural and educational factors. In sum, classroom activities such as the one demonstrated here can be a meaningful tool for developing metalinguistic awareness.

More case studies are needed for devising better activities and materials that articulate between mother tongue and foreign languages in different age groups. In doing so, it is recommended that further research be conducted to explore the processes by which increased metalinguistic awareness may potentially result in improved linguistic competency for both mother tongue and foreign language. This is an aspect that will be considered in future research.

7.5 Case Study of a Foreign Language Activity Class for Grade-4

In Japan, the implementation of foreign language activities and foreign language subjects in elementary schools has officially begun, and while English is mainly taught by classroom teachers, it is necessary to find an approach for foreign language education unique to elementary schools that can take advantage of classroom teachers' strengths. The aims of this case study are: to examine how the practice of elementary school-level foreign language education can generate among students an awareness of language features; how this might be applied towards the development of textbooks; and to examine the reflections of classroom teachers on their classroom practice. In a foreign language class for 32 fourth-graders at a public elementary school in Fukui Prefecture, the teacher and the author introduced an excerpt from a previously-used Japanese textbook; the excerpt is titled

Chapter 7／Towards an Approach for Enriching Learners' Metalinguistic Awareness   299

'Winter Landscape', and it was used to guide the students into thinking about Japanese, English, and Chinese, based on the combination of Chinese characters starting with the word 'white'. After they had finished comparing the three languages, we sought to identify the type of language awareness that the students had attained, by looking at their comments and self-reflections. In addition, judging from the reflective lesson practice records made by the teachers, we argued for the necessity of a meaningful, in-depth collaboration between in-service teachers and university researchers in order to tackle new challenges. However, the results also suggest that the current state of development of teaching materials for elementary school-level foreign language education, which incorporates multiple languages in tandem with Japanese language education, is still insufficient in some aspects.

In the new elementary school curriculum guidelines elaborated by MEXT (2017), there is a proposal calling for improvements in foreign language proficiency and the development of enhanced instruction methods in partnership with Japanese language education, which can bring attention to the characteristics of Japanese language and the richness of languages in general. In the elementary school foreign language section, there are phrases such as 'learning the differences between Japanese and English, and becoming aware of the fun and richness of language' or 'becoming aware of the differences in word order between Japanese and English'. As for elementary school Japanese, there is a proposal for 'improving the effectiveness of instruction, by actively linking it with other subjects such as foreign language activities and foreign language studies, from the viewpoint of improving overall language ability'. What these references all have in common is the existence of an understanding of the term 'language' that organically links Japanese and foreign languages in a synergistic manner. The word 'language' refers to the general mechanism that supports the individual languages that people can acquire; in other words, a system representing the universality of language (Otsu & Kubozono, 2008). Otsu (2014) pointed out that the reason why there are relatively few people in Japan who can use English, even if their TOEIC and TOEFL scores are high, is that there is a definite lack of an understanding of 'language' in which Japanese and foreign languages are seen as related aspects of the same entity. It is this understanding of 'language' or 'language education' that we sought to adopt in this study.

7.5.1 General Description of the Lesson

I was able to conduct this pilot lesson with a pre-service teacher in a public elementary school in Fukui Prefecture, whose name is Mr. Ikeda. Acknowledging the significance of metalinguistic awareness in language learning, Mr. Ikeda showed his interest in implementing a Japanese-English-Chinese language lesson in his class. In the past, he had obtained teaching certificates for both Chinese and English languages at the secondary school level during his bachelor studies (B.A.). Seeking to obtain the teaching certificate to become an elementary school teacher, Mr. Ikeda was enrolled in an educational studies course (M.Ed) at the time. He was doing an internship in a fourth-grade class of a public school, under the supervision of a mentor, and it was his third year of school internship as a pre-service teacher. As part of his duties as an intern, he went to school three times a week.

Mr. Ikeda and I planned the lesson, prepared mock lessons and had several discussion meetings before the actual lesson took place. In November

Chapter 7 / Towards an Approach for Enriching Learners' Metalinguistic Awareness   301

of 2017, the two of us conducted brainstorming sessions for the purpose of designing a lesson. Considering the season in which the class was expected to take place, we decided to introduce 'winter words' at the beginning of the class as an extension of a Japanese class devoted to 'seasonal words and winter scenery', since it would take place right after it. The goal of the class was for students to develop an interest in Japanese and foreign languages while trying to find similarities in the way words are combined in two-letter kanji phrases. We came up with a number of creative ideas, but also withheld a few others because they did not match up with the children's current situation at school. We further refined the lesson plan in December, and two days before the expected class in January, a mock class was held by the teacher and the author. In preparation for the class, we worked on the time allocation for each activity, the design of the board, and basic rehearsals regarding the general flow of the class.

After all preparations had taken place, the real lesson was conducted by Mr. Ikeda in a fourth-grade class at his elementary school in Fukui Prefecture. I was invited to attend as a guest teacher. The lesson was carried out in accordance with the lesson plan detailed below. Although this was merely a one-time teaching practice, a look at the reflective worksheets written by the pupils provided several positive comments, which revealed their language awareness towards word formation, and also their increased interest in knowing different languages (Wang, 2020).

Class 3 of Fourth Grade / Foreign Language Activity Lesson Plan

Date: January, 17th, 2018 / Third Period
Teacher: Mr. Ikeda
Guest Teacher: Wang Linfeng

1. Name of the Unit: Language Awareness

2. Contents of the Lesson:

① *Learning objectives:* to notice the common rules of word formation from two-kanji words, so as to make learners more interested in Japanese language and foreign languages.

② *Learning tools:* worksheet, thick white paper and marker pen.

③ *Lesson flow:* see Table 7.3 below.

④ *Evaluation point:* by paying attention to known Kanji combinations, this can help learners to notice that new words or phrases may be generated by combining different words or Kanji. This is a common rule which can be found in other languages.

Table 7.3: Lesson Flow and Sequence of Activities.

Description of procedures involved in the learning activity	Summary of teacher instructions & examples of learner responses	Types of support provided by the teacher
Get to know what students will learn in this lesson;	Review the last Japanese language lesson titled 'Winter view'; link white things with the Kanji 'white'.	Connect learners' experiences to the theme of 'white'.
> Confirm the lesson's objective;	> 「白」で始まる漢字の組み合わせから、日本語・英語・中国語について考えよう。 Lesson objective: thinking about Japanese, English and Chinese languages through combinations of the Kanji 'white' (白).	
> In groups, write down Kanji starting with 'white' (白);	> Use all the available resources to find the Kanji 'white' (白).	> Introduce the guest teacher;
> Each group shows their drawing papers and share their results to the whole class;	> Each group is asked to put their results on the blackboard. e.g. 白馬, 白紙, 白鳥, 白旗	

Chapter 7 / Towards an Approach for Enriching Learners' Metalinguistic Awareness

> Think about written phrases in two-Kanji combinations;	> What do you notice by looking at these Kanji combinations? e.g. *Two Kanji makes one phrase.*	> Write down learners' opinions on blackboard (See 7.5);
> Think about whether it makes sense or not in English;	> Do these literally-translated English words really exist in English language? e.g. *They all exist in English.* e.g. *Some of them have English versions, some of them don't have English expressions.*	
> Discuss answers with the whole class;	> Ask guest teacher if they exist in English language. e.g. *Yes.*	> Practice pronunciation with guest teacher;
> Think about whether it makes sense or not in Chinese;	> Do you think these Kanji also exist in Chinese? e.g. *Yes; or No.*	> Practice pronunciation with guest teacher;
> Discuss answers with the whole class;	> Ask guest teacher if they exist in Chinese language. e.g. *Yes.*	> Help learners to figure out similarities among languages in their own words;
> Individual thinking time: what have you noticed by now?	> Ask what have you learnt? e.g. *Color + thing pattern is common among three languages.*	> Promote learners to create phrases by combining Kanji or words;
> Use your creativity to make your own original phrase.	> Think up or make some words or phrases which also make sense in Japanese, English, and Chinese. Write down your questions or comments on the worksheet.	> Guest teacher's comment.

Figure 7.4: Image of classroom blackboard during the pilot lesson.

7.5.2 Results

This pilot lesson started by reviewing what had been studied in the last Japanese language class titled 'Sceneries of Winter'. It elicited children's interest in Kanji because of its inclusion of 'white' as relating to snow. After conducting an activity in which groups had to search for 'white Kanji', the children were presented with selected Kanji examples and worked with their English counterparts (Figure 7.4). Then, the Chinese counterparts were introduced, along with Japanese and English words.

To inquire what they had noticed by comparing the same words in three languages, children discussed in pairs. Most of them noticed the same function of 'shiro', 'white', and 'bai' at the beginning of the words. They were surprised to know that the same Japanese Kanji makes sense in Chinese language as well. When it was time to share their insights as a whole class, children pointed out that the single word for colour 'shiro/white/bai' + single word for animals/things can generate a new combined word, which is common to the three different languages. At the end of the class, children were asked to write down words that involve the formation of 'color + animals/things'.

In total, 120 words were written by 32 children in the class. Their reflective comments were also collected (Table 7.4) and analysed according to four categories of metalinguistic awareness (Tunmer & Bowey, 1984). It was found that phonological awareness, word awareness and pragmatic awareness were identified in children's reflections. In addition, according to children's voices during the class, their level of motivation and interest toward language awareness (such as other foreign languages) had increased.

Just like the previous pilot lesson, this lesson was shown to provide an opportunity for children to think attentively and creatively about word for-

Chapter 7／Towards an Approach for Enriching Learners' Metalinguistic Awareness   305

Table 7.4: Children's reflective comments written during the pilot lesson (Wang, 2020).

	Reflective Comments	Phonological	Word	Form	Pragmatic
1	色＋物で言葉ができることを始めて知りました。日本語は白，英語は white，中国語は bai など，白は外国語でも決まっているんだなと思いました。		○		
2	日本語，英語，中国語のいろいろな読み方があるとわかりました。中国語は難しいなと思いました。	○			
3	中国語は日本語とすこしにている部分がある事が分かりました。いただきます や こんにちは はどうやっているのかしりたいです。				○
4	かんこくごがなかった。				
5	日本語も英語も中国語も色に何かをたして発音することが分かりました。日本も中国も漢字を使うのは，いっしょなんだなあと思いました。		○		
6	日本と中国では，漢字を使うことが分かりました。色は読み方が別でも同じ言葉を使うということが分かりました。	○	○		
7	中国語，英語は日本と同じ最初の色とかの意味は同じということが分かりました。でもなんで外国や中国の字は全然違うんだなと思いました。		○		
8	日本語や英語中国語は日本語と読み方が違くてへーそうなんだなとお思いました。ファン先生は日本語英語中国語すべてしゃべれるので，すごいと思いました。大人になっても３つの語覚えたいです。	○			
9	えいごと中国語のいいかたがちがうことがわかりました。	○			
10	日本語や中国語英語を教わって私は，むずかしいことが分かりました。英語，中国語の言葉がつうじてすごいなーと思いました。				○
11	中国の漢字はなんで日本の漢字と違うのかなと思いました。		○		
12	中国のほとんどが最後に「一」になることが分かりました。ワン先生とわたしの滑舌が全然違いました。	○			
13	中国はすべて漢字ということをはじめて知りました。中国は私の知らない読み方ばっかりでした。	○			
14	中国語でもちょっと日本とちがうけど，漢字を使うとはしりませんでした。中国を書いたら何も関係のないことを書いていたので，これが中国語なんだなと思いました。		○		○
15	日本語と英語と中国語はぜんぜん違うなとおもいました。おぼえるのもたいへんだとおもいます。ワン先生は日本語も英語も中国語もしゃべれるのがすごいなとおもいました。		○		
16	日本語は漢字とひらがながまじって「今から遊びにいきます」とかになるけど，中国語は全て漢字なので，びっくりしました。		○		
17	中国では全部の文字が漢字なんだなとおもい，ぼくも中国の字をならってみてみたいです。発音もむずかしいからすごいです。	○	○		
18	日本語の漢字と中国語の漢字は少しちがうけどなんとなくわかるような漢字があったのでおもしろかったです。		○		
19	白鳥で中国語だったら別の意味のばいやニャオ べつべつの意味をつなげてすると白鳥と読めるなんてびっくりしました。	○	○		
20	わかったことは，かんじはおなじでもよみかたがちがうことです。	○	○		
21	うしろにもいろをかいていいのかわかりません。ほぼ２文字。		○		
22	日本語には白でも読み方はいろいろあるけど英語と中国語はよみかたが１種類しかないのが疑問におもいました。中国語は発音もちがうのでびっくりしました。	○			

23	ちゅうごくごは漢字はいっしょだけど読み方がちがうのは知りませんでした。	○	○		
24	日本語英語中国語の発音はむずかしいとおもいました。中国にいったときはしようできたらいいなとおもいました。	○			○
25	赤色や青色などの色はなにかを組み合わせて英語や中国語にできるなと思いました。		○		
26	中国や英語や漢字をつかっているのがわかりました。		○		
27	もっと中国語をもっとしりたい。		○		
28	中国でも漢字をかくなんてはじめてしりました。すこしずつ中国語を覚えたいです。		○		
29	中国でも英語がつたわるということがわかったし、外国でも中国語がつたわることが分かりました。				○
30	日本の漢字と中国の漢字はにているので、びっくりしました。中国語はあまり知らなかったけれどちょっと知れてよかったです。		○		
31	漢字は日本が中国どっちからきたのか疑問です。		○		
32	中国でもだいたいはなんてかいてあるかわかるんだなと思います。		○		

mation from a metalinguistic perspective by comparing three languages, while using the contents from the Japanese textbook as a basis. The results strongly suggest that it is feasible to include Japanese and English into a broader scope of language education at the elementary school level.

7.5.3 Reflections from the Teacher

The class instructor interpreted the emotions experienced by the children in this class as those of 'interest, increased interest, expression, confirmation, discovery, bewilderment, new discovery, formulation, understanding, and expressions of understanding'. Throughout the class, he reflected that he felt 'fulfilled but not satisfied. The reason for the sense of fulfilment was that we were able to carefully discuss the lesson the day before, simulate the time and prepare the questions. *I was able to see the children's behaviour and reactions during the class, and I was able to lead their impromptu comments in a meaningful direction'*. The compliments from the participants, such as 'a class I have never seen before', 'a class unique to

Chapter 7 / Towards an Approach for Enriching Learners' Metalinguistic Awareness   307

Mr. Ikeda', and 'a class that surprised even the participants', also contributed to his sense of fulfilment for having conducted this activity. The most
gratifying part was when the children said, 'I have never seen a class like
this before'. What made him most happy was that the children seemed to
enjoy the class and were surprised by it. In particular, according to him a
girl who usually fell asleep during Japanese language class shone brightly
in this class and said: 'They use Chinese characters in Korea and North
Korea too. Korean is read differently from Japanese, but in Chinese it is
read the same way? I was impressed by her enthusiasm for learning until
the end. At the very least, she must have developed an interest in foreign
languages'.

In addition, in his reflection, he was able to practice two things that he
had wanted to do but had been unable to until then. First, he was able to
teach a class involving the Chinese language. The author had thought that
Chinese might be a superfluous addition in that school setting, but by han-
dling three languages (Japanese, English, and Chinese) as examples of foreign language activities, this became an opportunity for the children to en-
counter 'language' in a general sense, and by having an extra language he
could come up with connections to other subjects more easily. The other
reason is that he had an insight on how to create a community where
teachers can learn from each other as professionals. He was able to work
as a team with the principal, mentor teachers, and university faculty. We
were able to create this kind of class as a result of the teachers (those
working in the school and at the university) sharing their opinions and repeatedly reassessing them. He realised the significance and importance of
collaborative practice, by means of organizing a small but solid community
of practice.

However, the reason why he felt unsatisfied was because there were many areas for improvement in the class. The use of 'words', 'vocabulary', and 'language' got mixed up in the class sometimes, confusing the children. He was not able to find words that were easy for the children to understand, so the questions became long and were not as sharp as they could be. In addition, when writing the children's comments on the board, he was thinking about the next step, so he did not always check the true meaning of the comments and sometimes misunderstood the meaning. In addition, he introduced group activities, but the class could have been more complete. For example, there was the possibility of discussing whether the Chinese characters that were mentioned in the group could be found in both English and Chinese, after which they would look for similarities and come to a conclusion.

Unlike the subject classes, this class did not have any solid answers. Nevertheless, it is a positive development if the children can develop their own interest in language through their encounters with words. At the end of the class, he felt it was difficult to summarize the lesson, but he also thought that the lesson would lead to real independent learning because the children struggled, became quiet, thought actively, and were engaged. Through this practice, he reflected that the value of this kind of language awareness classes in elementary schools (which incorporates different languages) is to foster an attitude of independent learning in which children are interested in various languages and language elements and want to know more about them.

7.5.4 Summary

In this study, from the perspective of 'language education', we have prac-

Chapter 7 / Towards an Approach for Enriching Learners' Metalinguistic Awareness   309

ticed elementary school-level foreign language education incorporating Japanese, English, and Chinese, while considering its potentials for the development of textbooks. This also involved the examination of children's awareness of language and their personal reflections regarding the lessons. By comparing the three languages, and focusing on the process of word formation (such as exploring different combinations of words), the children were able to notice a wide range of words. However, it remains to be verified how one's awareness of language eventually leads to the development of language skills.

Although there is a limit to the number of lessons that can be given in a single class, it is necessary to design language activities that can make use of the awareness of language in a single lesson. It is necessary to set up such activities in a systematic way with a clear vision. In order to do so, we should thoroughly research teaching materials in Japanese and foreign language education. It is desirable not only to add new contents, but also to make the best use of existing materials and to work together.

In addition to English, I would like to recommend the inclusion of a second foreign language. It is possible to mobilize resources that take advantage of local characteristics, such as foreign-speaking children with foreign roots, ALTs with multiple language skills, and multicultural communities. In order to promote a diverse range of classroom practices, there is an urgent need to develop teaching materials for elementary school-level foreign language education, by interrelating the mother tongue with multiple languages. In addition, the records of reflective teaching practice produced after the class suggest the necessity of further collaborative inquiry, especially in terms of creating an organization for cross-curricular collaborative practice.

7.6 Case Study of Online English Classes for Grade-7

The purpose of this case study is twofold: (1) to discuss its educational significance based on the practice of multilingual education in Japanese junior high schools, and (2) to discuss what is necessary for the sustainable inclusion of multilingual education in junior high schools.

The Japanese educational system is characterized by a double monolingualism, with secondary education being even more monolingual than primary and higher education. In secondary education, the subject framework is very clear. Teacher training is generally subject-specific, and even after becoming a teacher, there are few opportunities to collaborate with classes in other subjects.

On the other hand, it has been shown that there are certain pedagogical advantages to multilingual education. The problem is that even if its pedagogical significance is demonstrated, it is not always possible to counter the prevailing status quo, or monolingual habitus. Therefore, in order to consider what is necessary for the sustainable development of multilingual education despite this monolingual habitus, this section examines the practice of multilingual education in Grade-7 in a compulsory school. Here, only the Grade-7 lesson is shown, but a Grade-8 lesson was also carried out.

7.6.1 General Background

The lesson was originally planned to use one hour (45 minutes) of an English class (36 students) to invite several guest lecturers, divide the students into small groups, and teach a different foreign language to each guest lecturer. However, due to the spread of the new coronavirus, it was decided that the class would be held online, and each group of students

Chapter 7 / Towards an Approach for Enriching Learners' Metalinguistic Awareness   311

would have one iPad to participate in the lecture via Zoom. The English teacher, who had been observing the students' learning at the time, conceived a two-hour lesson based on this lesson, and conducted a follow-up lesson in the form of a report and cross-session. As a result, a total of three hours of multi-language project learning was accomplished.

In the following pages, I will give an overview of this educational project, including the profiles of the guest lecturers who participated, and then describe what was accomplished by means of multilingual education, by analysing the reflective records of the students and teachers. After that, I will analyse the transcripts of the students' and teachers' reflections and describe what was accomplished through this bilingual education. This is expected to provide useful suggestions for bilingual education in Japanese junior high schools.

The English textbook for first-year junior high school students included a unit on Chinese culture and language, titled 'Let's Go to Chinatown'. In response to a request from the English teachers at the school, I have been teaching a special one-hour lesson of this unit as a special guest since the 2018 school year. Specifically, activities such as 'Let's say your name in Chinese', 'Let's say the Chinese words you know', 'Let's find the city on the map of China', 'Let's listen to the Chinese words in the *karuta* game', and 'Let's guess the meaning of the Chinese words in the kanji quiz' were used to familiarize students with the Chinese language, and there was also a comparison activity aimed at finding the differences between the Chinese and Japanese versions. The students' learning and reflections showed that they were able to use their metalinguistic ability, which is the common foundation for general language ability (Wang, 2020).

I proposed the online multilingual approach to the class. We recruited several guest lecturers who could speak foreign languages, including Chinese, and each group of junior high school students chose one foreign language other than English that they wished to experience in order to develop an awareness of language. This class was conducted via Zoom due to restrictions posed by the corona virus pandemic.

7.6.2 Guest Teachers

The guest lecturers for each foreign language group were invited by us, and a total of nine members from eight language groups were gathered. Many of the guest lecturers came from a university background. We asked them to take charge of one language group in order to give Japanese junior high school students a chance to experience a foreign language other than English. The flow of the class began with self-introductions by the eight guest lecturers (10 minutes), followed by a group activity in each language (35 minutes), and a worksheet for reflection (5 minutes), for a total of 50 minutes of instruction. The guest lecturer distributed slides and worksheets for each language group to the students before the class. The basic language used in the groups was Japanese, but there was also a group that conducted activities in English.

After the class, in March 2021, the guest lecturers were interviewed about the reasons for their participation and their impressions. They provided a number of different reasons: an expectation that Japanese junior high school students would become interested in their own country and culture through exposure to their language; the fun of teaching a language to Japanese junior high school students as a foreigner; the desire to convey relevant historical and cultural ideas regardless of language; the importance of being a part of cultivating the qualities of a global citizen; and a

Chapter 7／Towards an Approach for Enriching Learners' Metalinguistic Awareness   313

perceived need to carry out multilingual activities for junior high school students.

7.6.3 Pre-lesson Phase

In the first half of the previous period, all students participated in a quiz session that was designed by referencing the Chinese Kanji quiz found in the textbook. Following the Chinese character quiz, I showed them some popular words that express current events and social trends, along with their Japanese translations, for them to match with each other.

In the latter half of the session, after distributing posters of the guest lecturers and language groups, including an introduction to the content of the session, the students were asked to freely choose their language groups. I instructed them not to have more than five students in each group, but as expected, there was a lot of variation.

Malay was the first language that no one wanted to choose. French and Portuguese were the most popular. When we asked the students who chose Portuguese, we found out that their language choice was influenced by their experiences and impressions of a particular language, such as 'there was a subject about Brazilians in my textbook', 'I had a child from Brazil in elementary school', or 'I wanted to choose Spanish, but it was not available, so I chose the closest language, Portuguese'. In the language group that was chosen by the largest number of people, the language of choice was Portuguese. In this case, we had planned to have the students give a speech stating why they chose the language they did, but due to time constraints, we did not implement the speech. Instead, I left it up to the students to either voluntarily change to another language group or decide by rock-paper-scissors.

7.6.4 Lesson Example: French

As a representative example of this case study, an outline for the French class is provided in this section. There were five participants in this group. For Japanese people who have never studied French, the image of France is often strongly influenced by high-class culture, such as paintings, architecture, gastronomy and fashion. In this class, we used the linguistic landscape as a visual resource to show French signs found in urban areas, and to raise awareness of the function of language by asking which language is used, and for what purpose.

Following this, I asked questions about where in the world French is spoken, and showed them a map, focusing on the various 'French languages' that extend beyond France and Europe to the rest of the world. Then, I presented a number of French vocabulary terms and asked the students to analogize what sounds they represent. The terms are shown in Figure 7.5.

The students tried to read these words based on their knowledge of English, but they could not understand what the nouns meant by themselves. However, when the teacher gave them a hint that these French words exist not only in English, but also in Japanese, the students began to discuss

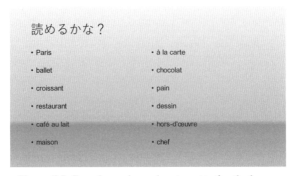

Figure 7.5: French words used as prompts for the lesson.

Chapter 7／Towards an Approach for Enriching Learners' Metalinguistic Awareness 315

and find the corresponding words in Japanese.

This was followed by an activity where they were asked to describe the pronunciation rules by themselves. Finally, I asked them how to say chocolate bread in French, and had them figure out that it is 'pain au chocolat'. At the end of the activity, I gave them a short introduction to the Norman Conquest and its subsequent influences, in order to understand historically why English and French vocabulary are so similar, by which time we had to conclude the class.

7.6.5 Selected Comments from Students

The following list contains a number of comments selected from the students' remark sheets.

① *I can write my name in Korean with Hangul. It is explained in detail why the sound matches the letter. There are three structures of Hangul, which are carefully written.*

② *I imagined the interaction between Portuguese and feudal lords and merchants.*

③ *Why did the word tsunami enter the Portuguese language?*

④ *Why are there different readings and meanings for the same kanji? I want to look it up. I want to know more.*

⑤ *I want to know more about it. [Felt] Respect for other languages, like Arabic speakers have a hard time (I thought so after only 30 minutes of learning about the language structure)?*

⑥ *Ukrainian. I didn't even know where the country was, but now I know about the place, the food, the culture, and even some of the language.*

⑦ *I was surprised, I want to know other languages, I want to learn more.*

⑧ *Listening to other languages has made me interested not only in languages but also in cultures and buildings.*

⑨ *I want to learn more about other languages.*

⑩ *I knew the language, but it was very different and interesting. It was interesting to see how different it is from Japanese ... There were similarities and differences, such as how to write words, which are similar to Japanese, and food, which is similar to Japanese.*

⑪ *All four of us said that the pronunciation of the Japanese language and the other language were similar or dissimilar, and we were divided in half, with two of us saying they were similar and two saying they were dissimilar.*

⑫ *I thought Portuguese was a little bit like Arabic from what I heard. The way men and women listen to each other is the same in both languages, and I thought there would be a lot of this in other languages if I learned them again.*

⑬ *The way men and women listen to each other is the same in both languages [Portuguese and Arabic], and I think there are a lot of things like this when you learn other languages again.*

⑭ *When I read that Korean and Arabic were 'similar to Portuguese', I thought I'd like to look up the languages that are the most similar.*

⑮ *I realized that there are many languages in the world, with cultures, pronunciations, and writing styles different from the French I studied. I realized that there are many languages in the world, and that Portuguese and Korean are similar to Japanese, and that there is a connection between them.*

7.6.6 Summary

The Japanese educational system is characterized by a very strong monolingualism, and there have long been objections to the overemphasis on English in foreign language education in particular. Monolingualism not

Chapter 7 ∕ Towards an Approach for Enriching Learners' Metalinguistic Awareness   317

only structurally deprives students of tolerance and interest in linguistic diversity, but also risks forming the representation that only the language they learn in school is an important language. To overcome this dual monolingualism in learning, it may be worthwhile to consider introducing multilingual education in schools.

In this case study, we interpret multilingual education as a type of language education in which reflective activities are conducted using multiple languages. At the core of bilingual education is the view of linguistic competence, that an individual is the sum of his or her repertoire in multiple languages. This view emerged from bilingual studies and was made clear within European language policy in the CEFR. Multilingual education, which is not limited to foreign language education, aims to equip all learners with the ability to approach things and social situations by mobilizing multiple language repertoires. In the modern Japanese education system, learning more than one foreign language has long been limited to the 'elites' of society. In contrast, bilingual education is aimed at general education, and furthermore, it aims to create citizens who will constitute a democratic society.

Research on bilingual education in Japan has developed around elementary school foreign language education (Yoshimura, Iwasaka, Abe & Oyama, 2020). Elementary school teachers usually do not specialize only in English, but are in charge of all subjects, and thus routinely engage in cross-disciplinary education. For this reason, they may be more familiar with the idea of mobilizing learners' multiple language abilities.

In contrast, secondary education has a very clear subject framework. Teacher training is generally conducted on a subject-by-subject basis. In other words, a teacher who teaches English as a foreign language receives training specific to English education, and a teacher of Japanese language receives training specific to Japanese education before entering the classroom. In addition, even after becoming a teacher, there are few opportunities to collaborate with classes in other subjects.

In Japan, English is still the only language taught in secondary education, and the educational goal is to pass the university entrance examination. In Europe, there is diversity in the foreign language examinations for university entrance qualifications. These curricular differences might lead one to believe that it would be easy for Europeans to have multilingual education at the secondary level, but in fact, even in the present Europe, the habitus of monolingualism in schools still exists, especially at the secondary level, where language education has become more normative and playful. It has been reported that there is a growing rejection of the playful curriculum.

So, how can we realize education that exposes students to multiple languages and reflective activities, and not merely English, even while considering the constraints posed by the curriculum? It is clear that teachers working in an organization are not able to change this situation by themselves. What might be done?

This chapter has sought to provide evidence for a pedagogical multilingual approach based on students' reflections, and reports from one-off activities. During these activities, we saw the demonstration of meta-linguistic skills by the students, along with an increased understanding and respect for the speakers of another language. By being exposed to a third language, they were able to say something new about the English and Japanese that they had become familiar with. Such exposure might not immediately provide them with full knowledge, or complete answers to their questions, but by doing this they were able to develop an interest in the unknown, and perhaps acquire a more proactive attitude towards learning by themselves.

Chapter 8 / Conclusion

8.1 Conclusion: Changes and Prospects for Newly-Revised Textbooks

The results of this entire study have brought about a few contentious issues that are still under debate in regards to the development of materials for foreign language learning. To address these issues, I have presented a methodology by which educational institutions can apply for textbook evaluation or selection, and by which teachers can produce their own supplementary teaching materials, besides those of textbooks.

In Chapter 1, I started my enquiry by pointing out the relevance and necessity of textbook research in regard to studies of curriculum and instruction; this was followed by a review of recent trends in English textbook research in an EFL context. It argued that authorized textbooks, seen as the materialized products of a national curriculum, are worth scrutinizing critically because they are assumed to impact heavily on classroom teaching and learning. A literature review of EFL textbook research suggested that a micro-approach towards examining unit designs was needed, so as to clarify the core traits of EFL textbooks.

With this in mind, a historical review of English textbooks development in both Japan and China was conducted, along with an analysis of current national curricula for junior high school. The history of English textbook development shows that both Japan and China went through a similar process of transitioning from imported textbooks to contextualized ones. Regarding the specific approaches used to achieve this contextualization, Japan sought to develop original textbooks with local publishers, while China tended to refer to globalized textbooks devised by international publishers. Furthermore, the present national curricula (which provide guidelines for textbooks currently in use) have served as the main reference points for interpreting which features are required for textbook compilation. Given its educational needs and overall objectives, Japan put an emphasis on balancing the four skills to achieve an all-round, general communication ability; as for China, it adapted the notion of task-based language use for developing comprehensive language competence.

By focusing on textbook research methods, this thesis intended to address three core research questions: is there a gap between authorized EFL textbooks and the national curriculum? What are the idiosyncrasies of EFL textbooks? What kind of fundamental issues or imbalances may be found in EFL textbooks, and how may we deal with them?

In Chapter 2, through the elaboration of different frameworks for language textbook analysis, I proposed a descriptive model for analysing learning units in detail. This model offers a cohesive way to take into account all of the three main components of a unit: metadiscourse, texts and practice activities. Metadiscourse analysis deals with information or messages that textbooks tend to send to learners, rather than the specific learning contents of the unit (Chapter 3). Rhetorical pattern analysis was applied to texts for the sake of clarifying text comprehensibility, with a particular focus on the linkage of each part within a unit (Chapter 4). Practice activities were analysed from a number of perspectives, namely: learners' initiative, focus of language contents, required mental processes, learners' interactions, and input & output contents; the aim is to infer (with as much precision as possible) what is implied within practice activities (Chapter 5). Three units, themed as 'school', 'family', and 'events', were chosen from each textbook compiled by all authorized publishers in both countries (6 from JP, 8 from CN), comprising 42 units in total.

In Chapter 3, the outcomes of the metadiscourse analysis reveal the ways in which textbooks guide learners' learning. The categories of analysis were divided into informational contents, attitudinal contents, and additional contents. I found that neither of the two countries used attitudinal metadiscourse in textbooks except for salience, and that none of them took into account the potential of promoting learners' metalinguistic ability, by using the mother tongue as a language learning material with which to help them apprehend key aspects of a foreign language.

In terms of informational metadiscourse contents, while Chinese textbooks lay weight on setting out the key objectives of learning contents, Japanese textbooks show an emphasis on providing introductions for both contextual situations and the learning contents themselves. Regarding the additional metadiscourse contents, Japanese was used as the instruction language using a first-person voice in Japanese textbooks, which could be inferred as emotionally supporting learners in their learning. In contrast, English was mainly used as the instruction language using a second-person voice in Chinese textbooks, which suggests an attempt to provide further language immersion and increase the learners' ability to focus on what is required of them.

Chapter 4 presents the progression of texts and text comprehensibility throughout a unit, by focusing on its rhetorical patterns. Rhetorical pattern analysis describes the linkage of parts through the use of diagrams, to show how (and to what extent) the various statements in texts are connected and developed. The matrix and hierarchy patterns (indicating tighter and denser relationships between statements) were rarely found in the EFL textbooks. Instead, the list pattern (which generates the least amount of relationships) was identified in the majority of units: this could be attributed to prioritizing a more pragmatic use of language structure, instead of producing more cohesive texts.

In Chapter 5, I carried out an examination of language practice activities, more specifically to understand what types of activities learners are required to do. This involved describing the explicit nature of 967 practice activities extracted from the textbooks. Through content analysis, it was found that practice activities are characterized by a high frequency of passive questions requiring 'meaning understanding' and 'information selection', related to learners' individual work (rather than pair or group work). Both countries also featured a good number of reproductive activities, by which learners are asked to reproduce what they are presented. Taken together, the findings in Chapters 3, 4 and 5 provide a convincing account for the essential features and character of learning units in EFL textbooks.

In Chapter 6, the outcomes from the various textbook analyses were summarized and mapped according to two key aspects:

① That of national curricula, involving the question of whether textbooks truly reflected the requirements of the curricula;
② That of EFL textbooks' characteristics, involving the question of what the fundamental issues and imbalances of EFL textbooks are.

Regarding ①, after checking the descriptions in national curricula and their requirements in terms of learning material contents, the discrepancies between textbook and curriculum were mainly discussed in terms of the teaching and learning of the four skills. As for ②, it was argued that the role of the mother tongue (L1) in developing metalinguistic awareness was undervalued. Therefore, as a starting point for an appropriate collaboration between L1 and FL in material development, two case studies were conducted in real class environments, so as to verify the validity and possibilities of interlinking both languages and boost metalinguistic awareness in learners.

Since it was found in Chapter 5 that practice activities were too focused on repetitive or reproductive actions as well as memorization on behalf of the learners, the other aim of these two case studies was to elicit learners to be more proactive, creative and use their own mental effort to link foreign language concepts with their previously-acquired mother tongue knowledge.

8.1.1 Significance of This Study

While this study recognizes the many positive outcomes, achievements and benefits that have been brought forth by the continuous development of the national curricula and textbooks over such a long period of time, it is also necessary to examine how they might be further improved. In terms of the methodological value of this research, it employs a detailed descriptive analysis of EFL textbook units at a micro-level, for the purpose of clarifying their key characteristics and potential insufficiencies. In addition, this study looks at textbooks from the unique perspective of an EFL researcher familiar with the shared linguistic and cultural heritage of both Japan and China (especially in terms of their usage of Kanji), in contrast to most of the prevailing textbook literature which is derived from ESL contexts. As a result, this study contributes an East-Asian dimension to the body of existing literature on English textbooks. I sought to clarify the core nature of these textbooks by looking in detail at their unit components, show how they are structured as a framework, and provide a constructive critique by comparing them against the requirements of the curricula in both countries. It is my belief that this analysis provides an opportunity to re-examine and re-evaluate current textbook authorizing procedures and compiling processes.

Regarding the theoretical value of this study, it includes a historical, socio-cultural and politico-economic view of how textbooks have been developed up until now, and serves as an example of how to explore EFL textbooks as a national curriculum artefact. In an attempt to better visualize the 'gap' between the curriculum and the EFL textbook, I have compared all of the authorized textbooks and national curricula in both Japan and China as holistically as possible within the bounds of the framework. Furthermore, it was demonstrated that this analysis framework is applicable to local textbooks in different countries.

As for the practical value of this research, its main contribution is to present the results of action research initiatives showcasing examples of lessons designed specifically for cultivating metalinguistic awareness. One of the main findings of this study is its claim that EFL textbooks are lacking in the aspect of metalinguistic development. To address this issue, it proposes a collaborative approach between L1 and FL classes, exemplified through a number of case studies. These helped to contextualize the study's findings, and shed further insights on other EFL contextual issues in language education.

8.1.2 Scope and Limitations of This Study

Throughout this work, the main focus and concern has been the national curriculum, which is the main force responsible for exerting an immediate influence on the preparation, compilation and evaluation of authorized EFL textbooks. It is acknowledged, however, that other factors and stakeholders should be accounted for in order to grasp the full breadth of textbooks as a research topic. Policy makers, publishers, parents, teachers and learners remain unexamined.

Furthermore, although Japan and China were selected for this study, other contexts such as Korea or Hong Kong are also worthy of consideration to draw a wider map of EFL teaching and learning environments, as well as to explore further synergies between mother tongues and FL. Finally, another limitation of this study is that the micro-analysis of units was only focused and carried out on currently-approved grade-7 textbooks published in 2012 along with the currently official curricula; this means that it is not possible to compare these textbooks and curricula with previous ones in full detail, or grasp their historic evolution using timelines. Furthermore, in order to conduct a thorough analysis regarding the adequacy of stipulations in the national curricula, it is also necessary to examine textbooks for higher grades, like the 9th grade representing the graduation level of junior high school.

8.1.3 Recommendations for Future Research

Given the limitations of this research, for the next step it is important to undertake classroom action research studies about textbook use and materials development. As one of the implications brought forth by the research results, there are potential merits in devising case studies in EFL contexts on how to use the mother tongue for foreign language learning. Both the acquisition of one's mother tongue and the learning of foreign languages require a level of metalinguistic development that provides a common ground for better proficiency (Cummins, 1978,1979) and operates as a fundamental central system for learning languages. In order to achieve the goal of metalinguistic development through a collaboration between mother tongue and foreign language education, I plan to pursue and carry out the following three research phases:

① To present the theoretical and practical bases, reasoning, and arguments for the significance and need of collaboration between mother tongue and foreign language education.

Method: I will investigate previous literature related to the necessity and theoretical grounds for collaboration between foreign and native languages. As a theoretical standpoint, I will rely on the theory of universal grammar (Chomsky, 1965; Samuels, 1979), Linguistic Interdependence Theory (Cummins, 1978), theory of 'language awareness' (Otsu, 1989; Schmidt, 1990) and the concept of 'pluralistic approaches to languages and cultures' (Candelier, 2007). I also intend to visit some schools in Europe that are conducting classes involving some form of collaboration between the teaching of mother tongue and foreign languages.

② To conduct a comparative analysis of textbooks, in order to select any linguistic items that are related to both mother tongue and foreign languages, and establish a tentative curriculum model that includes language activities.

Method: the framework for analysing textbooks is divided into four areas of meta-language awareness as defined by Ogose (2007) that give us the ability to consciously observe and operate language as an object. These are: awareness of phonology, awareness of words, awareness of language form and grammar, and operational awareness. Based on the results from a comparative analysis of elementary school textbooks (Wang, 2017), a number of language items and contents relevant to both national and foreign languages will be extracted. Based on this, I intend to design language activities that require 'observation, analysis, and reasoning' of multiple languages, and propose it as part of an integrated language curriculum.

③ To refine and verify the developed curriculum model (②) by conducting collaborative action research initiatives.

Method: put into practice the curriculum developed in ② and verify its applicability and educational effects. This practical research will be held in partner schools, where teachers are engaged in the process as active participants. In other words, this practical research will be conducted through a collaborative inquiry approach with classroom teachers, based on the theoretical framework developed by Schon (1983) known as 'reflective practitioner'.

This research also involves the domain of teacher education. The researchers and practicing teachers will act as collaborative explorers by conducting practical trials and practicing research that allows teachers to grow up as 'reflective practitioners'; in other words, teachers will be encouraged to look back on their actions and engage in a process of introspection and reflection, so as to open up new perspectives about teaching. The whole process can be considered as teachers' professional development story. Also, through gradual steps, there are plans for disseminating this collaborative foreign-native language class both inside and outside of the same school, by inviting class teachers of different grade classes as well as teachers from different types of schools to attend some classes and give their opinion.

8.1.4 Final Remarks

By acknowledging the textbook as a curriculum artifact, this study has clarified the essential characteristics of EFL textbooks from a micro-perspective, and by focusing on the issue of raising learners' metalinguistic awareness, suggested an approach for collaboration between mother tongue and foreign language in the classroom.

Based on the aforementioned findings, it can be affirmed that EFL textbook designs in both Japan and China do not yet fully meet the demands required by the currently-adopted teaching and learning principles, in spite of regular revisions in national curricula. Seeing as how authorized textbook publishers are expected to follow the new principle of balancing the so-called 'four skills', with the purpose of developing the comprehensive language capabilities of learners, these efforts have turned out to be partially flawed.

Until now, each country has chosen to take an isolated approach towards the development of textbooks, despite the fact that there are linguistic commonalities, and potential points of synergy. In particular, this study urges us to adopt a broader view on developing metalinguistic ability within EFL textbooks. This means that ESL textbooks and materials might not necessarily be the main point of reference for developing textbooks in an EFL context. Throughout these pages, it was demonstrated how this problem can be materialized from the conceptualization phase, up to the *insitu* context of classroom teaching and learning.

Even as textbooks move into the digital domain, their importance is unlikely to diminish in the near future, and international publishing companies are expected to maintain their strong presence and investments in attractive East Asian markets such as China and Japan. There is also a well-established market for English language tests, which pushes educators, parents and institutions to give extra importance to ESL materials. For all of these reasons, it is more crucial than ever to analyse in detail the deep contents of these learning materials, and provide a balanced critique so as to promote language learning in this region.

These external pressures might make it more challenging to develop textbook materials that integrate mother tongue and foreign language within EFL regions; thus, a continued collaboration between teachers and academics in different countries will be needed for pushing this early approach into a state of maturity. To conclude, it is hoped that the analytical framework presented in this study can help bridge the gaps between the deficiencies of EFL textbooks and the requirements of national curricula, and provide robust tools for teachers, textbook publishers and national textbook evaluation committees to achieve better results.

BIBLIOGRAPHY

List of government-approved EFL Japanese Textbooks analysed in this study

Sanseido (approved in 2015) *New Crown English Course 1*

Tokyo Shoseki (approved in 2015) *New Horizon English Course 1*

Kairyudo (approved in 2015) *Sunshine English Course 1*

Gakko Tosho (approved in 2015) *Total English Course 1*

Kyoiku Shuppan (approved in 2015) *One World English Course 1*

Mitsumura Tosho (approved in 2015) *Columbus 21 English Course 1*

List of government-approved EFL Chinese Textbooks analysed in this study

People's Educational Press (approved in 2012) *Renjiao ban English 7th grade (2 sets)*

Beijing Normal University (approved in 2013) *Beishida ban English 7th grade (2 sets)*

Popular Science Press (approved in 2012) *Ren'ai ban English 7th grade (2 sets)*

Yilin Press (approved in 2012) *Yilin ban English 7th grade (2 sets)*

Hebei Education Publishing House (approved in 2012) *Jijiao ban English 7th grade (2 sets)*

Foreign Language Teaching and Research Press (approved in 2012) *Waiyanshe ban English 7th grade (2 sets)*

Shanghai Foreign Language Educational Press (approved in 2012) *Shangwai ban English 7th grade (2 sets)*

Shanghai Educational Publishing House (approved in 2012) *Shangjiao ban English 7th grade (2 sets)*

List of Reference Works

Agirdag, O., & Vanlaar, G. (2016). *A hot piece of PISA: The relation between language use and academic achievement.* Paper presented at Cultural Diversity, Migration, and Education conference, Potsdam, Germany.

Aguilar, M. (2008). *Metadiscourse in academic speech: A relevance-theoretic ap-*

proach. European University Studies, vol. 317. Bern: Peter Lang.

Akita, K., Fujie, Y., Saito, Y., Fujimori, C., Sanpei, Y., Wang L.F., Tamiya, H. (2012). A Collaborative Action Research of Japanese and English Language Departments for Meta-Grammatical Lessons [in Japanese]. *Bulletin of the Graduate School of Education, the University of Tokyo,* 52, 337–366. 秋田喜代美；藤江康彦；斎藤兆史；藤森千尋；三瓶ゆき；王林鋒；柾木貴之；濱田秀行；越智豊＆田宮裕子.（2012）「国語科と英語科におけるメタ文法授業のアクションリサーチ」『東京大学大学院教育学研究科紀要』52, 337–366.

Akita, K., Saito & Y., Fujie. (Eds.). (2019). Teaching Grammar for Developing Meta-linguistic Abilities: Teachers of English and Japanese in Collaboration. Tokyo: Hitsuzi. [in Japanese]. 秋田喜代美・斎藤兆史・藤江康彦（編）（2019）『メタ言語能力を育てる文法授業：英語科と国語科の連携』東京：ひつじ書房.

Akita, K., Saito, Y., Fujie, Y., Fujimori, C., Masaki, T., Wang L.F., & Sanpei, Y. (2013). A Cross-Curricular Examination of the Factors Related to Grammar Learning: the Relationships among Meta-grammatical Ability, Feelings of Usefulness, Attitudes, and Learning Strategies [in Japanese]. *Bulletin of the Graduate School of Education, the University of Tokyo,* 53, 173–180. 秋田喜代美；斎藤兆史；藤江康彦；藤森千尋；柾木貴之；王林鋒 & 三瓶ゆき.（2013）「文法学習に関わる要因の教科横断的検討—文法課題遂行と有用感・好意度・学習方略間の関連—」『東京大学大学院教育学研究科紀要』53, 173–180.

Akita, K., Saito, Y., Fujie, Y., Fujimori, C., Masaki, T., Wang L.F., Oi, K. (2014). Developing a Curriculum for Training Meta-grammatical Abilities: Prospects of Meta-grammatical Curriculum in View of Practice and Teaching Material Development [in Japanese]. *Bulletin of the Graduate School of Education, the University of Tokyo,* 54, 355–388. 秋田喜代美；斎藤兆史；藤江康彦；藤森千尋；柾木貴之；王林鋒；三瓶ゆき & 大井和彦.（2014）「メタ文法能力育成をめざしたカリキュラム開発—実践と教材開発を通したメタ文法カリキュラムの展望」『東京大学大学院教育学研究科紀要』54, 355–388.

Apple, M. W. (1979). *Ideology and curriculum.* New York: Routledge & K. Paul.

Apple, M. W., & Christian-Smith, L. K. (1991). *The Politics of the Textbook.* London: Routledge.

Armbruster, B. B., & Anderson, T. H. (1985). Producing 'considerate' expository text: Or easy reading is damned hard writing. *Journal of Curriculum Studies,*

17(3), 247–274.

Bartlett, K. A. (2017). The divide between policy and practice in EFL high school classrooms in Japan. *PEOPLE: International Journal of Social Sciences, 3*(3).

Beckett, G., & Macpherson, S. (2008). The Hidden Curriculum of Assimilation in Modern Chinese Education: Fuelling Indigenous Tibetan and Uygur Cessation Movements. In Zvi Bekerman & Ezra Kopelowitz, eds. *Cultural Education-Cultural Sustainability: Minority, Diaspora, Indigenous and Ethno-Religious Groups in Multicultural Societies, 1st Edition*. New York: Routledge, 115–134.

Berg, B. L. & Lune, H. (2007). *Qualitative Research Methods for the Social Sciences*. USA: Pearson/Allyn & Bacon.

Bernstein, B. B. (1974). *Class, Codes and Control: Theoretical Studies Towards a Sociology of Language* (Vol. 3). London & New York: Routledge and Kegan Paul.

Block, E. (1986). The comprehension strategies of second language readers. *Tesol Quarterly, 20*(3), 463–494.

Bloom, B. S. (1956). *Taxonomy of Educational Objectives: The Classification of Educational Goals*. New York: Longmans, Green & Company.

Bolkan, J. (09/13/2017). IBM Rolls Out Free AI Tool for Math Teachers [Journalism]. In THE Journal: Transforming Education Through Technology. Retrieved October 25, 2018, from https://thejournal.com/articles/2017/09/13/ibm-rolls-out-free-ai-tool-for-math-teachers.aspx

Bransford, J. D., & Johnson, M. K. (1972). Contextual prerequisites for understanding: Some investigations of comprehension and recall. *Journal of Verbal Learning and Verbal Behavior, 11*(6), 717–726.

Breen, M. (1987). Learner contributions to task design. *Language Learning Tasks, 7*, 23–46.

Breen, M. P., & Candlin, C. N. (1980a). *A guide for the evaluation and design of materials*. Lancaster: Lancaster University, Department of Linguistics.

Breen, M. P., & Candlin, C. N. (1980b). The essentials of a communicative curriculum in language teaching. *Applied Linguistics, 1*(2), 89–112.

Breen, M. P., & Candlin, C. N. (1987). Which materials? A consumer's and designer's guide. In Leslie E. Sheldon, ed. *ELT Textbooks and Materials: Problems in*

Evaluation and Development. UK: Modern English Publications/The British Council, 13–28.

Britton, B. K., Woodward, A., & Binkley, M. (1993). *Learning from textbooks: Theory and practice.* USA: Lawrence Erlbaum Associates.

Bruce, N. J. (1989). The Roles of Metadiscourse, Speech Acts & the Language of Abstraction in a Top-Down Approach to Teaching English for Academic Purposes (or "Never Mind What He's Saying, What's He Doing?"). Paper presented at the European Languages for Special Purposes Symposium (7th, Budapest, Hungary, August 21–26, 1989).

Camiciottoli, B. C. (2003). Metadiscourse and ESP reading comprehension: An exploratory study. *Reading in a Foreign Language, 15*(1), 28.

Candelier, M., Camilleri-Grima, A., Castellotti, V., de Pietro, J.-F., Lörinez, I., Meissner, F.-J., Schröder-Sura, A. &. Artur, N. (2007). *Across languages and cultures: CARAP-framework of reference for pluralistic approaches to languages and cultures, Version 2 – July 2007.* Graz: European Centre for Modern Languages.

Celce-Murcia, M., & Olshtain, E. (2000). *Discourse and Context in Language Teaching: A Guide for Language Teachers.* Cambridge: Cambridge University Press.

Central Council for Education (2008) *Deliberation report from the Central Council for Education.* Retrieved from http://www.mext.go.jp/b_menu/shingi/chukyo/chukyo0/toushin/__icsFiles/afieldfile/2009/05/12/1216828_1.pdf

Chambliss, M. J. (1995). Text cues and strategies successful readers use to construct the gist of lengthy written arguments. *Reading Research Quarterly, 30*(4), 778–807.

Chambliss, M., & Calfee, R. (1998). *Textbooks for learning: Nurturing children's minds.* Oxford: Blackwell.

Chen, L. (2011) Revision and implementation of English curriculum: for learners' lifelong and full development. [in Chinese]. *Basic Foreign Language Education, 13*(04), 9–110. 陈琳. (2011)「通过英语教育为学生的终身发展和全面发展奠基——英语课标修订组组长陈琳教授谈《英语课程标准》的修订与实施」『基础英语教育』13(04), 9–11.

Chiswick, B.R. & Miller, P.W. (2004) Linguistic Distance: A Quantitative Measure of the Distance between English and Other Languages. Available at SSRN:

https://ssrn.com/abstract=575090

Chomsky, N. (1965). *Aspects of the Theory of Syntax*. Boston: MIT Press.

Chomsky, N. (1981). Knowledge of language: Its elements and origins. *Philosophical Transactions of the Royal Society of London B, 295*(1077), 223–234.

Cook, G. (1989). *Discourse*. Oxford: Oxford University Press.

Cook, G. (2010). *Translation in language teaching: An argument for reassessment.* Oxford: Oxford University Press.

Cook, L. K., & Mayer, R. E. (1988). Teaching readers about the structure of scientific text. *Journal of Educational Psychology, 80*(4), 448.

Cook, V. (2001). *Second Language Learning and Language Teaching* (3rd ed.). London: Arnold.

Corder, S. P. (1973). *Introducing applied linguistics*. Harmondsworth: Penguin Education.

Crismore, A. (1982). *The Metadiscourse Component: Understanding Writing about Reading Directives*. [Opinion Paper / Non-Journal]. Retrieved from https://eric.ed.gov/?id=ED217374

Crismore, A. (1983). *Metadiscourse: What It Is and How It Is Used in School and Non-School Social Science Texts*. Technical Report No. 273. USA: University of Illinois at Urbana-Champaign & Bolt, Beranek and Newman, Inc. Retrieved from https://eric.ed.gov/?id=ED229720

Crismore, A. (1984). The rhetoric of textbooks: Metadiscourse. *Journal of Curriculum Studies, 16*(3), 279–296.

Crismore, A. (1985). *Metadiscourse in social studies texts*. Technical Report No. 366. USA: University of Illinois at Urbana-Champaign & Bolt, Beranek and Newman, Inc. Retrieved from http://eric.ed.gov/?id=ED275986

Crismore, A. (1989). *Talking with Readers: Metadiscourse as Rhetorical Act*. New York: Peter Lang.

Crismore, A. (2000). *Helping ESL and EFL University Students Read Critically: A 2000's Challenge*. [Opinion Paper / Non-Journal]. Retrieved from https://eric.ed.gov/?id=ED450592

Cummins, J. (1978). Educational implications of mother tongue maintenance in minority-language groups. *Canadian Modern Language Review, 34*(3), 395–416.

Cummins, J. (1979). Linguistic interdependence and the educational development of bilingual children. *Review of Educational Research, 49*(2), 222–251.

Cunningsworth, A., & Tomlinson, B. (1984). *Evaluating and Selecting EFL Teaching Materials.* London: Heinemann Educational.

Davis, E. A., & Krajcik, J. S. (2005). Designing Educative Curriculum Materials to Promote Teacher Learning. *Educational Researcher, 34*(3), 3–14. https://doi.org/10.3102/0013189X034003003

Dijk, T. A. van, & Kintsch, W. (1983). *Strategies of discourse comprehension.* New York: Academic Press.

Dong, H. (2013) Historic review on English textbook in modern China [in Chinese]. *Lantai World,* 22, 113–114. 董辉. (2013)「近代中国英语教科书历史考察」『兰台世界』22, 113–114.

Dougill, J. (1987). Not So Obvious. In Leslie E. Sheldon, ed. *ELT Textbooks and Materials: Problems in Evaluation and Development.* UK: Modern English Publications/The British Council, 29–36.

Ellis, R. (2005). Principles of instructed language learning. *System: An International Journal of Educational Technology and Applied Linguistics, 33*(2), 209–224.

English Curriculum Revision Team (2012) *What is New in English Curriculum Revision* [in Chinese]. 课标修订组. (2012)『英语新课标，变在哪儿』. Retrieved from http://old.pep.com.cn/xe/jszx/jxyj/kcjcyj/201204/t20120406_1116959.htm

Erikawa H. (2003) *A Bibliographical Database on Foreign Language Textbooks* [in Japanese]. 江利川春雄. (2003)『明治以降外国語教科書データベース』. Retrieved from http://www.wakayama-u.ac.jp/~erikawa/

Erikawa, H. (2008) *A socio-cultural history of English language education in Japan.* [in Japanese] Tokyo: Kenkyusha. 江利川春雄. (2008)『日本人は英語をどう学んできたか：英語教育の社会文化史』東京：研究社.

Erikawa, H. (2012) *Towards cooperative learning in English classes* [in Japanese]. Tokyo: Taishūkan Shoten. 江利川春雄. (2012)『協同学習を取り入れた英語授業のすすめ』東京：大修館書店.

Fitzgerald, J. (1995) English-as-a-second-language learners' cognitive reading processes: A review of research in the United States. *Review of Educational Research, 65*(2), 145–190.

FSI (2020) FSI's Experience with Language Learning. Retrieved from https://www.state.gov/foreign-language-training/

Fukaya, Y., Ohkouchi, Y. & Akita, K. (2000) Influence of reminder signals towards relevant information on the way of reading history textbooks [in Japanese]. *Reading Science, 44*(4), 125–129. 深谷優子；大河内祐子 & 秋田喜代美.（2000）「関連する情報への注意喚起の信号が歴史教科書の読み方に及ぼす影響」『読書科学』44(4), 125–129.

Garner, R., Gillingham, M. G., & White, C. S. (1989). Effects of "seductive details" on macroprocessing and microprocessing in adults and children. *Cognition and Instruction, 6*(1), 41–57.

Gorbutt, D. (1972). Education as the Control of Knowledge: The New Sociology of Education. *Education for Teaching,* (89), 3–11.

Graddol, D. (2008). *English Next. Why global English may mean the end of 'English as a foreign language'*. Report. UK: British Council.

Gray, J. (2010). *The construction of English: culture, consumerism and promotion in the ELT global coursebook*. Basingstoke: Palgrave Macmillan.

Gu, Y. (2012). English curriculum and assessment for basic education in China. In Jiening Ruan & Cynthia Leung, eds. *Perspectives on teaching and learning English literacy in China.* New York: Springer, 35–50.

Guilloteaux, M. J. (2013). Language textbook selection: Using materials analysis from the perspective of SLA principles. *The Asia-Pacific Education Researcher, 22*(3), 231–239.

Hare, V. C., Rabinowitz, M., & Schieble, K. M. (1989). Text effects on main idea comprehension. *Reading Research Quarterly, 24*(1), 72–88.

Harmer, J. (1983). *The practice of English language teaching*. London & New York: Longman.

Harmer, J. (2001). *The practice of English language teaching, 3rd Edition*. Essex: Longman.

Hawkins, E. (1984). *Awareness of Language: An Introduction*. Cambridge: Cambridge University Press

Hill, A. A. (1970). The hypothesis of deep structure. *Studia Linguistica, 24*(1), 1–16.

Hishikari, T. (2018) Curriculum and New Course of Study: Focusing on Elementary School [in Japanese]. *Primary Education,* 19, 1–17. 菱刈晃夫.（2018）「教育課程と新学習指導要領：小学校を中心に」『初等教育論集』19, 1–17.

Hobbs, J. R. (1985). *On the coherence and structure of discourse*. Technical Report

No. CSLI-85-37 USA: Center for the Study of Language and Information. Retrieved from https://www.hf.uio.no/ilos/forskning/prosjekter/sprik/pdf/ocsd. pdf

Holliday, A. (1994a). *Appropriate Methodology and Social Context*. Cambridge: Cambridge University Press.

Holliday, A. (1994b). The house of TESEP and the communicative approach: the special needs of state English language education. *ELT Journal*, *48*(1), 3–11.

Horiba, Y. & Araki, K. (2002) Language Proficiency [in Japanese]. In Tsuda College Language and Culture Research Institute Reading Research Group, eds. *Process and Guidance for English Reading*. Japan: Taishūkan Shoten, 166–184. 堀場裕紀江 & 荒木和美. (2002)「言語習熟度」『英文読解のプロセスと指導』(津田塾大学　言語文化研究所読解研究グループ編著) 東京：大修館書店, 166–184.

Horiba, Y., van den Broek, P. W., & Fletcher, C. R. (1993). Second Language Readers' Memory for Narrative Texts: Evidence for Structure-Preserving Top-Down Processing. *Language Learning*, *43*(3), 345–372.

Hu, G.W. (2005a) English language education in China: policies, progress, and problems. *Language Policy 4*(5), 5–24.

Hu, R., & Adamson, B. (2012). Social ideologies and the English curriculum in China: A historical overview. In Jiening Ruan & Cynthia Leung, eds. *Perspectives on teaching and learning English literacy in China*. New York: Springer, 1–17.

Hyland, K. (2000). *Disciplinary Discourses: Social Interactions in Academic Writing*. Harlow: Longman.

Hyland, K. (2005). *Metadiscourse: Exploring interaction in writing*. London & New York: Continuum.

Imura M. (2003). *200 Years of English Education in Japan* [in Japanese]. Tokyo: TaishukanShoten. 伊村元道 (2003)『日本の英語教育200年』東京：大修館書店.

Iori, I. (2007) *A study on the cohesiveness of texts in Japanese* [in Japanese]. Tokyo: Kuroshio Publishing. 庵功雄. (2007)『日本語におけるテキストの結束性の研究』東京：くろしお出版.

Ishii, T. (2002) Structure of National Readers and language materials [in Japanese] *HiSET Journal*, 17, 77–93. 石井俊彦. (2002)「『ナショナル第一読本』の構成と言語材料」『日本英語教育史研究』17, 77–93.

Ito, H. (2003) A Consideration of Past and Current Problems regarding the Teaching of English Grammar in Schools and Universities [in Japanese]. *Language studies*, 102, 93–135. 伊藤裕道.（2003）「英文法教育の歴史と大学における英文法教育の今日的課題」『語学研究』102, 93–135.

Ito, T., Kubota, K., & Ohtake, F. (2015). *The hidden curriculum and social preferences* (Working Paper No. 954). ISER Discussion Paper, Institute of Social and Economic Research, Osaka University. Retrieved from https://www.econstor.eu/handle/10419/127063

Japan Textbook Research Centre (2020) International Textbook Research Survey Reports [in Japanese]. 教科書研究センター（2020）海外教科書制度調査研究報告書　Retrieved from https://textbook-rc.or.jp/kaigai/

Johnson, M. (1977). *Intentionality in Education: A Conceptual Model of Curricular and Instructional Planning and Evaluation*. New York: Center for Curriculum Research and Services.

Kachru, B. B. (1982). *The other tongue: English across cultures*. Champaign: University of Illinois Press.

Kachru, B. B. (1992). World Englishes: approaches, issues and resources. *Language Teaching*, 25(1), 1–14. https://doi.org/10.1017/S0261444800006583

Kiai, A.W. (2012) Biography of an English language textbook in Kenya: a journey from conceptualization to the classroom. (Doctoral dissertation, The University of Warwick, U.K.). Retrieved from http://go.warwick.ac.uk/wrap/49465

Kihei, K. (1988) Americanization in Japan after the Second World War: on Jack and Betty [in Japanese] *HiSET Journal*, 3, 169–205. 紀平健一.（1988）「戦後英語教育におけるJack and Bettyの位置」『日本英語教育史研究』3, 169–205.

Kogushi, M. (2011) *English test textbooks: institutions, teaching materials, and utilization* [in Japanese]. Tokyo: Sanseido. 小串雅則.（2011）『英語検定教科書：制度，教材，そして活用』東京：三省堂.

Kopple, V., & J, W. (1997). *Refining and Applying Views of Metadiscourse*. [Opinion Paper / Non-Journal]. Retrieved from https://eric.ed.gov/?id=ED411539

Krashen, S. D. (1985). *The input hypothesis: issues and implications*. London & New York: Addison-Wesley Longman Ltd.

Kuhn, M. R., & Stahl, S. A. (2003). Fluency: A review of developmental and remedial practices. *Journal of Educational Psychology*, 95(1), 3.

Kumaravadivelu, B. (2001). Toward a postmethod pedagogy. *TESOL Quarterly*,

35(4), 537–560.

Lee, J. F. (2014). A hidden curriculum in Japanese EFL textbooks: Gender representation. *Linguistics and Education, 27*(1), 39–53.

Li, L.Y., Zhang R.S., & Liu, L. (1988). *A history of English language teaching in China* [in Chinese]. Shanghai: Shanghai Foreign Language Education Press. 李良佑：张日昇 & 刘犁. (1988)『中国英语教学史』上海外语教育出版社.

Li, Y.J. (2001) CLT research in China: Problems and reflections [in Chinese]. *Foreign Language World, 2*, 13–19. 李予军. (2001)「交际法研究在中国:问题与思考」『外语界』(02), 13–19.

Littlejohn, A. (1988). How to Fail Interviews. In Andrew Littlejohn & Mohammed Melouk, eds. *Research Methods and Processes*. Lancaster, UK: Lancaster University, 67–75.

Littlejohn, A. (1998). The analysis of language teaching materials: Inside the Trojan Horse. In Brian Tomlinson, ed. *Materials Development in Language Teaching*. Cambridge: Cambridge University Press, 190–216.

Littlejohn, A. (2012). Language teaching materials and the (very) big picture. *Electronic Journal of Foreign Language Teaching, 9*(1), 283–297.

Littlejohn, A. P. (1992). *Why are English Language Teaching materials the way they are?* [PhD Thesis]. UK: University of Lancaster.

Liu, D.Y. & Wu, Z.Y. (2015) *English language education in China: past and present.* Beijing: People's Education Press.

Liu, D.Y., Gong, Y.F., & Zhang, X.C. (2011) The historical experiences and enlightenments of primary and secondary school English textbook construction in China. [in Chinese] *Curriculum, Teaching Material, and Method, 31*(1), 69–75. 刘道义；龚亚夫 & 张献臣. (2011)「我国中小学英语教材建设的历史经验及启示」『课程教材教法』31(1), 69–75.

Liu, H.N. (2011). A 150-year history of English textbooks in China: past and future. [in Chinese] *Shandong Foreign Language Teaching Journal, 145,* 61–66. 柳华妮. (2011)「国内英语教材发展150年回顾与启示」『山东外语教学』145, 61–66.

Long, M. H. (1985). Input and second language acquisition theory. In Susan Gass & Carolyn Madden, eds. *Input in Second Language Acquisition,* Rowley, Mass: Newbury House, 377–393.

MEXT (2006) *Basic Act on Education.* Retrieved from http://www.mext.go.jp/en/

policy/education/lawandplan/title01/detail01/1373798.htm

MEXT (2008a) *Tentative English translation of the guide to course of study: Foreign language.* 文部科学省.（2008a）『中学校学習指導要領英訳版（仮訳）：外国語』. Retrieved from http://www.mext.go.jp/

MEXT (2008b) *The guide to course of study: Foreign language* [in Japanese]. Tokyo: Kairyudo. 文部科学省.（2008）『中学校学習指導要領解説：外国語編』東京：開隆堂.

MEXT, Expert Panel on English Education, & Office for Promoting Foreign Language Education. (2014). *Report on the Future Improvement and Enhancement of English Education (Outline): Five Recommendations on the English Education Reform Plan Responding to the Rapid Globalization.* Retrieved October 25, 2018, from http://www.mext.go.jp/en/news/topics/detail/1372625.htm

MOE (2001) *English curriculum standards for full time compulsory education and senior high schools (Experiential edition)* [in Chinese]. Beijing: Beijing Normal University Press. 中华人民共和国教育部.（2001）『全日制义务教育普通高级中学英语课程标准（实验稿）』北京：北京师范大学.

MOE (2012a) *English curriculum standards for compulsory education (2011 edition)* [in Chinese]. Beijing: Beijing Normal University Press. 中华人民共和国教育部.（2012a）『义务教育英语课程标准（2011年版）』北京：北京师范大学.

MOE (2012b) *Explanation of 2011 English national curriculum for compulsory education (2011 edition)* [in Chinese]. Beijing: Beijing Normal University Press. 中华人民共和国教育部.（2012b）『义务教育英语课程标准（2011年版）』北京：北京师范大学.

MacKay, D. G. (1987). Constraints on theories of sequencing and timing in language perception and production. In Alan Allport et al., eds. *Language Perception and Production: Relationships between Listening, Speaking, Reading and Writing*, Cognitive Science Series, London: Academic Press Inc, 407–429.

Mackey, W. F. (1965). *Language teaching analysis.* London: Longmans Green & Co.

Macnamara, J. (1966). *Bilingualism and Primary Education: A Study of Irish Experience.* Edinburgh: Edinburgh University Press.

Mann, W. C., & Thompson, S. A. (1986). Relational propositions in discourse. *Discourse Processes, 9*(1), 57–90.

Masaki, T. (2012) History of Collaboration Between Japanese education With English Education in 1970s (in Japanese). Language and Information Sciences, 10, 125–141. 柾木貴之 (2012).「国語教育と英語教育の連携史－1970年代・英語教育雑誌における議論を中心に」『言語情報科学』10, 125–141.

Masaki, T. (2015) History of Collaboration Between Japanese education With English Education 1901–1945 (in Japanese). *Language and Information Sciences*, 13, 67–84. 柾木貴之 (2015).「国語教育と英語教育の連携前史－1901年から戦前までを対象に」『言語情報科学』13, 67–84.

Masaki, T. (2016) History of Collaboration Between Japanese education With English Education 1945–1960 (in Japanese). *Language and Information Sciences*, 14, 71–87. 柾木貴之 (2016).「国語教育と英語教育の連携前史－戦後から1960年代までを対象に」『言語情報科学』14, 71–87.

Masuhara, H. (2003). Materials for developing reading skills. In Brian Tomlinson, ed. *Developing materials for language teaching.* London: Continuum, 340–363.

Mauranen, A. (1993). Contrastive ESP rhetoric: metatext in Finnish-English economics texts. *English for Specific Purposes, 12*(1), 3–22.

Mayer, R. E. (1985). Structural analysis of science prose: Can we increase problem-solving performance? In Bruce Britton & John Black, eds. *Understanding expository text: a theoretical and practical handbook for analyzing explanatory text.* Hillsdale, NJ: L. Erlbaum Associates, 65–87.

McDonough, J., & Shaw, C. (2003). *Materials and Methods in ELT: A Teacher's Guide. Second Edition.* Chichester: Wiley-Blackwell.

Meyer, B. J., & Freedle, R. O. (1984). Effects of discourse type on recall. *American Educational Research Journal, 21*(1), 121–143.

Miller, G. A. (1956). The magical number seven, plus or minus two: some limits on our capacity for processing information. *Psychological Review, 63*(2), 81.

Minhui, Q. (2007). Discontinuity and reconstruction: The hidden curriculum in schoolroom instruction in minority-nationality areas. *Chinese Education & Society, 40*(2), 60–76.

Miyaura, K. (2002) Text Type [in Japanese]. In Tsuda College Language and Culture Research Institute Reading Research Group, eds. *Process and Guidance for English Reading.* Japan: Taishūkan Shoten, 118–136. 宮浦国江. (2002)「テクスト・タイプ」『英文読解のプロセスと指導』(津田塾大学　言語文化研究所読解研究グループ編著) 東京：大修館書店, 118–136.

Morris, P., & Adamson, B. (2010). *Curriculum, Schooling and Society in Hong Kong*. Hong Kong: Hong Kong University Press.

Nakamura, K., Minemura, M. & Takashiba, H. (2014). *Broken of English education myth: why this textbook now* [in Japanese]. Tokyo: Sangensha. 中村敬・高柴浩・峯村勝（2014）『「英語教育神話」の解体―今なぜこの教科書か』東京：三元社.

Nation, I. S. P. (1996). The four strands of a language course. *TESOL in Context*, *6*(1), 7.

Nation, I. S. P. (2001). *Learning vocabulary in another language*. Stuttgart: Ernst Klett Sprachen.

Nation, I. S. P. (2007). The four strands. *International Journal of Innovation in Language Learning and Teaching*, *1*(1), 2–13.

Nation, I. S. P. (2008). *Teaching ESL/EFL reading and writing*. New York & London: Routledge.

Nation, I. S. P., & Yamamoto, A. (2012). Applying the four strands to language learning. *International Journal of Innovation in English Language Teaching and Research*, *1*(2), 173.

Nikkei Asian Review (11/19/2016). Japan's Diet votes yes to more foreign care workers. [Journalism]. Retrieved October 25, 2018, from https://asia.nikkei.com/Politics-Economy/Policy-Politics/Japan-s-Diet-votes-yes-to-more-foreign-care-workers

Nunan, D. (1985). Content Familiarity and the Perception of Textual Relationships in Second Language Reading. *RELC Journal*, *16*(1), 43–51. https://doi.org/10.1177/003368828501600104

Nunan, D. (2001). Aspects of Task-Based Syllabus Design. [Opinion / Non-Journal]. Retrieved from http://www.seasite.niu.edu/tagalog/teachers_page/language_learning_articles/aspects_of_taskbased_syllabus.htm

Oates, T. (2014). New research shows why textbooks count. Retrieved October 24, 2018, from http://www.cambridgeassessment.org.uk/news/new-research-shows-why-textbooks-count-tim-oates/

Oates, T. (2014). *Why textbooks count. A Policy Paper.* Report. Cambridge: University of Cambridge. Retrieved from http://www.cambridgeassessment.org.uk/Images/181744-why-textbooks-count-tim-oates.pdf

Ogose, H. (2007). Cultivating metalinguistic ability in Japanese language education in elementary school [in Japanese]. *The National Association of College Teachers for Japanese Language and Literature Education Conference Programme,* 13–16. 生越秀子.（2007）「メタ言語能力を育てる小学校国語教育についての一考察－「伝えあう力」育成を視座に－」『全国大学国語教育学会発表要旨集』13–16.

Ojima, S., Nagai, A., Taya, F., Otsu, Y., & Watanabe, S. (2011). Correlates of high foreign-language proficiency in adults' mother-tongue processing: An event-related potential (ERP) study. *Neuroscience Research. Supplement: Abstracts of the 34th Annual Meeting of the Japan Neuroscience Society, 71*(1), e285.

Okido, A. (2018, September 4). The Spartan Education of AI Teachers that won't let slide a 'don't understand' response [in Japanese] *Forbes Japan.* 大木戸歩.（2018）「「わかったふり」が通用しないAI先生のスパルタ教育」 [Journalism]. Retrieved October 25, 2018, from https://forbesjapan.com/articles/detail/22736

Okihara, K. (2011) On the distinction between EFL and ESL [in Japanese] *Bulletin of Kyoto Notre-Dame University* 41, 69–80. 沖原勝昭.（2011）「英語教育におけるEFLとESLの違いについて」『京都ノートルダム女子大学研究紀要』41, 69–80.

Omura, K., Takanashi K. & Deki S. (eds) (1980) *Handbook of English education history* [in Japanese]. Tokyo: Tokyo Hōrei Publishing. 大村喜吉；高梨健吉 & 出来成訓（編）.（1980）『英語教育史資料』東京：東京法令出版.

Ortega, L. (2018). What is SLA research good for, anyway? Plenary talk delivered at the 52nd Annual International. IATEFL Conference and Exhibition. Brighton, UK, April 10–13. 2017. *The 52th International IATEFL Conference Programme*, 52.

Otsu, Y. & Torikai, K. (2002) *Why English in elementary schools: thinking about school English education* [in Japanese]. Tokyo: Iwanami. 大津由紀雄・鳥飼玖美子（2002）『小学校でなぜ英語？－学校英語教育を考える』東京：岩波書店.

Otsu, Y. (2009) Metalinguistic awareness in TEFL: preliminary notes. *Reports of the Keio Institute of Cultural and Linguistic Studies*, (40), 179–187.

Otsu, Y. (2010). Metalinguistic awareness in TEFL : preliminary notes (2). *Reports of the Keio Institute of Cultural and Linguistic Studies*, (41), 165–174.

Otsu, Y. (2011) Development of metalinguistic awareness: a case study. *Reports of the Keio Institute of Cultural and Linguistic Studies*, (42), 219–225.

Otsu, Y. (2017) On the New Course of Study: Towards Integrating Japanese Language "Kokugo" Teaching and English Language Teaching [in Japanese]. Trends in the sciences, 22(11), 101–103. 大津由紀雄. (2017)「次期学習指導要領から見た英語教育の今後の課題」『学術の動向』22(11), 101–103.

Otsu. Y, & Kubozono, H. (2008) *Cultivating language competence* [in Japanese]. Tokyo: Keio University Press. 大津由紀雄・窪薗晴夫. (2008)『ことばの力を育む』東京：慶應義塾大学出版会.

Otsu. Y. (1989) Meta-linguistic ability development and language education: from the perspective of linguistic psychology [in Japanese]. *Language*, 18(10), 26–34. 大津由紀雄. (1989)「メタ言語能力の発達と言語教育－言語心理学研究からみたことばの教育」『月刊言語』18(10), 26–34.

Oyama. M. (2016) *Awakening to Languages* [in Japanese]. Tokyo: Kurosio Publishers. 大山万容. (2016)『言語への目覚め活動－複言語主義に基づく教授法』東京：くろしお出版.

Ozasa, T. & Erikawa H, eds. (2004) *Research on history of English textbooks.* [in Japanese] Tokyo: Jiyūsha. 小篠敏明・江利川春雄 (編). (2004)『英語教科書の歴史的研究』東京：辞游社.

Ozasa, T. (1995) *Teaching method of Harold E. Palmer: its development in Japan* [in Japanese]. Hiroshima: Daiichi Gakushūsha. 小篠敏明. (1995)『Harold E. Palmerの英語教授法に関する研究：日本における展開を中心として』広島：第一学習社.

O'Malley, J. M., Chamot, A. U., Stewner-Manzanares, G., Russo, R. P., & Küpper, L. (1985). Learning strategy applications with students of English as a second language. *TESOL Quarterly, 19*(3), 557–584.

Pinker, S. (2015). The Sense of Style: The Thinking Person's Guide to Writing in the 21st Century. Penguin Publishing Group.

Posner, G. J. (1995). *Analyzing the Curriculum*. New York: McGraw-Hill.

Qin X.D. (2014) Literature view of English textbook research in and out of China. [in Chinese] *Journal of Mudanjiang University, 23*(12), 169–172. 秦希笛. (2014)「国内外英语教科书研究述评」『牡丹江大学学报』23(12), 169–172.

Remillard, J. T. (2005). Examining Key Concepts in Research on Teachers' Use of Mathematics Curricula. *Review of Educational Research, 75*(2), 211–246. https://doi.org/10.3102/00346543075002211

Richards, J. C., & Rodgers, T. (1982). Method: approach, design, and procedure. *Tesol Quarterly, 16*(2), 153–168.

Richards, J. C., & Rodgers, T. S. (2001). *Approaches and methods in language teaching.* Cambridge: Cambridge University Press.

Rivers, W. M. (1981). *Teaching Foreign Language Skills* (3rd ed.). Chicago: University of Chicago Press.

Saito, Y. (2000). *The art of English* [in Japanese]. Tokyo: University of Tokyo Press. 斎藤兆史（2002）『英語の作法』東京：東京大学出版会.

Saito, Y. (2003). *English masters' learning methods* [in Japanese]. Tokyo: Chukoshinsho. 斎藤兆史（2003）『英語達人塾：極めるための独習法指南』東京：中公新書.

Saito, Y. (2006) *English learning method for Japanese: why people in Meiji could do it* [in Japanese]. Tokyo: Shodensha. 斎藤兆史（2006）『日本人に一番合った英語学習法:明治の人は、なぜあれほどできたのか』東京：祥伝社.

Saito, Y. (2007) *Japanese people and English language: the other 100-year of English* [in Japanese]. Tokyo: Kenkyūsha. 斎藤兆史（2007）『日本人と英語：もうひとつの英語百年史』東京：研究社.

Saito, Y., Akita, K., Fujie, Y., Fujimori, C., Masaki, T., Wang, L.F., & Sanpei, Y. (2013). Developing a Curriculum for Meta-Grammar Teaching: Cross-Curricular Grammar Teaching in Japanese and English Classrooms in the Secondary School [in Japanese]. *Bulletin of the Graduate School of Education, the University of Tokyo,* 53, 255–272. 斎藤兆史；秋田喜代美；藤江康彦；藤森千尋；柾木貴之；王林鋒 & 三瓶ゆき．（2013）「メタ文法カリキュラムの開発：中等教育における国語科と英語科を繋ぐ教科横断カリキュラムの試み」『東京大学大学院教育学研究科紀要』53, 255–272.

Saito, Y., Hamada H., Masaki, T., Akita, K., Fujie, Y., Fujimori, C., Wang, L.F. (2012). The Prospect and Challenge of Developing Students' Meta-Grammatical Abilities in Grammar Teaching at the Level of Secondary Education [in Japanese]. *Bulletin of the Graduate School of Education, the University of Tokyo,* 52, 467–478. 斎藤兆史；濱田秀行；柾木貴之；秋田喜代美；藤江康彦；藤森千尋；三瓶ゆき & 王林鋒．（2012）「メタ文法能力の育成から見る中等教育段階での文法指導の展望と課題」『東京大学大学院教育学研究科紀要』52, 467–478.

Samuels, S. J. (1979). The Method of Repeated Readings. *The Reading Teacher, 32*(4), 403–408.

Satō, M. (2012) *School reform: vision and practice of learning communities.* [in Japanese]. Tokyo: Iwanami Shoten. 佐藤学．(2012)『学校を改革する：学びの共同体の構想と実践』東京：岩波書店．

Satō, M. (2012b) Thinking about English Textbooks [in Japanese] *Textbook Forum: Bulletin of the Chuo Education Institute,* (10), 74–76. 佐藤学．(2012b)「英語教科書を考える」『教科書フォーラム：中研紀要』(10), 74–76.

Sarkar Arani, M. (2014). Meaning of lesson study in teaching script changes: focusing on teachers' teaching beliefs on subject contents and materials. [in Japanese]. Journal of the Faculty of Education, Teikyo University (2), 171–185. サルカール アラニ モハメッド レザ (2014)「ティーチング・スクリプトの変容をもたらす授業研究の意義：教科内容と教材に関する教師の授業観を中心に」『帝京大学教育学部紀要』2, 171–185.

Schmidt, R. (1992). Psychological mechanisms underlying second language fluency. *Studies in Second Language Acquisition, 14*(4), 357–385.

Schmidt, R. W. (1990). The Role of Consciousness in Second Language Learning. *Applied Linguistics, 11*(2), 129–158. https://doi.org/10.1093/applin/11.2.129

Schwab, J. J. (1971). The Practical: Arts of Eclectic. *The School Review, 79*(4), 493–542.

Schön, D. (1983). *The reflective practitioner.* New York: Basic Books.

Scruggs, T. E., Mastropieri, M. A., Berkeley, S. L., & Marshak, L. (2010). Mnemonic strategies: Evidence-based practice and practice-based evidence. *Intervention in School and Clinic, 46*(2), 79–86.

Sercu, L. (2000). *Acquiring Intercultural Communicative Competence from Textbooks: The Case of Flemish Adolescent Pupils Learning German.* Leuven: Leuven University Press.

Sheldon, L. E. (1988). Evaluating ELT textbooks and materials. *ELT Journal, 42*(4), 237–246. https://doi.org/10.1093/elt/42.4.237

Sheng J. (2016) Impact of postmodernism on English textbooks in china [in Chinese]. *Shanghai Research on Education,* 4, 52–57. 盛静．(2016)「后现代主义教育思潮对我国中小学英语教科书的影响」『上海教育科研』4, 52–57.

Shi, G. (2010). An Examination of Hidden Curriculum in Foreign Language Education [in Chinese]. *Technology Enhanced Foreign Language Education,* (3). 史光孝．(2010)「外语隐性课程的审视与思考」『外语电化教学』(3), 30–33. Retrieved from http://en.cnki.com.cn/Article_en/CJFDTOTAL-WYDH201003009.htm

Skierso, A. (1991). Textbook Selection and Evaluation. In Marianne Celce-Murcia, ed. *Teaching English as a Second or Foreign Language*. Boston, MA: Heinle and Heinle, 432–453.

State Council (2010) *Outline of China's National Plan for Medium and Long-term Education Reform and Development (2010–2020)* [in Chinese]. 国务院. (2010) 『国家中长期教育改革和发展规划纲要（2010–2020年）』. Retrieved from http://www.gov.cn/jrzg/2010-07/29/content_1667143.htm

Storch, N., & Wigglesworth, G. (2007). Writing tasks: The effects of collaboration. In María del Pilar García Mayo, ed. *Investigating Tasks in Formal Language Learning*. Clevedon: Multilingual Matters, 157–177.

Swain, M. (1985). Communicative competence : Some roles of comprehensible input and comprehensible output in its development. *Input in Second Language Acquisition*, 15, 165–179.

Swain, M. (1995) Three functions of output in second language learning. In Guy Cook & Barbara Seidlhofer, eds. *Principles and practice in applied linguistics: Studies in honor of H. G. Widdowson*, Oxford: Oxford University Press, 125–144.

Swan, M., & Smith, B. (2001). *Learner English: A Teacher's Guide to Interference and Other Problems*. Cambridge: Cambridge University Press.

Takanashi, K., Deki S. (1992) *Selections of English Textbooks*. [in Japanese] Tokyo: Ozorasha. 高梨健吉；出来成訓. (1992)『英語教科書名著選集』東京：大空社.

Takanashi, K., Deki S. (1993) *History and problems of English textbooks*. [in Japanese] Tokyo: Ozorasha. 高梨健吉；出来成訓. (1992)『英語教科書の歴史と解題』東京：大空社.

Tanabe, K. (1991) Teaching the connective relations of sentences: Teaching logical consonants [in Japanese]. *Naruto English Research*, (5), 27–35. 田鍋薫. (1991)「文の連接関係を読む指導：論理的連結語句の指導」『鳴門英語研究』(5), 27–35.

Tomlinson, B. (2012). Materials development for language learning and teaching. *Language Teaching*, 45(2), 143–179.

Torikai, K. (2012) "Teaching about textbooks"? "Teaching through textbooks"? (Considering English textbooks) [in Japanese]. *Textbook Forum: Bulletin of the Chuo Education Institute*, (10), 76–78. 鳥飼玖美子. (2012)「「教科書を教える」？

「教科書で教える」? (英語教科書を考える)」『教科書フォーラム：中研紀要』(10), 76–78.

Toulmin, S. E. (1958). *The Uses of Argument*. Cambridge: Cambridge University Press.

Tufte, E. R. (1990). *Envisioning information*. Cheshire, CT: Graphics Press.

Tunmer, W.E., & Bowey, C. (1984) "Metalinguistic awareness and reading acquisition." In Tunmer, W.E. et al (eds.) Metalinguistic Awareness in Children: Theory, Research, and Implications. Berlin; New York: Springer-Verlag, pp.144–168.

Turula, T. (2018, March 23). A 21-year-old Swedish AI prodigy wants to revolutionize the $6 trillion education industry – and Tim Cook is impressed [Journalism]. Retrieved October 25, 2018, from https://nordic.businessinsider.com/a-21-year-old-ai-prodigy-sweden-sana-labs-wants-to-revolutionize-the-$5-trillion-education-industry--heres-why-mark-zuckerberg-and-tim-cook-seem-convinced--/

Tyler, R. W. (1949). *Basic principles of curriculum and instruction*. Chicago : University of Chicago Press.

Ujihara, Y. (2011) A study on the transmission of gendered messages through the hidden curriculum [in Japanese]. *Journal of Nagoya Women's University: Home Economics, Natural Science, Humanities, Social Science*. (57), 151–160. 氏原陽子. (2011)「隠れたカリキュラムによるジェンダー・メッセージの伝達に関する研究」『名古屋女子大学紀要 家政・自然編, 人文・社会編』(57), 151–160.

Ujihara, Y. (2013) Intentional Hidden Curriculum [in Japanese]. *Journal of Nagoya Women's University*, (59), 149–159. 氏原陽子. (2013)「意図的な隠れたカリキュラム」『名古屋女子大学紀要』(59), 149–159.

Underwood, P. (2012). The Course of Study for senior high school English: recent developments, implementation to date, and considerations for future research. *Toyo Eiwa University Journal of Humanities and Social Sciences*（東洋英和女学院人文社会科学論集）, *30*, 115–145.

Urata, Y. & Kojima, Y. (2016). Cultivating Globally Competent Human Resources with a "Presentation": the Case of the Foreign Language Presentation Event [in Japanese]. *The Journal of Community Design Studies* (4), 13–26. 浦田葉子 & 小島由美. (2016)「「発表」が促すグローバル人材育成：外国語発表会が培ったもの」『地域社会デザイン研究』(4), 13–26.

Valero-Garcés, C. (1996). Contrastive ESP rhetoric: Metatext in Spanish-English economics texts. *English for Specific Purposes, 15*(4), 279–294.

Wang, L.F. (2012). A Comparative Study of the Metadiscourse Analysis in EFL Textbooks in Japan and China. *Journal of Textbook Research, 5*(2), 103–123.

Wang, L.F. (2014). The Prospect and Challenge of Textbook Research in English Language Education [in Japanese]. *Bulletin of the Graduate School of Education of the University of Tokyo,* (53), 247–254. 王林鋒.（2014）「英語教育における教科書研究の展望と課題」『東京大学大学院教育学研究科紀要』(53), 247–254.

Wang, L.F. (2015). Gap between English authorized textbooks and national English curriculum: focusing on the balance of the four skills [in Japanese]. *Textbook Forum: Bulletin of the Central Education Research Center,* (14), 2–10. 王林鋒.（2015）「英語検定教科書の練習活動から求められる能力と学習指導要領目標の乖離：四技能のバランスに焦点をあてて」『教科書フォーラム：中研紀要』(14), 2–10.

Wang, L.F. (2017). The Possibility of Collaboration among Japanese, English and Chinese in Foreign Language Education in Elementary School: from the Perspective of Language Awareness, *Primary Education Research,* Fukui University, (3), 25–32. [in Japanese] 王林鋒.（2017）「小学校外国語教育における国語・英語・中国語の連携の可能性：ことばへの気づきに着目して」『福井大学初等教育研究』(3), 25–32.

Wang, L.F. (2018a). Collaboration between L1 and EFL education in Japan. Paper Presentation, The 52nd Annual International. IATEFL Conference and Exhibition. Brighton, UK, April 10–13. 2017. In *The 52th IATEFL International Conference Programme,* 208.

Wang, L.F. (2018b). How Mother Tongues Are Dealt with in Elementary English Textbooks in Mainland China, Taiwan, Japan, and South Korea. Paper Presentation, Siem Reap, Cambodia, 2008-05-11. In *The 11ᵗʰ Comparative Education Society of Asia (CESA) Conference Programme,* 65.

Wang, L.F. (2018c). Incorporating L1 in EFL Classes in Primary Schools. Paper Presentation, Kyoto, Japan, 2018-08-26. *The 44ᵗʰ Japan Society of English Language Education (JASELE) Conference Programme,* 330–331.

Wang, L.F. (2019a). Collaborative Practice Research on Incorporating Japanese and Foreign Language Education in Materials Development: Case Studies of Textbook Use in Classrooms [in Japanese] *Teacher Education Research,* 12, 181–

193. 王林鋒. (2019a)「母語と連携する外国語教育の教材開発に関わる協働的実践研究：教科書を生かした授業実践事例を通して」『教師教育研究』12, 181–193.

Wang, L.F. (2019b). Action Research towards Partnering L1 with EFL & CFL in Japanese Schools. Paper Presentation, Bangkok, Thailand, 2019-06-29. *The 17th Asia TEFL International Conference.*

Wang, L.F. (2019c). Incorporating L1 and Multiple Languages in EFL Classes in East Asian Countries. Paper Presentation, Tokyo, Japan, 2019-08-08. *World Education Research Association 2019.*

Wang, L.F. (2019d). Action Researches on Incorporating Japanese and Chinese in EFL Classes. Paper Presentation, Nagoya, Japan, 2019-08-28. *The 58th JACET International Convention.*

Wang, L.F. (2020a). Practice Research on Incorporating Japanese and Foreign Language Education in Elementary Schools: A Case Study of Material Development [in Japanese] *JES Journal*, 20, 100–114. 王林鋒.（2020）「ことばの教育として国語と連携する小学校外国語教育の実践研究：教科書開発を見据えて」『JES Journal』20, 100–114.

Wang, L.F. (2020b). Action Research on Collaborating Mother Tongue and Foreign Languages in EFL Materials Development. *The Journal of East Asian Educational Research*, 10, 82–93.

Wang, L.F., & Akita, K. (2014). An Analysis of Rhetorical Patterns within English Textbooks for Junior High-Schools: from the perspective of textual connectivity [in Japanese] *The Science of Reading, 56*(1), 26–36. 王林鋒. (2014)「中学校英語教科書本文内容の記述における修辞パターンの分析：テキストのつながりに焦点を当てて」『読書科学』56(1), 26–36.

Wang, Q. (2012). Meaning of learning English for learner development: explanation of revised English curriculum [in Chinese]. *Basic Foreign Language Education,14*(2), 3–10. 王蔷.（2012)「凸显英语学习对于学生健康成长的意义——英语课程标准修订解读」『基础英语教育』14(2), 3–10.

Wen, Q.F. (2016). Framework of teaching Lingua Franca in China. [in Chinese] *Linguistic Science, 15*(04), 354–355 文秋芳. (2016)「英语通用语的教学框架」『语言科学』15(04), 354–355.

Williams, D. (1983). Developing criteria for textbook evaluation. *ELT Journal*, 37(3), 251–255. https://doi.org/10.1093/elt/37.3.251

Williams, J. (2005). Form-focused instruction. In Eli Hinkel, ed. *Handbook of Research in Second Language Teaching and Learning*. Mahwah, NJ: L. Erlbaum Associates, 671–691.

Yamada, G. (1998). The meanings of transition from Jack and Betty to New Prince [in Japanese] *HiSET Journal*, (13), 123–152. 山田豪. (1998)「Jack and Bettyの時代性をいかに評価するか—教科書としての内容検討を踏まえて」『日本英語教育史研究』(13), 123–152.

Yoshitome, F. (2010). Effects of Guidance on Reading Comprehension of English Texts from the Viewpoint of Textual Structure [in Japanese]. *Japan Educational Society Conference Presentation Summary, 69*, 164–165. 吉留文男. (2010)「テキスト構造に焦点を当てた英文読解指導の効果」『日本教育学会大會研究発表要項』69, 164–165.

Young, M. F. D. (1971). *Knowledge and control: new directions for the sociology of education*. London: Collier-Macmillan.

Zhang L.Z. (2011). New standard and new curriculum [in Chinese]. *Basic Foreign Language Education, 13*(04), 111–112. 张连仲. (2011)「新标准与《新标准》」『基础英语教育』13(04), 111–112.

Zhang, D. & Luo, Y. (2016). Social exclusion and the hidden curriculum: The schooling experiences of Chinese rural migrant children in an urban public school. *British Journal of Educational Studies, 64*(2), 215–234.

Zhang, Z.D. (2005). Reconsidering the purpose of English curriculum [in Chinese] *Curriculum, Teaching Material, and Method* , (09), 55–61. 张正东. (2005)「探讨我国英语课程的目标」『课程. 教材. 教法』(09), 55–61.

ACKNOWLEDGEMENTS

This publication was supported by JSPS KAKENHI Grant Number JP24HP5150.

Any opinions, findings, and conclusions or recommendations expressed in this material are those of the author and do not necessarily reflect the views of the authors' organization, JSPS or MEXT.

This book originates from my doctorate studies. All in all, it has been roughly thirteen years since I entered the Ph.D. course at the University of Tokyo in 2011. During this long journey, there were moments when I would not have been able to push forward without the help of numerous kind and patient people, too many to cite here in full. There are, however, a few to whom I have become particularly indebted for the continued support and insights they have shared with me during these years. It is these people that I wish to briefly acknowledge here, by sending them a heartfelt 'Thank You'.

Firstly, my former supervisor at Southwest University in China, Prof. Dr. Yule Jin, with whom I took my first steps in academic research, who inspired me to feel excited about making new discoveries, and who encouraged me to pursue my studies abroad. Secondly, my parents, from whom I learned the value of being independent.

Finally, and most importantly, to Prof. Dr. Kiyomi Akita, my supervisor at the University of Tokyo, a life mentor and a role model, under whose influence I feel continually encouraged to better myself.

【著者略歴】

王　林鋒（わん　りんふぉん）

学歴
2008年　西南大学大学院教育学研究科カリキュラム及び教授法専攻修士
課程修了〈中国・重慶〉
2015年　東京大学大学院教育学研究科教職開発専攻博士課程満期退学
博士（教育学）

主な経歴
2017年4月—2022年3月　福井大学連合教職大学院　特命助教
2022年4月—現在　　　　大阪教育大学多文化教育系　特任准教授

著書に『メタ言語能力を育てる文法授業—英語科と国語科の連携』（分担
執筆, 2019, ひつじ書房）,『辞書引き学習、海を渡る：汎用的語彙学習方略
モデルの開発』（分担執筆, 2024, 三省堂）など

A Plurilingual Approach for Foreign Language Education in Japan
Enriching Learners' Metalinguistic Awareness through
Comparative Sino-Japanese EFL Textbook Research

2025 年 2 月 5 日　初版第 1 刷発行

著　者　王　　　林　　鋒

発行者　風　間　敬　子

発行所　株式会社　風　間　書　房

〒 101- 0051　東京都千代田区神田神保町 1-34
電話 03（3291）5729　FAX 03（3291）5757
振替 00110 -5 -1853

印刷　太平印刷社　製本　井上製本所

©2025　Linfeng WANG　　　　　　　　　NDC分類：375.893
ISBN978-4-7599-2528-9　　Printed in Japan
[JCOPY]〈出版者著作権管理機構 委託出版物〉
本書の無断複製は、著作権法上での例外を除き禁じられています。複製される
場合は、そのつど事前に出版者著作権管理機構（電話 03-5244-5088、FAX
03-5244-5089、e-mail: info@jcopy.or.jp）の許諾を得て下さい。